KNITTING BY DESIGN

A STEP-BY-STEP GUIDE TO DESIGNING AND KNITTING YOUR OWN CLOTHES

MARY ANNE ERICKSON AND EVE COHEN

BANTAM BOOKS
TORONTO · NEW YORK · LONDON · SYDNEY · AUCKLAND

KNITTING BY DESIGN
A Bantam Book / September 1986

Art Direction and Design: Eve Cohen
Illustration: Mary Anne Erickson
Design Assistant: Monica Kowarick

Cover Photograph: Tim Geaney
Cover Model: Nancy De Weir

Library of Congress Cataloging-in-Publication Data

Erickson, Mary Anne.
   Knitting by design.

   1. Knitting—Patterns. 2. Knit goods. I. Cohen, Eve.
II. Title.
TT825.E75   1986   746.9′2   86-47582

ISBN 0-553-34271-1
Published simultaneously in the United States and Canada

Bantam Books are published by Bantam Books, Inc. Its trademark, consist-
ing of the words "Bantam Books" and the portrayal of a rooster, is
Registered in U.S. Patent and Trademark Office and in other countries.
Marca Registrada. Bantam Books, Inc., 666 Fifth Avenue, New York, New
York 10103.

PRINTED IN THE UNITED STATES OF AMERICA

KP   0 9 8 7 6 5 4 3 2 1

Dedication

From Mary Anne, to my dear Auntie, who taught me about knitting and love.
From Eve, to my Mother and Father, for their love and encouragement.

Acknowledgments

Many thanks to my parents Marge and Rollie Neibauer, for their strong support, encouragement, and love. To Marge Edris for everything. To Julie Winter for showing me that everything is possible. To my dearest husband, Richard, for trusting and loving me.

Mary Anne

To my friends for their patience. To Richard Carey for his love and support.
To Monica, for her dedication to this project and especially her friendship.

Eve

Special thanks and love to those who believed in our project and helped us realize it: Andrea Cirillo, Coleen O'Shea, Allan Eaglesham, Dorothy Parrish, Teri Whitcraft, Lola Erlich, Nancy De Weir, Tim Geaney, Candi Jensen, Valerie Green, Scott Jacobson, Pam Choy, Doug Raimer, Larry Katz, Neil Gorman, Gary Brofermaker, Wanda Slomiany, Ron Leighton, Doris and Al Erickson and Becky Cabaza.

CONTENTS

INTRODUCTION

Are you tired of searching knitting stores for the sweater pattern you really like? And what are you going to do with that great yarn you got on sale last year when you still haven't found the right pattern for it? We've all felt that sense of exasperation at seeing a gorgeous designer sweater in a magazine or store window and wishing that we could find a similar pattern to make for ourselves. Well, now you can!

Our book will provide you with all the information you need to begin designing your own garments. Turn your measurements into instructions for sweaters, skirts, and dresses with little more than a measuring tape and simple arithmetic.

We'll take you through the basic knitting skills in Chapter One, in case you're just learning how to knit, or need a little brushing up to get you started. We've provided measurement charts for you to record your own measurements and those of family and friends, a quick reference file for when you begin those special gifts.

And we've supplied many simple stitches that you can combine for instant designs in your own creations. Imagine, being able to call yourself a designer! After reading and practicing the various techniques we're presenting, that's just what you'll be able to do.

In Chapter Two, "How To . . .," you'll find lots of step-by-step instructions for everything from choosing a figure-flattering style, to drawing schematic diagrams, to charting techniques for different styles. Charting is a way of writing instructions so that you can look at your pattern and immediately see whatever you need to know to knit your garment. If you like pictorial sweaters, you will learn how to plot and enlarge realistic images onto your favorite sweater shape. We've made this easier by giving different examples of images, starting simply and getting progressively more complex. This way, you can practice with an image that feels comfortable and move on to more difficult designs as you advance in knowledge and confidence. Your choice of yarn colors and textures will make the design your own.

Some of you may be more interested in traditional sweater designs. Aran sweaters offer a great opportunity for experimentation with stitches and texture. We've provided a complete menu of ideas, as well as the basic ingredients that make up an Aran and the simplest stitches you can use to achieve these effects.

In Chapter Three we have included 32 of our own designs for you to knit, pointing out connections between various techniques described in the text and those in the designs so you can see how they look when finished. We show you how to modify the patterns to make them simple or complex.

Let's face it. We all run into problems from time to time on knitting projects. Chapter Four, "Knitting Psychology," will help bail you out when you get stuck. You'll find practical, as well as silly, ways to get yourself out of the knitting doldrums and back in action! After all, you've spent your hard-earned money on that yarn and your valuable time working on what you had hoped would be your next masterpiece! It can be very demoralizing to wonder whether you're going to have to scrap the whole thing and start over again.

Finishing techniques are essential skills. They can make all the difference in the look of your completed garment. If you knew of an invisible way to sew up your shoulder seam, wouldn't you prefer it to one that appears bulky? In Chapter Five, we've provided helpful information that will give your next sweater, skirt, or dress that enviable finished designer quality.

The Workbook chapter (Chapter Six) is the heart of the book. We encourage you to start a Workbook binder of your own and use it as a way to teach yourself what it is you really like in styles of knitted garments, as well as what you prefer to spend your time working on. As you begin to keep a record of your preferences, you'll find design ideas much easier to create.

Also in this chapter are many fill-in pages to help simplify your new skills as a designer. You'll find pages to record your pattern instructions, knitter's graph paper, Prep Pages (for designing sweaters you've admired), and cut-out pages, an alternative to drawing. Last but not least, the Fiber File is a way to keep track of all the little odds and ends of yarn you might have from old knitting projects. The Fiber File can be a tool in the designing process and also a way to make a sweater for very little money—something we're all interested in!

If you live in a rural or remote area, or even in a thriving metropolis, the Resource Section should be helpful in ordering unique and one-of-a-kind yarns and related products through the mail. Often yarn stores can stock only a limited amount of yarn, so you may have only a limited idea about what's available. There are countless small companies and individuals all over the world who make yarns of outstanding character. Each company listed has provided a description of what they have to offer, so consider sending away for that exotic, handmade silk next time you want to make yourself a sumptuous masterpiece!

We hope you enjoy learning how to design your own garments. Remember, be patient with yourself. Know that each new skill you master will bring you one step closer to realizing your knitting fantasies!

CHAPTER ONE
THE BASICS

This chapter will give you a good foundation in the fundamental knitting skills. For beginners, we have provided the basic stitches you need to get started knitting today. The more experienced knitter will also find many valuable technique-sharpening tools.

We take you through the basics of knitting supplies, how to measure your gauge, how to "swatch" for experimenting with new stitch patterns, how to take your own measurements, how to follow knitting instructions or alter them when necessary, shorthand symbols for pattern stitches, and instructions for many interesting stitch patterns.

The Knitter's Guide Charts in this chapter are an essential tool for anyone who wants to design sweaters. These charts provide standard measurements for every design, and using the charts will make your designing process much simpler.

Knitting in the round is explained in detail, as are several attractive ways to increase and decrease to achieve a more decorative look on your next raglan.

Now you're ready to approach knitting as an art! First, let's talk about supplies . . . .

NEEDLES

If knitting is an art—and we think it is—then needles and yarn are the brushes and palette. Like any artist, a knitter knows her tools well.

✔ CHECKLIST OF KNITTING TOOLS

- ☐ Single-Pointed Needles
- ☐ Double-Pointed Needles
- ☐ Circular Needle
- ☐ Cable Needle
- ☐ Tapestry Needle
- ☐ Crochet Hook
- ☐ Bobbins
- ☐ Row Counter
- ☐ Scissors
- ☐ Stitch Markers
- ☐ Tape Measure
- ☐ Stitch Holders

TIPS

• *Your choice of needle size and yarn weight will be a major factor in how long it takes you to complete a project. If you want to make a sweater over a weekend, use large needles (#13–#35) and bulky yarn, and you'll have it done in no time. If you want a finer, more delicate garment, use smaller needles (#2–#8), lightweight yarn, and remember it will take more time.*

• *A row counter is a very useful tool for pattern stitches, cables, and multicolored knitting. It is a small device which you slip on the needle at the beginning of the first row (or whenever you're ready to begin counting). You manually rotate a dial to change numbers, which keep track of the finished rows. When you get to the end of a row, transfer the counter to the other needle and continue knitting, making sure to change the number after each row.*

There are basically three types of needles: single-pointed, double-pointed, and circular. Straight needles (single-pointed or double-pointed) are available in plastic, in lightweight nickel-coated aluminum, and in wood. Each material has distinct qualities. As the lightest weight, plastic needles are good to learn on, but they are not as "fast" as aluminum needles, which are better balanced. The metal tips though can sometimes poke holes in wider material such as knitting ribbon. Wood and bamboo may look more "natural," but the needles are more prone to break and splinter, which can snag or split the yarn. Once you invest in good needles, take care to store them carefully so they don't get bent or damaged.

Needles are sized by their diameter; however, there are three different methods of labeling them: U.S., metric, and old U.K. Most yarn stores in the United States sell both U.S. and metric sizes. If you are following a European pattern, the needle sizes will often be old U.K. or metric. The chart shows how the different sizes all relate.

INTERNATIONAL NEEDLE SIZES																				
U.S.	000	00	0	1	2	3	—	4	—	5	6	7	8	9	10	—	10½	—	11	—	13
Metric(mm)	1.75	2	2.25	2.5	2.75	3	3.25	3.5	3.75	4	4.25	4.5	5	5.5	6	6.5	7	7.5	8	9	10
Old U.K.	—	14	13	—	12	11	10	—	9	8	—	7	6	5	4	3	2	1	0	00	000

EXPERIMENTING WITH YARN

There are some important considerations to remember when choosing yarn for a special project, as each yarn has unique characteristics. Some homespun yarns are loosely twisted, which gives the garment a distinctive handcrafted quality. If you're interested in a highly polished look, this would be an inappropriate choice. In that case you would look for a tightly twisted, smoother yarn, which would be excellent for stitch patterns or multicolored knitting.

Pay attention to the yarn's "ply" and "weight." "Ply" refers to the number of strands that are twisted together, and "weight" refers to the thickness of the yarn. A "three-ply" yarn could be either lightweight or bulky. Generally weights fall into four categories: baby weight, sport weight, worsted weight, and rug weight. Look for this information on the yarn label.

WOOL

Derived from sheep, wool is our most enduring fiber, with the longest history. For over 2,000 years wool has been harvested and spun as a natural insulation from the cold. Today there are over 200 different breeds of sheep that are raised commercially for their fleece. Wool's unique qualities include superior elasticity, which contributes to its bulkiness, to its stretch and recovery abilities, and to its moisture absorption.

COTTON

This plant fiber is used in the brightest and most subtle color combinations. It is far less elastic than any other yarn, so be sure to knit a gauge swatch to see how much it stretches. (This is especially important for ribbing, which needs to have plenty of "give.") Although not as warm as wool, it has become a year-round favorite for handmade garments.

LINEN

Another plant fiber, linen has qualities similar to cotton, and the two are often combined. Linen is absorbent, comfortable, and extremely durable. Another plus, it's moth- and perspiration-resistant. Hand-washing is recommended for linen garments that have intense colors, as the dyes may bleed.

Baby weight wool

Sport weight wool

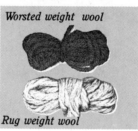

Worsted weight wool

Rug weight wool

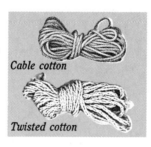

Cable cotton

Twisted cotton

Mercerized cotton

Cotton and linen blend

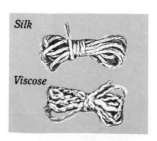

Silk

Viscose

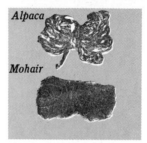

Alpaca

Mohair

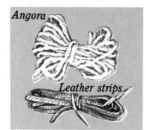

Angora

Leather strips

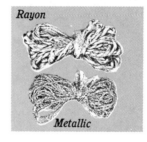

Rayon

Metallic

Ribbon

Paper

Silk and wool blend

Bouclé

SILK

Spun by a worm fed on mulberry leaves, silk has always been a luxury yarn. Silk breathes well yet retains heat for warmth. Silk stays elastic when wet or dry. To remove the wrinkles from a silk garment, drape it over a soft hanger and the wrinkles will fall out.

OTHER LUXURY YARNS

Mohair, angora, and alpaca come from goats, rabbits, and alpacas (a breed of llama) respectively. Lightweight mohair has remarkable body, but is relatively inelastic. Angora and alpaca are incredibly soft, but somewhat fragile and have a tendency to shed. Because they are expensive, consider using them in combination with other common yarns to add a touch of luxury to any garment.

ACRYLIC OR MANMADE YARNS

Many yarns combine manmade fibers such as acrylic with natural fibers to give added strength and elasticity. Far less expensive than natural fibers, manmade yarns come in a wide variety of weights and textures and are usually machine washable.

NOVELTY YARNS

Be prepared to find anything in a yarn store these days. This includes paper strands, tube, string, and cord yarns, metallics, leather tapes, ribbons, fur, fabric with fringes or frayed edges, and chainettes.

BLENDS

Many manufacturers are combining some of the more classic fibers, such as linen/cotton, silk/angora, and wool/linen. Many of these blends have separate strands of each fiber that twist around to make wonderful touches of color and texture. This type of texture,

Bouclé

called "bouclé", is created when strands of different sizes are combined at different speeds in the manufacturing process.

GETTING STARTED

There are many questions to consider when you begin to design your own garments. What do I want to make? In what style? In what color? With what type of yarn? All of these questions can be intimidating and leave you feeling a bit lost. A great way to overcome this anxiety is a trip to a favorite yarn store. We all know how easy it is to fall in love with a particular type of yarn. Once you've discovered you can't live without it, you'll be amazed at the inspiration that yarn can provide. We'll give you lots of instructions about how to proceed with the designing process later in the book; for now you've got a great way to begin, with some yarn you really love.

One of the critical questions you will want to ask yourself before you buy the yarn is, How much time do I want to spend knitting this garment? This is very important because the weight of the yarn and the needle size will determine how long the project will take. If you want to

make a sweater vest over the weekend, buy some bulky yarn and knit it on very large needles (#13–#35). If you want a tailored or more complex garment, choose a lighter weight yarn and smaller needles (#2–#8). The main thing to remember is that the size of the needles and weight of the yarn determine how long you'll be knitting.

Also consider the difference in textures and elasticity. Tightly twisted yarns are smooth, easy to work with, durable, and good for pattern stitches or pictorial designs. Loosely twisted or handspun yarns are less durable and more likely to lose their shape, but they often have more texture and give a garment a unique, handcrafted look. Once you have the skein in hand, knit a test swatch and explore the yarn's characteristics (see page 17, Swatching). The swatch helps you visualize the sort of stitch pattern and garment which will work best with the yarn and to calculate the amount of yarn you need.

COMBINING YARNS

Many beautiful yarns are delicate and require small needles and therefore take a great deal of time to knit as is. Consider combining several different yarns that will allow you to use larger needles and knit faster. For example, a strand of mohair or metallic yarn can accent linen or wool. Expensive angora mixes well with wool to make a

luxurious but affordable sweater.

There are several ways to combine yarns. The easiest and fastest way is simply to twist the strands together as you knit. However, if you want to avoid working with several balls of yarn at once, simply roll a single new ball of yarn which incorporates the two, three, or four strands twisted together.

SUBSTITUTING YARNS

When you can't find the exact yarn called for in a pattern, don't despair—substitute. It's possible to substitute one yarn for another as long as the gauge is the same. (The gauge is the number of stitches in one inch across and the number of rows in one inch length.) Remember, you can always increase or decrease the needle size to give your swatch the same gauge called for in the pattern. Check yarn labels to find a recommended gauge which is similar to your pattern and make a test swatch to check it. Yarn with a different weight or texture (like a novelty yarn) can change the gauge a great deal. So keep the original yarn's characteristics in mind. If you do choose a yarn of a different weight, you may have to rework the pattern. (See page 12 for an explanation of this process.)

FABRIC AS YARN

Did you ever think to knit with fabric? You don't have to go to the yarn store to get the materials for your next sweater, they could be as close as the trunk in your closet.

Cutting Fabric on the Bias

Lay your preshrunk fabric on a flat surface and cut several large bias sections out of it, using as much of the fabric as possible. A good width for this large strip is 12″–18″. With right sides together, bring the two diagonal ends of the strip together and sew a ¼″ seam. Begin cutting at any point on the surface of the strip to your predetermined width.(Remember, the width of the strip will determine the weight of the yarn.) Continue cutting in a spiral direction, forming one long strip. When you have cut all the fabric, either tie or sew the ends together and roll into balls. Now you're ready to knit up your fabric.

HOW MUCH YARN DO YOU NEED?

Most patterns tell you how much yarn is called for to complete the project. But what if you're designing your own garment? You certainly don't want to run out of yarn on the last half of the second sleeve! Make sure you know all the important information about your garment, such as size, shape, and measurements.

If you have picked a project from a pattern book and use yarn with the same gauge called for in the pattern, you can simply follow the pattern's instructions. Or you could find a pattern similar in size and shape to the one you yourself plan to design and assume that the quantities will be about the same. When in doubt, ask the salesperson's advice.

Most experienced knitters overbuy yarn. Dye lots change and yarn sells out quickly, so to be safe, buy a skein or two more than you think you'll need.

To calculate your yarn needs there are two methods: one based on yardage (length), and the other based on weight. Both figures are printed on the label of most skeins.

YARN BY YARDAGE

Step 1 —Draw each section of the garment (front, back, sleeve, and any collar or pockets), noting the number of inches for the width and depth of each piece. Write these measurements next to each section they represent, as shown below.

```
1      22
    25        25     18        16
                          9
    21        21         2
```

Step 2 —Find the <u>total square inches of the garment</u> (the <u>grand total</u>) by multiplying the length by the width of each piece and adding the sums together.

This works easily on the front and back, which are basically rectangular shapes. The sleeves require additional explanation. To determine square inches you need to work with a rectangular shape, use the widest measure of the sleeve as the width of the rectangle and draw dotted lines to the longest point of the sleeve, which will be the length of the rectangle. (This does not include the cuff, which is calculated as a separate rectangle.)

```
2     25   Front and Back   25      525  front
     ×21                    ×21     +525  back
      525                   525    1050  square inches
```

a)Multiply the width and length of the center rectangle.

b)Subtract the width of the center rectangle from the total width of the sleeve. Divide by two to get the width of each side rectangle.

c)Multiply the width and length of one side rectangle.

(The triangular section of the sleeve cuts this rectangle in half. We have just determined the square inches for two halves, therefore we have the square inches for the whole sleeve.)

d)Add the square inches from the center rectangle to the square inches from the side rectangle to get the square inches for one sleeve. Multiply this figure by two to get the figure for two sleeves.

```
a)  18″              b)  22″  (total width)
    ×9″                  -9″  (center rectangle)
   162 (center rectangle)  13″ ÷ 2 = 6 ½″ (width of each rectangle)

c)    16″            d)  162″          266″
    × 6.5″              +104″          ×  2
   104.0 (one side rectangle)  266″ (one sleeve)  532″ (two sleeves)
```

Step 3 —Add the total inches for the front and back to the total inches for both sleeves (plus whatever other pieces you might have on your garment) to get the <u>grand total</u>.

```
3        1050″ (front and back)
        +532″ (two sleeves)
        1582″ (total square inches in sweater)
```

Step 4 —Knit a 4″x 4″ swatch with the yarn you've chosen for your garment. Lay it on a flat surface and carefully measure the length and width to get an accurate measure of the square inches. Then, unravel the swatch and keep track of how many yards of yarn have been used.

```
4      4″           16 square inches
      ×4″           contains 10 yards     4″ × 4″ swatch
      16″ = swatch
```

Step 5 —Next find out how many swatches equal the sweater. Divide the <u>grand total</u> (total square inches in sweater) by the number of square inches in the swatch.

```
5          1582 ÷ 16 = 97.62 or 98 swatches
```

Step 6 —Multiply that figure by the amount of yardage in the swatch to find out the amount of yarn needed to knit the sweater.

```
6          10 (yards)
         ×98 (swatches)
         980 (total yards needed)
```

YARN BY WEIGHT

This method works almost the same way.

Step 1 —Find the <u>grand total</u> of square inches for the garment. See Steps 1 and 2 in Yarn by Yardage

Step 2 —Find the square inches for the swatch.
4″ × 4″ = 16″ swatch   4″ × 4″ swatch

Step 3 —Divide the <u>grand total</u> by the square inches of the swatch to determine the number of swatches which would make your garment. See Step 5 in Yarn by Yardage

Step 4 —Instead of unraveling your swatch, weigh it on a postal or kitchen scale. Multiply the weight of the swatch by the number of swatches you need and you'll have the total weight.
33 ×.04 = 13.2 total oz.

BASIC STITCHES

The art of knitting is based on two simple stitches: the knit stitch and the purl stitch. If you know these two stitches, you can knit almost anything. This section provides a quick refresher course on the six basic knitting skills: knitting and purling, casting on and binding off, increasing and decreasing. We are presenting the basic approaches to these skills, so you can learn quickly and get on to the more exciting part—knitting!

THE KNIT STITCH

The knit stitch is vertical and V-shaped. It is usually found on the right side of a garment. Every knit stitch is a purl stitch on its reverse side.

This is a knit stitch

THE PURL STITCH

The purl stitch is a horizontal raised loop. Every purl stitch is a knit stitch on its reverse side.

This is a purl stitch

Step 1 —Begin by holding the needle with the cast-on stitches in your left hand. Take the yarn in your right hand as shown above. (You can hold the yarn in either your left or right hand, whichever is more comfortable for you.)

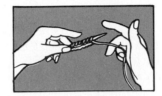

Step 1 —Hold the needle with the cast-on stitches in your left hand. Take the yarn in your right hand as shown above, holding it in whatever way feels most comfortable.

Step 2 —Pick up the other needle with your right hand. With the yarn held in back, insert the needle through the front of the stitch and under the needle held in your left hand. Using your right index finger, wrap the yarn around the back of the right needle in a counterclockwise motion. The yarn is now between the two needles. Pull it tight.

Step 2 —Pick up the other needle in your right hand. Hold the yarn to the front and insert the needle into the front of the stitch. Wrap the yarn around the back of the right needle counterclockwise. The yarn is now between the needles. Pull the yarn tight.

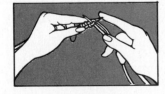

Step 3 —Bring the loop on the right needle forward and through the stitch. Pull the stitch off the left needle. This loop forms the first knit stitch. (Although this may seem awkward at first, you will gain speed with practice, and soon it will become second nature.)

Step 3 —Now there is a loop around both needles. Move the right needle under the left needle and through the loop. Pull the left needle out of the stitch. This loop forms the first purl stitch.

A KNITTING SECRET

Have you ever wondered how people can knit while "juggling" two needles and wrapping the yarn at the same time? There are many ways to hold the needles and yarn, but the goal is to find the way which is most comfortable for you. We both taught ourselves how to knit, and for many years have used a technique which is unique but works well for us.

Here's what we do. Rest the righthand needle on your right leg. This way the needle is stationary and the weight is on the leg instead of the arms. Since you're not worried about juggling both needles, you can focus on wrapping the yarn around the needles, and the knitting will go much faster.

CASTING ON

Casting on is the process of forming the loops which become the first row of stitches. These will be the bottom edge of the garment.

Step 1 —Form a loop (a slip knot) and hold it in your left hand. Insert the needle held in your right hand through the loop. Pull tight.

Step 2 —Grasp the two yarn strands with your left hand, separate the two strands with your thumb and index finger. Pull the needle downward to form a V-shape with the yarn. Keep the tension tight.

Step 3 —With the needle, pick up the yarn that is closest to you, from your thumb (outside strand).

Step 4 —Now pick up the yarn strand that is farthest away from you off your index finger.

 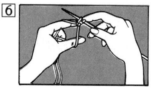

Step 5 —Pull the needle toward you and through the loop extending off your thumb to form the second stitch on the needle.

Step 6 —With the thumb and index finger of your left hand, pull the loop tight against the needle. (Make sure the cast-on stitches are pulled tight, so the bottom edge of the garment isn't loose and baggy.)

TIP
• *Generally, cast on with a needle that is two sizes smaller than the ones used to knit the body of the garment. (This is the same size needle you'll use to knit the ribbing.) If you find that the first row is too loose after you've knit the ribbing, rip it out and cast on using an even smaller size. Just be sure to transfer the stitches to the proper needle when you begin knitting.*

For example, if you're knitting the ribbing with #8 needles and find that the first row isn't tight enough, go down to a #6 for the cast-on row. Be sure to transfer back to the #8 needle when you begin to knit the ribbing.

BINDING OFF

Binding off is a way of eliminating stitches from a row. This can be done at any time within a sweater and is usually done on the final row.

You can bind off on a knit or purl row; however, if you bind off on a purl row, hold the yarn at the back of the needle for Steps 2 and 3 .

Step 1 —Knit the first two stitches on the needle.

Step 2 —With the lefthand needle, pick up the first knit stitch.

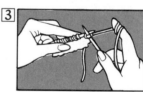

Step 3 —Making sure to hold the yarn tightly at the back, slip the first stitch over the second stitch and off the needle. This will leave one stitch on the righthand needle. Continue this process until you have removed as many stitches as you desire. Be sure to keep an even tension to create a good edge.

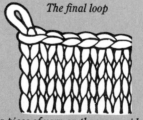 

The final loop

Tie a piece of yarn on the wrong side. With a needle, pull the yarn through the final loop and secure to the seam edge

TIP
• *For a tighter bind-off edge, rather than knitting the bind-off row, simply transfer the first two stitches to the right needle (as if to purl) and lift the first stitch over the second (as in Step 2). Continue this process of lifting the first stitch over the second until all the stitches are removed. The final loop should be secured, or it will unravel. This method of binding off is especially good for cottons and for other yarns that don't have much elasticity.*

INCREASING

Increasing is a way to add stitches to a row to create shaping. This usually occurs on the outer edges of a flat piece, at the armhole, shoulder, and neck shaping. For circular knitting, all increasing occurs within the garment, as there are no outer edges.

SINGLE INCREASES

Bar increase—This is the easiest way to add a stitch to a row. Knit a stitch, but instead of removing it from the needle, knit into the back of the original stitch again.

Single "bar" increase on a knit row

M1 (make one or raised increase)—Pick up the horizontal strand of yarn between stitches and put it on the lefthand needle to form a new loop. Knit into the back of the loop to create a stitch that doesn't leave a hole in the fabric. Knitting or purling into the front of the stitch leaves a hole beneath, which works nicely for lace stitches.

Single "bar" increase on a purl row

yo (yarn over)—Wrap yarn over (or around) needle. This forms a hole in the fabric. This is sometimes shown as "yrn" for "yarn round needle."

DOUBLE INCREASES

When you have to increase many stitches within a small section of a garment, it's best to use double increases. These are paired additions that are made on either side of a center stitch and are more visible and decorative than a single increase.

K1, yo—Good for garments with lace patterns because there is a line of double holes on each side of the seam stitch. The seam stitch remains constant.

K1-B—Take stitch from the row below the seam stitch and put it on the left needle and knit into it. Knit seam stitch itself.

M1, and knit into back of it.

DECREASING

Decreasing is a way of removing stitches from a row to create shaping. This usually occurs on the outer edges of a flat piece, at the armhole, shoulder, and neck shaping. It's only advisable to decrease one or two stitches at the beginning or end of a row. If you have many stitches to remove, bind them off. For circular knitting, all decreasing occurs within the garment, as there are no outer edges.

SINGLE DECREASES

K2tog—The simplest decrease is to knit two stitches together. If you insert the right needle through the front of the two stitches, the decrease will slant toward the right. If you knit through the back of the two stitches, the decrease will slant toward the left.

Single decrease to the right

s1 1, K1, psso—Slip stitch from lefthand needle without knitting it, knit the following stitch, pull the slipped stitch over the knit stitch and off the righthand needle. This decrease will create a slant to the left.

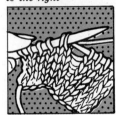

Single decrease to the left

TIP
• *A good rule of thumb to remember if you're using stockinette stitch is to s1 1, K1, psso at the beginning of the row to create a slant to the left. K2tog at the end of the row to create a slant to the right.*

DOUBLE DECREASES

Vertical—Slip 2 stitches knitwise, inserting needle into second stitch, then first one; knit next stitch, then pass 2 slipped stitches over knitted one (great for V-neckline).

K3tog, tbl—Knit 3 stitches together through back of all 3 loops.

s1 1, K2tog, psso—Slip stitch knitwise, knit next 2 stitches together, pass the slipped stitch over the knitted ones.

KNITTING IN THE ROUND

Circular knitting, or knitting in the round, is a technique that has long been a part of the knitting tradition.

Whether you decide to knit from the bottom up or from the top down, you can create some very interesting and unusual designs using circular knitting. Working from the top down is the perfect way to make a skirt, for instance. What could be more convenient than being able to try the garment on as you knit, making sure the waist and hips fit, and finally settling on a length by actually seeing how it looks! (Not to mention the joy of not having to put in a zipper, buttonholes, flaps, or darts.) Of course, you can add all of these details if you wish, but for those who like simplicity, this method is easy. All you need to do is add elastic to the waist (see page 79).

There are two different ways to knit in the round. You can use a large circular needle, which is made of two straight needles connected by a flexible nylon wire. It's a great tool for any large item (either tubular or flat) because it can hold a lot of stitches and allow the weight of the garment to be supported on your lap instead of by your arms.

The other method is to use double-pointed needles, which are usually sold in sets of four and are all the same size. These sets are available in various lengths.

CIRCULAR NEEDLES

Let's explore the difference of knitting with circular needles as opposed to double-pointed needles. Although the approach is basically the same, the techniques are very different. You may find circular needles much easier to knit with because you don't have to change needles. When you reach the end of the first row, or "round," you simply knit the very first stitch next, creating the beginning of the tube. This point of combining the last stitch and the first stitch is also where you would place a marker, indicating the beginning of the round. Slip the marker to the next round after completing each round; that way the marker won't get "stuck" in the knitted fabric.

To knit successfully on circular needles the stitches should reach between the needle tips without stretching the fabric. You will know when the circumference of the needle is too large because you will find it is difficult to work the stitches. If there are no needles available that are short enough to allow you to work the stitches comfortably, change to double-pointed needles to complete the knitting. (This may happen if you are knitting a ribbed cuff off a dolman sweater. Often you will be instructed to decrease stitches as the cuff progresses, and as a result you will have fewer stitches to work and a harder time knitting them.)

DOUBLE-POINTED NEEDLES

With double-pointed needles you can cast on in two ways. If you are a beginner, start by casting all of your stitches onto a straight double-pointed needle, count the total, and divide by three. Place the first third onto the first needle, the second third onto the second needle, and the third, onto the third needle to form a triangle. The fourth needle will be the free needle. It's important that all the stitches are kept facing the center on the first row. If any stitches are twisted, adjust at this point; you won't be able to change them later. Knit the first round, and when you come to the strand of yarn that indicates the beginning of the row, place a marker. You have now completed your first row or "round." As you move from one needle to the next, be sure to pull the thread tightly to avoid slack stitches which would show on the finished garment.

TIPS

- *Knitting in the round can be used when making a crew or turtleneck collar, or when picking up stitches to knit cuffs off the sleeve of a dolman sweater.*
- *Needle markers keep your place within a row: a marker will tell you when it's the end of one round and the beginning of another, or the point of increase or decrease.*

PROS AND CONS

There are a few real bonuses to knitting in the round, aside from not having to sew side seams! You are always working on the right side of the fabric, which is wonderful for working jacquard stitches. It's less confusing when you can see the right side of what you are working on. If you are knitting stripes, realize that they will be slightly staggered at the marker point (where one round meets the next).

Circular knitting is not well suited for patterns that call for bobbins, such as argyles and plaids, because these patterns depend on carrying colors from one point to another on a row to create the design. The only way to achieve these motifs is to knit on straight needles and use bobbins (see page 62).

Because you are always knitting on the right side of the fabric, many of the basic stitches are changed. You must remember that you will be knitting the knit stitches and purling the purl stitches. For stockinette stitch, knit every round; garter stitch (which is normally knit every row) is created by knitting one round, purling the next, and so on.

The only way to achieve shaping with circular knitting is through increasing and decreasing within the garment. Single increasing and decreasing will give a more gradual line of increase than will double, although double has a more decorative quality, which works well for shoulder seams on raglans and semiraglans.

WHAT IS GAUGE?

Gauge is one of the most important words in the knitter's vocabulary, and it is *the* one concept that you must understand to design and knit your own garments successfully. Gauge refers to the number of stitches (horizontal) in one inch and the number of rows (vertical) in one inch. You measure the gauge by knitting a 4″ × 4″ square, a "swatch," with your chosen yarn and needles. Cast on enough stitches to knit at least a four-inch row. Begin knitting in a stockinette stitch (knit one row, purl one row, and repeat). When the piece measures at least four inches long, bind off loosely. Lay the swatch on a flat surface and pin the corners, making sure the swatch isn't stretched. Take a measuring tape and count the number of stitches across and the number of rows lengthwise within the four inches of the swatch. Divide by four (the number of inches) to see how many stitches and rows there are within one inch. This is your gauge.

WHY KNIT A GAUGE SWATCH?

Knitting a swatch may seem like a waste of time, but this step ensures an accurate fit for the garment. Remember the warning you've seen printed in bold type on most patterns, Be sure to check gauge. This is not to scare you but to indicate the importance of taking the time to knit your test swatch.

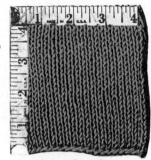
Gauge Swatch

If you multiply the gauge by the number of inches in either the horizontal or vertical measurements of your garment, you will know how many stitches or rows you have to knit. For example, if you decide that you want your sweater to be 40″ wide at the hipline, take half this measurement to get the number of inches for the front and back (20″). If your gauge is 4sts = 1″ (stitch gauge), multiply 20 by 4. This will give you 80 stitches, the number of stitches to cast on.

This also applies to the vertical measurement, or the "row gauge." If you decide you want your sweater to be 24″ long and your gauge is 5rws = 1″, multiply 24 by 5 to get 120, the number of rows in the sweater.

For example, in the illustration above, there are 16 stitches and 20 rows in the four-inch measurement. When you divide each number by four you get four stitches per inch and five rows per inch.

EVERY FRACTION OF A STITCH IS IMPORTANT

Occasionally, you may not have an even number of stitches and rows per inch in the gauge swatch. For instance, there may be 22 stitches across a four-inch horizontal measure. You would divide 22 by 4 and see that you have 5.5 stitches per inch. It's very important not to round off any fraction of a stitch for the

Stitch change

Stitch change

Stitch change and needle change

Swatching

following reason: correct fit! Let's say your gauge is 5.5 stitches per inch and you want to make each front and back piece of your sweater 20 inches wide. To determine the proper number of stitches to cast on, multiply the stitch gauge (5.5sts = 1″) by the number of inches (20) to get a total of 110 stitches. But what if you weren't careful when you were measuring and said, "Oh well, I'll just round it to 6 stitches to the inch: 6 × 20 = 120 stitches. The difference is 10 stitches or almost two inches difference! And this is just for the front! If you knit the back the same way, you would have four inches more than you had originally planned on. You can imagine the surprise of trying on your sweater to discover the fit was four inches too big. So be as careful as you can when measuring your gauge. Every fraction of a stitch is important.

TENSION AND SWATCHING

Several other issues are directly related to gauge: tension and swatching. Tension refers to how much you "pull" on the yarn as you knit, that is, how tight or loose your knitting appears. It's important to develop a consistent tension with the yarn to ensure a consistent gauge. You'll know you're applying the right amount of tension when the stitches can be worked easily. If the stitches are too tight, it will be difficult to insert the righthand needle, and your project will go slowly. If the stitches are too loose, they can slip off the needle too soon, and the piece will not hold its shape.

Most of the adventure in knitting comes with experimenting. This is what "swatching" is all about. When you find a yarn you like, buy one skein and make some test swatches. We like to try the same yarn with several different-size needles (based on the size recommended on the yarn label) to see which swatch we like best. Begin by knitting a 4″ × 4″ swatch. If you prefer, bind off and start a new swatch with a different needle size, or simply switch from one needle size to another and continue knitting up the swatch with a new set of needles. Try several different stitches if you like. Remember, the gauge of each stitch pattern is different, so it's important to knit your gauge swatch in the stitch you will be using for your garment.

TIP
• *Ribbing gauge is different from stockinette gauge. That's why the ribbing is usually knit on smaller needles. You may want to begin your gauge swatch with ribbing to determine the gauge, then switch to a larger needle size for testing your pattern stitches.*

HOW TO TAKE YOUR MEASUREMENTS

Taking measurements often makes people feel self-conscious and uncomfortable, but it's the only way to ensure that your garment will fit properly. Try to take measurements in front of a mirror. A mirror helps you to check your posture and to see that the measuring tape falls where it should. If you're measuring someone else, have the person stand in front of you, facing the mirror, and take his or her measurements from the side. To record measurements, use the charts on page 160.

Wear the appropriate undergarments and, if the measurements include skirt length, the shoes to be worn with the skirt. Hold the tape taut, but not tight, against the body. It's a good idea to take your measurements regularly to keep track of changes. And never fudge the numbers—after all, only you know them.

For sweaters you need these measurements: (a) neck, circumference at the base (or see Knitter's Guide Charts on pages 19-20); (b) shoulder width, length from neck base to shoulder bone; (c) chest, (or bust), measure at fullest point, keeping tape horizontal; (d) waist, put tape measure around midriff, holding the ends together, and measure where it falls naturally; (e) hip, measure at fullest point, usually eight inches below the waistline; (f) bicep, measure fullest part of upper arm; (g) armlength, bend arm slightly, take from shoulder bone to elbow, then from elbow to wrist; (h) wrist, measure slightly above wrist bone.

The style you choose will determine the armhole depth and garment length, but have these measurements handy as a reference: (i) underarm to waist, placing the tape two or three inches below the top of the armpit, measure to waist; (j) shoulder to waist, measure from shoulder bone to waist; (k) skirt length, measure from waist to whatever finished length you desire.

STANDARD BODY MEASUREMENTS

Here is a chart of standard body measurements to help you if you are working on a garment for another person and know his or her approximate size but not specific measurements. It's always better to take actual measurements, but this reference will help fill in the gaps.

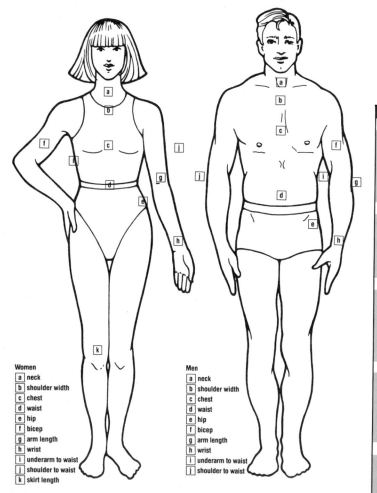

Women
- a neck
- b shoulder width
- c chest
- d waist
- e hip
- f bicep
- g arm length
- h wrist
- i underarm to waist
- j shoulder to waist
- k skirt length

Men
- a neck
- b shoulder width
- c chest
- d waist
- e hip
- f bicep
- g arm length
- h wrist
- i underarm to waist
- j shoulder to waist

Size					
Infants	6 mos.	12 mos.	18 mos.	2	4
Chest	19	20	21	22	23
Shoulder width	7¾	8	8½	9¼	9¾
Shoulder length	2¼	2¼	2½	2¾	3
Back of neck	3¼	3½	3½	3¾	3¾
Armhole depth	3¾	4	4¼	4½	4¾
Sleeve upper arm	6	6½	7	7½	8
Sleeve seam length	6½	7½	8½	9½	10½
Crotch length	6½	7	7½	8	8½
Children	4	6	8	10	12
Chest	24	25	26	28	30
Shoulder width	9¾	10½	11	11¾	12¼
Shoulder length	3	3¼	3½	3¾	4
Back of neck	3¾	4	4	4¼	4¼
Armhole depth	5	5¼	5½	6	6½
Sleeve upper arm	8½	9	9½	10½	11
Sleeve seam length	11½	12	13	14	15

Teenage Girls/Women	6	8	10	12	14	16
Bust	30½	31½	32½	34	36	38
Shoulder width	12¼	12½	13	13¼	14	14¾
Shoulder length	4	4⅛	4¼	4¼	4½	4¾
Back of neck	4¼	4¼	4½	4¾	5	5¼
Armhole depth	6½	6¾	7	7¼	7½	7¾
Underarm to waist	7	7¼	7½	7¾	8	8¼
Sleeve upper arm	11¼	11½	12	12½	13	13½
Sleeve seam length	16½	16¾	17	17¼	17½	18
	18	20	40	42	44	46
Bust	40	42	44	46	48	50
Shoulder width	15½	16	16¾	17¼	18¼	18½
Shoulder length	5	5⅛	5¼	5¼	5½	5½
Back of neck	5½	5¾	6¼	6¾	7¼	7½
Armhole depth	8	8¼	8½	9	9¼	9½
Underarm to waist	8¼	8½	8½	8¾	8¾	9
Sleeve upper arm	14	14½	15	15½	16	16½
Sleeve seam length	18	18¼	18¼	18½	18½	18½
Teenage Boys/Men	30-32	32-34	36-38	40-42	44-46	48-50
Chest	31	33	37	41	45	49
Shoulder width	13	14	16	17	18¼	19¼
Shoulder length	4¼	4½	5¼	5¼	6	6¼
Back of neck	4½	5	5½	6	6¼	6¾
Armhole depth	7½	8	8½	9	9½	10
Sleeve upper arm	12½	13	14½	15½	16½	17½
Sleeve seam length	16	17½	19	19½	20	20½

WHAT IS EASE?

A sweater made to exactly the same size as your measurements would be extremely uncomfortable to wear. The garment would cling to your chest, and you wouldn't be able to move your arms. Those extra inches you need in a pattern are for ease. Designers use ease two ways, for movement and for style. Every pattern needs ease for movement. How much ease you want for style is up to you. You can choose whether you want a close-fitting set-in sleeve sweater or a loose-fitting dolman sleeve. You can also judge how much ease a pattern has by its description and measurements. The Ease Chart gives you the relative amounts of ease to use.

Bust Measurements	32	34	36	38	40
Converted to sweater measurements					
Very tight fit	30	32	34	36	38
Tight fit	32–33	34–35	36–37	38–39	40–41
Standard fit	34	36	38	40	42
Comfortable fit	36	38	40	42	44
Roomy fit	37	39+	41+	43+	45+

TIPS

• *Choose your style and remember your personal preferences. Do you like clothing which is loose, tight, or somewhere in between? Keep in mind whether the garment will be worn next to the skin or over other clothing. Also, take into account the kind of yarn you will be using. Wool has far more elasticity than linen or cotton and will hold its shape differently even using the same pattern.*

• *To get an idea of what ease you prefer, try on your favorite clothes, then measure them on a flat surface, comparing the clothes measurements against your own body measurements. If you have a garment with just the style you want, copy its measurements.*

• *For a more complex garment, one with a collar or lapels, buy a sewing pattern in your size and measure the pattern pieces (minus the seam allowances). When you're knitting the garment, you can check the fit by comparing the knitted piece against your full-size pattern piece.*

• *Keep a file of the measurements of family and friends in your Workbook so you'll be prepared when a holiday or birthday is approaching. A yearly update might be a good idea.*

KNITTER'S GUIDE CHARTS

These charts will be an invaluable tool and a necessary part of the designing process. You will refer to them at various points when writing and charting your pattern to determine the measurements for the back of the neck, the underarm to shoulder measurement, the shoulder shaping, round neck shaping, and sleeve cap shaping. The measurement charts included are standard clothing sizes for men, women, and children.

These measurements vary with the age of the person for whom you are designing the sweater. It is important to use these charts as a guide, but remember, they are not absolute. You may want to add or subtract from them to suit your own particular needs.

UNDERARM TO SHOULDER

This measurement refers to the distance between the first armhole decrease and the shoulder and is used for a standard-fitting sweater. It would not apply in making a dolman-type sleeve or any other style with an extremely low armhole. Remember always to measure from the shoulder straight down to the point of the armhole decrease, not along the curve of the armhole, which would give you a longer measurement.

FOR STANDARD-FITTING GARMENTS

	Chest size	Number of inches
Child	20–23	5½"
Child	24–27	6"
Child	28–31	6½"
Female	32–35	7"
Female	36–39	7½"
Female/Male	40–43/32–35	8"
Female/Male	44–47/36–39	9"
Female/Male	48+/40–43	9½"
Male	44–47	10"
Male	48+	10½"

FOR BULKY GARMENTS

If you are making garments to be worn over other clothing, you will have to increase all the measurements (see Ease Chart above). This chart should help you determine how many more inches to allot for the underarm to shoulder.

	Chest size	Number of inches
All sizes/children		add ½"
Female/Male	32–39	add 1"
Female/Male	40–47	add 1½"
Female/Male	48+	add 2"

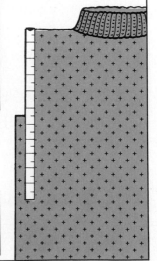

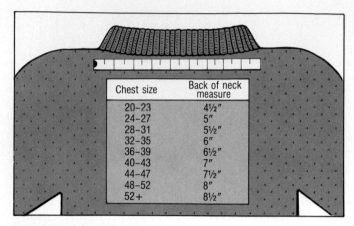

Chest size	Back of neck measure
20–23	4½″
24–27	5″
28–31	5½″
32–35	6″
36–39	6½″
40–43	7″
44–47	7½″
48–52	8″
52+	8½″

BACK OF NECK

Because the neck can be measured at different points, this chart will help to create more "standard" measurements. It's fine to allot a slightly larger amount of space for the neck opening, because most necklines are ribbed, which will pull the neckline in considerably. Sizes for men and women are the same, but pay attention when making a sweater for someone with a large neck. In that case it would be best to measure the neck and divide in half for each front and back.

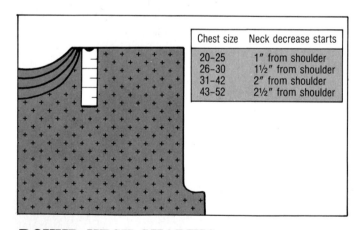

Chest size	Neck decrease starts
20–25	1″ from shoulder
26–30	1½″ from shoulder
31–42	2″ from shoulder
43–52	2½″ from shoulder

ROUND NECK SHAPING

When designing a round neck sweater, you have to determine at what point the first neck decreases will occur. This chart is a guide for a standard type of crew neck, which is high. For a lower round neck, use your own judgment.

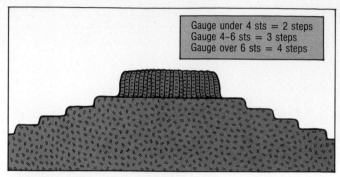

| Gauge under 4 sts = 2 steps |
| Gauge 4–6 sts = 3 steps |
| Gauge over 6 sts = 4 steps |

SHOULDER SHAPING

This chart applies to a sloped shoulder, as opposed to a shoulder which you bind off all in one row. For a sloped shoulder, bind off in steps to create the proper fit. The number of steps used for decreasing will depend on the stitch gauge.

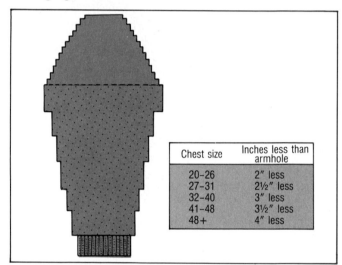

Chest size	Inches less than armhole
20–26	2″ less
27–31	2½″ less
32–40	3″ less
41–48	3½″ less
48+	4″ less

SLEEVE CAP SHAPING

The length of the sleeve cap has to be several inches shorter than the underarm to shoulder measure of the front and back to ensure that the sleeve fits into the body of the sweater. This chart will tell you how many inches less the sleeve cap should be. For instance, if you are a size 32″ bust, you already know that you should allow 7″ for the underarm to shoulder measurement. The sleeve cap should be 3″ shorter than the armhole measurement, 7 − 3 = 4. Therefore, your sleeve cap should be 4″ long.

FOLLOWING KNITTING INSTRUCTIONS

Most knitting instructions could confuse anyone. At first glance a knitting pattern looks like a foreign language; at second glance you still may not be able to decipher that particular pattern stitch. Don't despair. Take our page on abbreviations (see page 175) and use it. Try translating the instructions and look on the bright side—the more you use the abbreviations, the easier it will be to remember them. When you write your own patterns, the abbreviations will save you a lot of time.

MULTIPLES AND REPEATS

Pattern stitches repeat a sequence of stitches shown between two asterisks. That sequence is called a multiple. Here's an example of a multiple of six stitches plus three selvedge (or border) stitches.

Row 1 *P3, K1, P1, K1*, P3
Row 2 K3, *P3, K3*
Row 3 Repeat from row 1

The six stitches between the asterisks make up the multiple. The three stitches before and after the asterisks are selvedge stitches which create a flat border on each edge of the knitted piece.

When designing your own garment, the multiple of a pattern stitch is very important. The total number of stitches on the needle should be divisible by the multiple or the pattern won't work. You should use a multiple that divides into the total number of stitches there are in the first row of the body of the garment. For instance, if the design calls for 100 stitches, a multiple of 12 wouldn't work, but a multiple of 10 would. Figure this out by dividing the number of stitches in the multiple into the total number of stitches. Realize that adding stitches to shape the garment will change its size, although you may add several selvedge stitches on each side of the garment if you want to fill out a measurement. These stitches can be used to create the seam, and don't have to show on the right side of the garment.

The section on Shorthand Symbols presents another method of reading multiple and repeat patterns, which uses a visual graph.

ADAPTING KNITTING INSTRUCTIONS

Have you ever found a great pattern for a sweater and set out to buy the yarn, only to discover the yarn is out of stock or discontinued? What do you do?

You can either find another yarn that has the same gauge and knit it according to the pattern, or you can choose an entirely different yarn and adjust the pattern. (This is only necessary if the yarn you choose has a different gauge.)

Here's how to adapt a pattern for a yarn of a different weight:

Step 1 —Choose your yarn and knit a 4″ × 4″ swatch to get the gauge.

gauge
swatch
4sts = 1″
5rws = 1″

Step 2 —Draw a schematic diagram (see page 34) of the pattern (there may be one provided), and put down the dimensions you want.

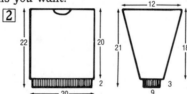

Step 3a —Multiply the "stitch gauge" (stitches per inch) by the horizontal measurements on your schematic.

3a	20″ ×4sts 80 sts	9″ ×4sts 36 sts	12″ ×4sts 48 sts

Step 3b —Multiply the "row gauge" (rows per inch) by the vertical measurement.

3b	2″ rib ×5rws 10rws	22″ ×5rws 110rws	20″ ×5rws 100rws	3″ rib ×5rws 15rws	18″ ×5rws 90rws	21″ ×5rws 105rws

Step 4 —Write down these totals on your drawing. Now you have the number of stitches and rows you need to work your pattern. Be sure to adapt the increases and decreases to your gauge.

This can be done by taking the original gauge and the new gauge and figuring out the percentage of increase or decrease you'll be dealing with. For example, if the original gauge was 3sts = 1″ and the new gauge is 6sts = 1″, we can see that the new gauge is twice as many stitches per inch. If the original instructions called for us to bind off four stitches for the underarm, we would have to double that number for our new pattern.

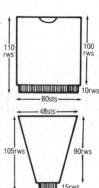

TIP
• *To avoid confusion, photocopy the pattern, white out all the printed numbers, and replace them with your new figures.*

SYMBOLCRAFT

If you feel confused or uncomfortable about reading abbreviations for stitch patterns, take heart! There is another way. Many knitters now use symbolcraft to chart their stitch patterns (multiple and repeats) instead of written instructions, because with symbolcraft it's often much easier to visualize where you are and what you're doing. Symbolcraft assigns a symbol to each type of stitch. The Japanese developed the system as a way of translating Western patterns; other designers took the idea and created their own set of symbols. Knitters like symbolcraft because it guides them through the work visually, row by row.

WHAT IT LOOKS LIKE

Patterns are drawn on a grid—one stitch and one row equals one box. The bottom line of the grid is the first row and right side of the work; the first stitch is in the righthand corner. All odd-numbered rows are marked on the right and move right to left. The even-numbered rows are the wrong side of the work. They are marked on the left and move left to right. As you can see from the illustration, the grid lets you know exactly where you are—the right or wrong side, and which row.

There is no universal symbolcraft. Often you'll see this symbol (|) for knit and this symbol (-) for purl. We've included examples of other commonly used symbols for your use. After practicing with them, you may want to create whatever symbols work best for your pattern.

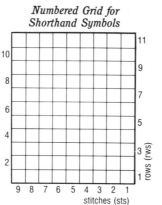

Numbered Grid for Shorthand Symbols

MULTIPLES AND REPEATS

We've also included symbols that represent pattern stitches, such as a cable stitch. At first, it may seem difficult to have an arrow represent a sequence of stitches. However, most of your knitting patterns will have a pattern stitch repeat several times in the work. You'll learn the pattern stitch fairly quickly and not have to refer to written instructions. At that point symbols can guide you to put the pattern stitch in the proper place. If your pattern stitch does not change in the piece, you probably won't have to plot a grid of the whole front, back, sleeve, and so on. If you have several pattern stitches, a grid of your whole work will save you from frustrating mistakes.

SYMBOLCRAFT CHART

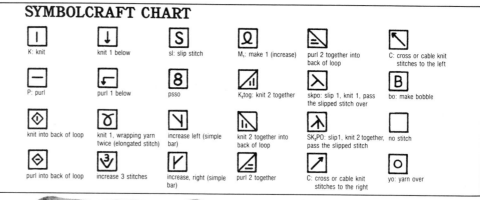

K: knit	knit 1 below	sl: slip stitch	M₁: make 1 (increase)	purl 2 together into back of loop	C: cross or cable knit stitches to the left
P: purl	purl 1 below	psso	K₂tog: knit 2 together	skpo: slip 1, knit 1, pass the slipped stitch over	bo: make bobble
knit into back of loop	knit 1, wrapping yarn twice (elongated stitch)	increase left (simple bar)	knit 2 together into back of loop	SK₂PO: slip1, knit 2 together, pass the slipped stitch	no stitch
purl into back of loop	increase 3 stitches	increase, right (simple bar)	purl 2 together	C: cross or cable knit stitches to the right	yo: yarn over

A CHARTED AND WRITTEN PATTERN

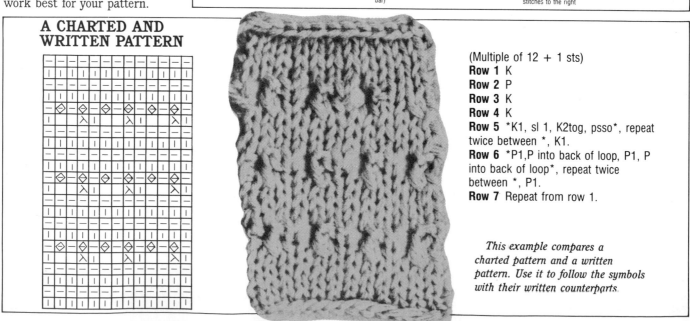

(Multiple of 12 + 1 sts)
Row 1 K
Row 2 P
Row 3 K
Row 4 K
Row 5 *K1, sl 1, K2tog, psso*, repeat twice between *, K1.
Row 6 *P1,P into back of loop, P1, P into back of loop*, repeat twice between *, P1.
Row 7 Repeat from row 1.

This example compares a charted pattern and a written pattern. Use it to follow the symbols with their written counterparts.

SIMPLE STITCHES

Now that you know the basics of how to knit and purl, why not expand your vocabulary and try some combinations of the two? It's amazing what fun and attractive stitches you can make using only the knit stitch and the purl stitch. In this section, we're presenting some of our favorite simple stitches. When you're comfortable with these, why not try a cable, openwork, or Aran stitch, which you'll find in the pages that follow.

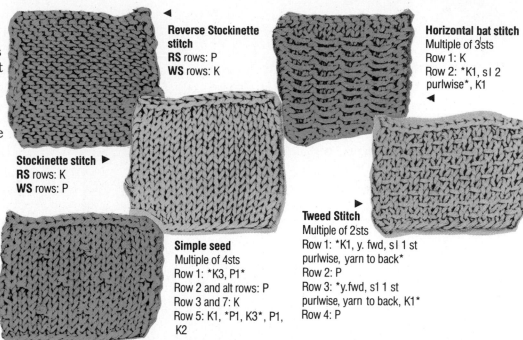

Reverse Stockinette stitch
RS rows: P
WS rows: K

Stockinette stitch ►
RS rows: K
WS rows: P

Horizontal bat stitch
Multiple of 3 sts
Row 1: K
Row 2: *K1, sl 2 purlwise*, K1

Simple seed
Multiple of 4 sts
Row 1: *K3, P1*
Row 2 and alt rows: P
Row 3 and 7: K
Row 5: K1, *P1, K3*, P1, K2

Tweed Stitch
Multiple of 2 sts
Row 1: *K1, y. fwd, sl 1 st purlwise, yarn to back*
Row 2: P
Row 3: *y.fwd, sl 1 st purlwise, yarn to back, K1*
Row 4: P

Basket stitch Multiple of 10 sts ▲
Rows 1-6: *K5, P5*
Rows 7-12: *P5, K5*

Pique Diamonds: ▲
Multiple of 10 sts
Row 1: *K9, P1*
Row 2 and 8: K2, *P7, K3*, P7, K1
Row 3 and 7: P2, *K5, P5*, K5, P3
Row 4 and 6: K4, *P3, K7*, P3, K3
Row 5: P4, *K1, P9*, K1, P5

▲
Triangles on Pleats
Multiple of 10 sts
Row 1: *P2, K8*
Row 2 and 12: *P7, K3*
Row 3 and 11: *P4, K6*
Row 4 and 10: *P5, K5*
Row 5 and 9: *P6, K4*
Row 6 and 8: *P3, K7*
Row 7: *P8, K2*

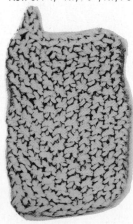

◄ **Moss or Rice Stitch**
Multiple of any number of sts
Row 1: *K1, P1*
Row 2 and following rows: K the purl sts and P the knit sts

OPENWORK OR LACE STITCHES

These delicate stitches often look more complicated than they really are. They are created by increasing and decreasing frequently within the same row, to create holes in the fabric. Practice reading over one pattern, with the abbreviations page at hand, and you will soon find that these patterns can be quite enjoyable.

◄
Lacy Entrelacs Multiple of 13 + 1 st
Row 1: K1, *K2, skpo, K4, K2tog, K2, yon, K1, yon*, K1
Row 2 and alt rows: K1, * P *, K1
Row 3: K1, *yon, K2, skpo, K2, K2tog, K2, yon, K3*, K1
Row 5: K1, *K1, yon, K2, skpo, K2tog, K2, yon, K4*, K1
Row 7: K1, *yon, K1, yon, K2, skpo, K4, K2tog, K2*, K1
Row 9: K1, *K3, yon, K2, skpo, K2, K2tog, K2, yon*, K1
Row 11: K1, *K4, yon, K2, skpo, K2tog, K2, yon, K1*, K1
Row 13: repeat from row 1

►
Broken and lacy diagonals Multiple of 12 + 2 sts
Row 1: K1, *y.fwd, K2tog, y.fwd, K2tog, K8*, K1
Row 2 and alt. rows: K1, * P *, K1
Row 3: K2, *y.fwd, K2tog, y.fwd, K2tog, K8*, y. fwd, K2 tog, y.fwd, K2tog, K8
Row 5: K3* y.fwd, K2tog, y.fwd, K2tog, K8*, y. fwd, K2tog, y.fwd, K2tog, K7
Row 7: K4, *y.fwd, K2tog, y.fwd, K2tog, K8*, y.fwd, K2tog, y.fwd, K2tog, K6
Row 9: K
Row 11: K9, *sl 1, K1, psso, y.fwd, skpo, y.fwd, K8*, skpo, y.fwd, sl 1, K1, psso, y.fwd, K1
Row 13: K8*, sl 1, K1, psso, y.fwd, skpo, y.fwd, K8*, skpo, y.fwd, sl 1, K1, psso, y. fwd, K2
Row 15: K7, *sl 1, K1, psso, y.fwd, skpo, y.fwd, K8*, skpo, y.fwd, sl 1, K1, psso, y.fwd, K3
Row 17: K6, *sl 1, K1, psso, y.fwd, skpo, y.fwd, K8*, sl 1, K1, psso, y.fwd, skpo, y.fwd, K4
Row 19: K

CABLES

A cable is usually knit in stockinette stitch and looks like a series of twists or intertwining stitches. This effect is created by moving the first group of stitches behind the next group to create the repositioning and twist. Use a short double-pointed needle in a slightly smaller size, or a cable needle to hold the stitches you're transferring until you are ready to work them. If the stitches are held to the front, the cable twists to the left, if held to the back it twists to the right.

Cables usually show up best against simple backgrounds such as reverse stockinette stitch or garter stitch. The look of the cable will vary with the number of stitches transferred, the number of rows worked between the twists, and the direction of the twist itself. Have fun experimenting with your own cable designs by adding stitches to make them wider, or by adding rows between twists to make them longer.

It's best not to have too much shaping (increasing or decreasing) when you're knitting cables, so try to plan your design so you can knit straight up.

You can also use cables to spark up ribbed borders. Simply insert small two-stitch cables at regular intervals, for an elegant and different look.

Braided Cable ▶
Multiple of 9sts
Row 1: (RS) K9
Row 2: P9
Row 3: sl 3sts onto cn and hold to back of work, K3, then K the 3sts from cn (called C6B), K3
Row 4: P9
Row 5–6: repeat rows 1 and 2
Row 7: K3, sl 3sts onto cn and hold to front of work, K3, K 3sts from cn (called C6F)
Row 8: P9

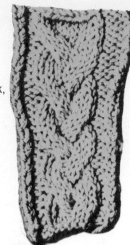

◀ **Interwoven cables**
Multiple of 29sts
Row 1: K1, P1, K3, *(P4, K6) twice, *P3, K1
Row 2 and alt rows: Knit the K sts, Purl the P sts
Row 3: K1, P1, K3, *P4, sl 3sts on cn and hold to front, K3, then K3 from cn ; rep from * once, P3, K1
Row 5: K1, P1; *sl 3sts on cn and hold to front, P2, then K3 from cn (called "cross 5 left"); sl next 2sts on cn and hold to back, K3, then P2 from cn (called "cross 5 right");* rep from * once, cross 5 left, P1, K1.
Row 7: K1, P3, *sl 3sts on cn and hold to back, K3, then K3 from cn , P4*; rep from * once, K3, P1, K1.
Row 9: K1, P1, *cross 5 right, cross 5 left;* rep from * once, cross 5 right, P1, K1

Cabled braid Multiple of 10sts
Row 1: (RS) K10
Row 2: P10
Row 3: K2, *sl 2sts onto cn and hold to front of work, K2, K2 from cn (called C4F), rep from * once more
Row 4: P10
Row 5: *sl 2sts onto cn and hold to back of work, K2, K2 from cn (called C4B), rep from * once more, K2
Row 6: P10
Repeat rows 3–6 for pattern.

◀ **Crowned cable**
Multiple of 14 + 5sts
Row 1: *P5, K9*, P5
Row 2 and alt rows: Knit the K sts, Purl the P sts
Row 3: *P5, sl 2sts onto cn and hold to front, K next 2sts, K 2sts from cn , K1, sl 2sts onto cn and hold to back, K next 2sts, then K the 2sts from cn*, P5

Horseshoe cable ▶
Multiple of 12sts
Row 1: (RS) K12
Row 2: P12 Row 3–4: repeat rows 1 and 2
Row 5: sl 3sts onto cn and hold to back of work, K3, K3 sts from cn (called C6B), sl 3sts onto cn and hold to front of work, K3, then K3sts from cn (C6F)
Row 6: P12
Row 7–8: repeat rows 1 and 2
Pattern repeat is 8 rows.

Cable twist to right or left Multiple of 6sts
Row 1: (RS) K6, P4, K6
Row 2 and alt rows: Knit the K sts, Purl the P sts
Row 3–4: repeat rows 1 and 2
Row 5: sl 3sts onto cn and hold to back, K3, then K 3sts from cn, P4, sl 3sts onto cn and hold to front, K3, then K 3sts from cn
Row 7–8: repeat rows 1 and 2

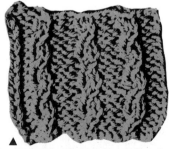

Corded cable rib Multiple of 9 + 3sts
Row 1: *P3, K6*, P3
Row 2, 3, and 4: Knit the K sts and Purl the P sts
Row 5: *P3, sl 3sts to cn and hold to back, K3, K the 3sts from cn *, P3
Row 6–10: repeat rows 2–5

ARAN STITCH PATTERNS

This is just a small sampling of some Aran patterns. Most of these involve crossing stitches to create mock-cable effects.

To cross two sts to the right (called "cross 2R"), pass righthand needle in front of first stitch, knit the second stitch, then knit the first stitch and drop both stitches off lefthand needle together.

To cross two stitches to the left (called "cross 2L"), pass righthand needle behind first stitch, knit the second stitch through the back of the loop, then knit the first stitch and drop both stitches off lefthand needle together.

Try your hand at one of the smaller multiple patterns to begin, and work up to the more complex as you feel comfortable.

Oblique bobble stitch Multiple of 6 + 2sts
Row 1:   K1*, K2, 1 bobble (K 6 in 1 st working alternately through front of loop and back of loop; pass 1 st, 2nd, 3rd, 4th, and 5th sts over the 6th st) P3*, K1
Row 2 Knit the K sts and Purl the P sts
Row 3: K1, *P1, K2, 1 bobble, P 2*, K1
Row 4 Knit the K sts and Purl the P sts. Continue in this way offsetting 1 st to the left at beg of each odd-numbered row

Bobble stitch Make 5 sts in 1 st
Row 1: K2, yfwd, K1 but don't remove st from LH needle, K into st 4 more times
Row 2 turn work to other side, sl 1 st purlwise onto RH needle, P4
Row 3 turn, sl 1 st knitwise onto RH needle, K4
Row 4 turn, P2tog (2 times), P1
Row 5 turn, sl 1 st knitwise, K2tog, psso, 1 st rem on needle

Lattice stitch Multiple of 12sts
Row 1: *K4, P2*
Row 2 and alt rows: Knit the K sts and Purl the P sts
Row 3: *sl 2 to cn and hold to back, K2, K2 from cn, *P2
Row 5: P2, *K2, sl 2 to cn and hold to back, K2, P2 from cn*, K4
Row 7: *P2, sl 2 to cn and hold to front, K2, K2 from cn*
Row 9: K4, *sl 2 to cn and hold to front, P2, K2 from cn, K2*, P2

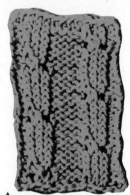

Little Bells Multiple of 14sts
Row 1 and 5: *P2, K3 tb1, P4, K3 tb1, P2*
Row 2 and 6: *K2, P3 tb1, K4, P3 tb1, K2*
Row 3: *P2, K3 tb1, P4, wrn to M1, sl 1, K2tog, psso, M1, P2*
Row 4: *K2, P1, P1, tb1, P1, K4, P3 tb1, K2*
Row 7: *P2, wrn to M1, sl 1, K2tog, psso, M1, P4, K3 tb1, P2*
Row 8: *K2, P3 tb1, K4, P1, P1 tb1, P1, K2*

Twigs ▶
Multiple of 13 sts + 4sts
Row 1: K2, *K1, cross 2 R, K2, cross 2 R, K1, cross 2 L, K3*, K2
Row 2 and alt rows: P
Row 3: K2, *K4, cross 2 R, K3, cross 2 L, K2*, K2
Row 5: K2, *K3, cross 2 R, K1, cross 2 L, K2, cross 2 L, K1*, K2
Row 7: K2, *K2, cross 2 R, K3, cross 2 L, K4*, K2

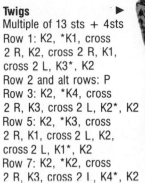

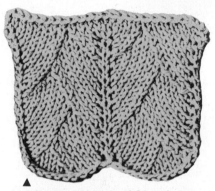

Leaf pattern Multiple of 24 + 1 st
Row 1: (RS) K1, *M1, skpo, K4, K2tog, K3, M1, K1, M1, K3, skpo, K4, K2tog, M1, K1*
Row 2 and alt rows: P
Row 3: K1, *M1, K1, skpo, K2, K2tog, K4, M1, K1, M1, K4, skpo, K2, K2tog, K1, M1, K1*
Row 5: K1, *M1, K2, skpo, K2tog, K5, M1, K1, M1, K5, skpo, K2tog, K2, M1, K1*
Row 7: K1, *M1, K3, skpo, K4, K2tog, M1, K1, M1, skpo, K4, K2tog, K3, M1, K1*
Row 9: K1, *M1, K4, skpo, K2, K2tog, K1, M1, K1, M1, K1, skpo, K2, K2tog, K4, M1, K1*
Row 11: K1, *M1, K5, skpo, K2tog, K2, M1, K1, M1, K2, skpo, K2tog, K5, M1, K1*

Wasp's nest stitch
Multiple of 4sts
Row 1: *cross 2R, cross 2L*
Row 2: P
Row 3: *cross 2L, cross 2R*
Row 4: P

Woven basket stitch ▶
Multiple of 2sts
Row 1: *cross 2L*
Row 2: P1, *of the next 2 sts, P the 2nd, then P the first*, P1

CHAPTER TWO
HOW TO...

Now that you understand the basics, you're ready to get down to the real "knitty gritty"!

We'll teach you how to design your own garments based on a photographed piece or on an actual sweater that you may want to adapt. What could be better than having that expensive-looking designer sweater without having to pay the high price? Pick out the yarn you like, and for much less money you can have a sweater that will stand up against the most expensive one!

The designing process begins with a small drawing, called a schematic diagram, which has all the important information you'll need to knit your garment. This is your blueprint, something that will become an integral part of the designing process. We'll explain all you need to know about schematics, and soon you'll be drawing your own.

You'll learn how to choose styles that are flattering to your figure, and also get a brief rundown of all the basic sweater shapes. If you've never heard of "charting" before, you'll soon know that this is how you create the shape of your garment on graph paper. Once you've mastered this skill, you'll be able to work from a chart instead of having to read complicated written instructions. We'll also take you through the process of how to write your own instructions, a necessary skill.

One of the joys of knitting is challenging yourself to learn new skills. Multicolored knitting is a fun way to expand your knowledge without having to learn complex stitch patterns. Our term for this, "pictorial sweaters," refers basically to any design that has more than one color and uses images or motifs for interest. Here is an area where you can really let your imagination go wild! What could be more fun than splashing some grafitti across the front of your next sweater, or enlarging a section of your favorite comic strip? Perhaps you have a favorite photograph or postcard you could envision as a vest. We'll teach you how to translate these images or shapes onto a graph paper chart (called "charting"), and before you know it you'll be thinking of all sorts of projects to use up those odds and ends of colored yarn you've been saving.

For those of us who love the traditional look of sweaters with lots of different stitch patterns, Aran sweaters are a good choice. You'll learn the basic ingredients that make up an Aran and how you can mix and match different simple stitch patterns with only one color of yarn to create a sweater that looks complex but really isn't.

Today knit skirts and dresses have become as popular as sweaters. Although many people shy away from them because they seem like a lot of work, these garments can be quite simple. We'll take you through the step-by-step process to create your own patterns for several different styles of skirts and dresses.

There's a lot of information in this chapter, so take it slowly and focus on what especially interests you. As you integrate the new information, you'll be amazed at how it all makes sense. Be patient, and realize that you have the ability to do whatever you set your mind to.

CREATE YOUR OWN DESIGNER ORIGINALS

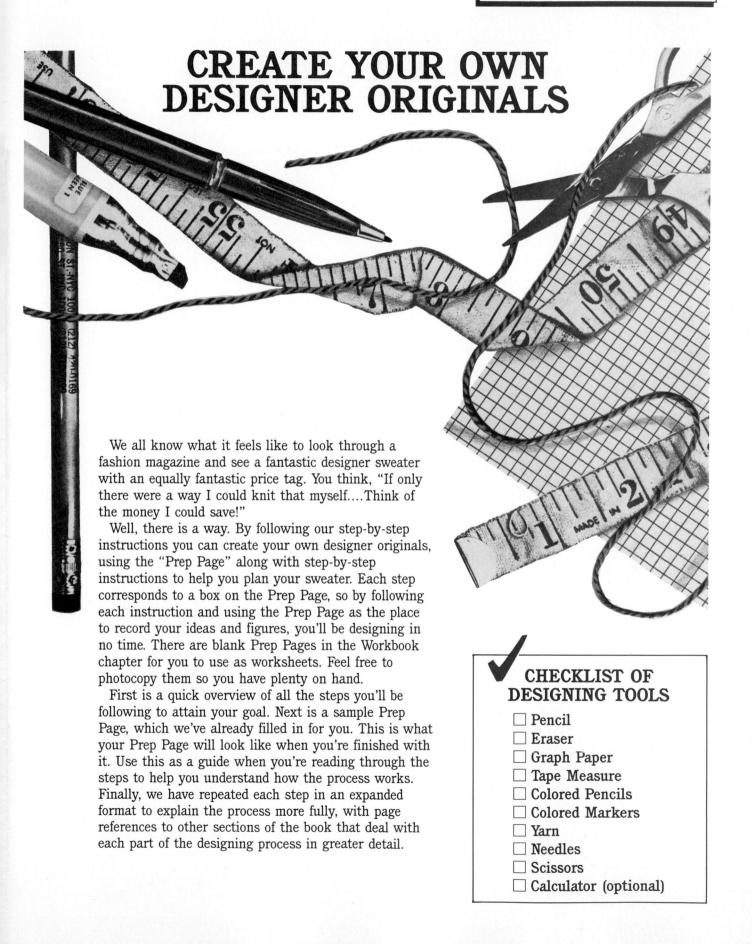

We all know what it feels like to look through a fashion magazine and see a fantastic designer sweater with an equally fantastic price tag. You think, "If only there were a way I could knit that myself....Think of the money I could save!"

Well, there is a way. By following our step-by-step instructions you can create your own designer originals, using the "Prep Page" along with step-by-step instructions to help you plan your sweater. Each step corresponds to a box on the Prep Page, so by following each instruction and using the Prep Page as the place to record your ideas and figures, you'll be designing in no time. There are blank Prep Pages in the Workbook chapter for you to use as worksheets. Feel free to photocopy them so you have plenty on hand.

First is a quick overview of all the steps you'll be following to attain your goal. Next is a sample Prep Page, which we've already filled in for you. This is what your Prep Page will look like when you're finished with it. Use this as a guide when you're reading through the steps to help you understand how the process works. Finally, we have repeated each step in an expanded format to explain the process more fully, with page references to other sections of the book that deal with each part of the designing process in greater detail.

✔ CHECKLIST OF DESIGNING TOOLS

- ☐ Pencil
- ☐ Eraser
- ☐ Graph Paper
- ☐ Tape Measure
- ☐ Colored Pencils
- ☐ Colored Markers
- ☐ Yarn
- ☐ Needles
- ☐ Scissors
- ☐ Calculator (optional)

HOW TO USE THE PREP PAGE

Step ☐1 —Make a small thumbnail sketch of the sweater with a pencil, cut out and tape into box #1.

Step ☐2 —Draw a schematic diagram of each section of the sweater in box #2.

Step ☐3 —Take the measurements you will need for this sweater, making sure to include the "ease" you want for style and fit, and record them in box #3.

Step ☐4 —Record the measurements taken in Step ☐3 on the schematic in box #4.

Step ☐5 —Identify and record the stitch pattern in box #5.

Step ☐6 —Choose the yarn and attach it to the Prep Page in box #6.

Step ☐7 —Choose the needle size and record in box #7.

Step ☐8 —Knit a 4″ x 4″ gauge swatch, and be sure to test your ribbing on smaller size needles. Staple the swatch to box #8.

Step ☐9 —Determine the gauge by measuring the stitches and rows per inch, and record in box #9.

Step ☐10 —To determine the number of stitches or rows for each measurement on the schematic, multiply the number of inches in each measurement by the gauge. Do this math in the spaces provided in box #10.

Step ☐11 —Write your final figures for stitches and rows in the appropriate spaces in box #11.

Step ☐12 —Determine what type of neckline, sleeve cap, closure, and details you will use.

Step ☐13 —Record your pattern instructions on a blank sheet of paper, or chart them on graph paper.

Step ☐14 —Begin knitting!

THE PREP PAGE

BOX#1 THUMBNAIL SKETCH

BOX#2 AND BOX#4 SCHEMATIC WITH MEASUREMENTS

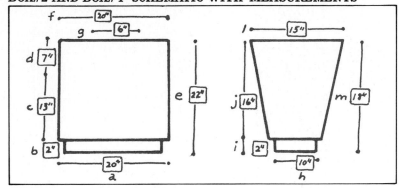

BOX#3

	MEASUREMENTS	
a	Baseline: ½ of hip or waist measurement	20"
b	length of ribbing	2"
c	length of ribbing to underarm	13"
d	length of armhole to shoulder	7"
e	total length	22"
f	shoulder width	20"
g	neck width	6"
h	width of sleeve at cuff	10"
i	length of cuff ribbing	2"
j	length of top of cuff ribbing to underarm	16"
k	sleeve cap length	—
l	width of upper arm at armhole	15"
m	total length of sleeve	18"

BOX#5 STITCH PATTERN

SYMBOLCRAFT CHART

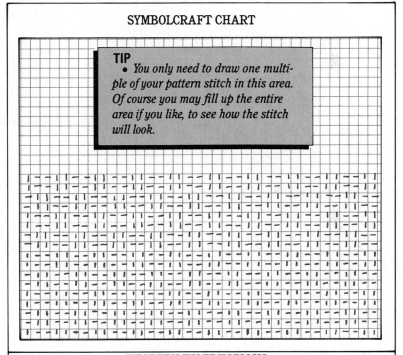

TIP
• *You only need to draw one multiple of your pattern stitch in this area. Of course you may fill up the entire area if you like, to see how the stitch will look.*

WRITTEN INSTRUCTIONS

Irish Moss Stitch (multiple of 2 st)

Rw 1: * K1, P1 *

Rw 2: K the knit sts, and P the purl sts

Rw 3: * P1, K1 *

Rw 4: K the knit sts, and P the purl sts

BOX#6 YARN

Bernat knitting worsted 3.5 oz balls

BOX#7 NEEDLE SIZES

8 and #10

BOX#8   4" × 4" GAUGE SWATCH + RIBBING

BOX#9

GAUGE	
_4_ sts =1"	_5_ rws =1"

BOX#10   MATH

MEASUREMENTS × GAUGE = STITCHES + ROWS		
STITCHES PER ROW (HORIZONTAL MEASUREMENTS)		**ROWS PER INCH (VERTICAL MEASUREMENTS)**
a	20" × 4 sts / 80 sts	**b**	2" ×5 rws / 10 rws
		c	13" × 5 rws / 65 rws
f	20" × 4 sts / 80 sts	**d**	7" ×5 rws / 35 rws
g	6" × 4 sts / 24 sts	**e**	22" × 5 rws / 110 rws
		i	2" ×5 rws / 10 rws
h	10" × 4 sts / 40 sts	**j**	16" × 5 rws / 80 rws
		k	———
l	15" × 4 sts / 60 sts	**m**	18" × 5 rws / 90 rws

BOX#11

		STITCHES/INCH ROWS/INCH
a	Baseline: ½ of hip or waist measurement	80 sts
b	length of ribbing	10 rws
c	length of ribbing to underarm	65 rws
d	length of armhole to shoulder	35 rws
e	total length	110 rws
f	shoulder width	80 rws
g	neck width	24 sts
h	width of sleeve at cuff	40 sts
i	length of cuff ribbing	10 rws
j	length of top of cuff ribbing to underarm	80 rws
k	sleeve cap length	———
l	width of upper arm at armhole	60 sts
m	total length of sleeve	90 rws

BOX#12 AND BOX#13 YOU WILL FILL IN ON YOUR OWN BLANK SHEET OF PAPER

AN IN-DEPTH LOOK
AT THE PREP PAGE

Before you actually begin, it's important to have a style in mind for the sweater you would like to make. This may be a sweater you've seen in a store window and drawn a sketch of, or a photograph from a magazine. What you want to do is capture the qualities that you like about the sweater because it's almost impossible to duplicate it precisely. If you have a photograph of the garment, you may want to photocopy it, making it easier to write on it with pencil or markers.

Step 1 —Make a small thumbnail sketch of the sweater with a pencil, cut out and tape into box #1.

Include whatever details you can see: perhaps an interesting collar treatment, the way the neckline is shaped, an unusual cuff, or anything that makes the garment special. It's always best to draw first in pencil, then with a pen later when you know you've captured the look of the sweater. If you feel uncomfortable about drawing, refer to the "Cut-Outs" section in the Workbook chapter, where we've provided the basic shapes which you can use (see page 159).

In our example (in box #1), we've drawn a boat neck pullover with a drop shoulder (which means that the sleeves aren't fitted, so there is no need for an armhole decrease). As you can see, this drawing doesn't have to be finished-looking, but it should include the basic style considerations.

Step 2 —Draw a schematic diagram of each section of the sweater in box #2.

Photographs often don't show a sweater in its entirety. It may be difficult to see how it's constructed in certain areas, such as the underarm, the cuff, or the ribbing. The more you observe sweaters and understand how they are constructed, the easier it will be to diagram a schematic. We recommend that beginners choose a simple sweater to copy. You will know when you're ready to tackle more complex garments (see page 34).

In our example (in box #2), we've drawn the shape of the front (or back) and one sleeve. Generally both front and back are the same shape and dimensions; the same is true for the sleeves, therefore you only need to show one of each.

Step 3 —Take the measurements you will need for this sweater, making sure to include the "ease" you want for style and fit, and record them in box #3 (see page 18).

Each letter in box #3 relates to the corresponding letter on the schematic (box #2). For example, (a) represents the measurement for the bottom edge or baseline. When you've determined that measurement for your sweater design (making sure to include ease), enter the measurement onto line (a) in box #3.

Letter (b) refers to the length of the ribbing. Once you've determined how long you want the ribbing to be, enter the measurement onto line (b) in box #3. And so on.

In box #3 you will see the letters "a-m" with their corresponding measurements. We are creating this pattern for a woman with a size 34″ bust and 36″ hips. We want the sweater to have ease of movement, so we're allowing 2″ of ease on each side of the hips: 36″ + 4″ = 40″, which is the total hip measurement. Because the schematic shows only one-half of the sweater, either the front or the back, we have to divide each total measurement in half: 40″ ÷ 2″ = 20″. So we record "20" in the space for the baseline measurement.

The length of the ribbing and the length of the sweater are subjective measurements. You will want to ask yourself, "How long do I want my sweater to be?" and "How much ribbing do I want at the bottom of the sweater, at the cuffs, at the neck?" Take a look at other sweaters you like, and see how long they are, what ribbing styles they have. The more observant you become about how other people design, the quicker you'll be making those decisions for yourself.

For the underarm to shoulder measurement, we turned to the Knitter's Guide Chart on page 19 and determined that for a size 34″ bust, we would have a 7″ measurement here. So we entered 7″ on line (d). The same is true for the neck measurement. Turn to the Knitter's Guide Chart on page 20 and you will see that for a size 34″ bust, the neck measurement would be 6″.

Step 4 —Record the measurements taken in Step 3 on the schematic in box #4 (see page 34).

We have used the design of the schematic shown on page 34 as the basis for the way we've entered our measurements in box #4. You may want to photocopy that design and use it as a guide when you're working with the Prep Page. Enter each measurement in the appropriate area, so you will have an immediate picture of the dimensions of your sweater design.

The first measurement is for the baseline, so it should go at the bottom of the diagram. The second is for the ribbing, so it should go next to the ribbing. And so on. It helps to draw arrows to show the points at which each measurement begins and ends.

Step 5 —Identify and record the stitch pattern in box #5.

If you are using a photograph and cannot be sure what stitch is used, look at the textural quality and decide on a stitch that resembles it. For beginners, it's best to stay with simple stitches such as stockinette, garter, moss, and seed (see pages 23–25, Stitch Patterns; see page 22, Symbolcraft).

We have chosen Irish Moss Stitch for our sample design. We have both written out the instructions and charted them visually through symbolcraft. The page numbers above will give you more detail on how to proceed with both.

Step 6 —Choose the yarn and attach it to the Prep Page in box #6.

Take the photograph to the yarn store and ask the salesperson to help you determine what type of yarn was used in the original. You can usually tell the weight of the yarn by the bulkiness of the sweater. Once you determine the weight, there may be several yarns that you could choose to achieve the same effect (see page 11).

Either tape or staple your yarn samples in this box and write in the brand name, the number of ounces in each skein, and the number of yards in each skein, if that information is available.

Step 7 —Choose the needle size and record it in box #7.

Usually needle sizes are recommended on the yarn label. We recommend using a needle size that is two sizes smaller for the ribbing. If in doubt, ask the salesperson (see page 9).

Step 8 —Knit a 4″ × 4″ gauge swatch, and be sure to test your ribbing on smaller size needles. Staple it to box #8.

Test the yarn with larger or smaller needles to get the proper tension (see page 17).

Step 9 —Determine the gauge by measuring the stitches and rows per inch and record it in box #9 (see page 17).

Our gauge is four stitches equal one inch and five rows equal one inch. The abbreviation that is commonly used is 4sts = 1″, 5rws = 1″.

Step 10 —To determine the number of stitches or rows for each measurement on the schematic, multiply the number of inches in each measurement by the gauge. Do this math in the spaces provided in box #10.

In our example, the first measurement we want to convert to stitches is the baseline, so we multiply the number of inches (20) by the stitch gauge (4) and get 80. This is the number of stitches to cast on for our first row. The second measurement is the length of the ribbing, which is a vertical measurement. We would multiply the length of the ribbing (2) by the row gauge (5) and determine that the ribbing should be 10 rows.

All the measurements that are horizontal are in the lefthand column and will all be multiplied by the stitch gauge (in this case, 4). All the vertical measurements are in the righthand column and should be multiplied by the row gauge (in this case, 5).

> **TIP**
> • *We cannot overemphasize the importance of entering this math on the same page with all the other information. You may have to go back and recheck certain figures, so it's essential to know where to find your calculations. For instance, you may realize that the sweater is not as long as you want it to be, and you have already figured out the number of rows for the length. If you have your math handy, you can go back, erase, refigure, and correct the measurements on your schematic.*

Step 11 —Write your final figures for stitches and rows in the appropriate spaces in box #11.

Box #3 and box #11 are placed next to each other to make it easier for you to understand their connection. Box #3 contains your measurements in inches (both horizontal and vertical measurements). You have just multiplied each measurement by your gauge to determine how many stitches and rows equal those measurements. Now you are entering in box #11 the corresponding figures next to the original measurements in box #3.

All you have to do here is take the math you've just done and write the figures into the appropriate spaces in box #11. We see that the baseline (line [a]) is 20″ and 80 stitches. The ribbing is 2″ and 10 rows. And so on.

Step 12 —Determine what type of design variations and details you will use.

You may have already decided on a basic neckline style or a certain type of sleeve cap when you drew your schematic diagram. This step will help you to further your understanding of exactly how to execute your design.

Step 13 —Record your pattern instructions on a blank sheet of paper, or chart them on graph paper (see pages 50–52, "How To Write a Pattern"; see pages 42–44, "Charting a Pattern").

If this is your first time reading through this process, you are not going to know how to write your own pattern or how to draw a chart for your design. These skills are still to come in this chapter. Once you've learned and practiced doing this several times, you will find it much easier than it may now appear. Be patient, and keep it simple in the beginning!

Here are the written instructions for our sample pattern. All we've done is taken the measurements, stitches, and rows from the schematic and used them as our guide for creating this pattern.

Back—With #8 needles, cast on 80 stitches. Work in K1, P1 ribbing for 10 rows (2″). Change to #10 needles. Work straight up in the pattern stitch (Irish Moss Stitch) until piece measures 22″. Bind off all stitches.

Front—Work same as for back.

Sleeves—With #8 needles, cast on 40 stitches. Work in K1, P1 ribbing for 10 rows (2″). Change to #10 needles. Work in pattern stitch (Irish Moss Stitch), increasing as follows: increase one stitch each end of first row. Increase one stitch at each end of every eighth row (nine times). Your knitted piece should measure 18″ and should have 60 stitches. Bind off all stitches.

Finishing—Block all pieces. Sew up shoulder and side seams. Sew up sleeve seam. Sew sleeves into the body of the sweater. If you like, add one or two rows of single crochet around neckline, or with a #8 circular needle pick up all the stitches at the neck edge and work several rows of ribbing, to desired length.

Step 14 —Begin knitting!

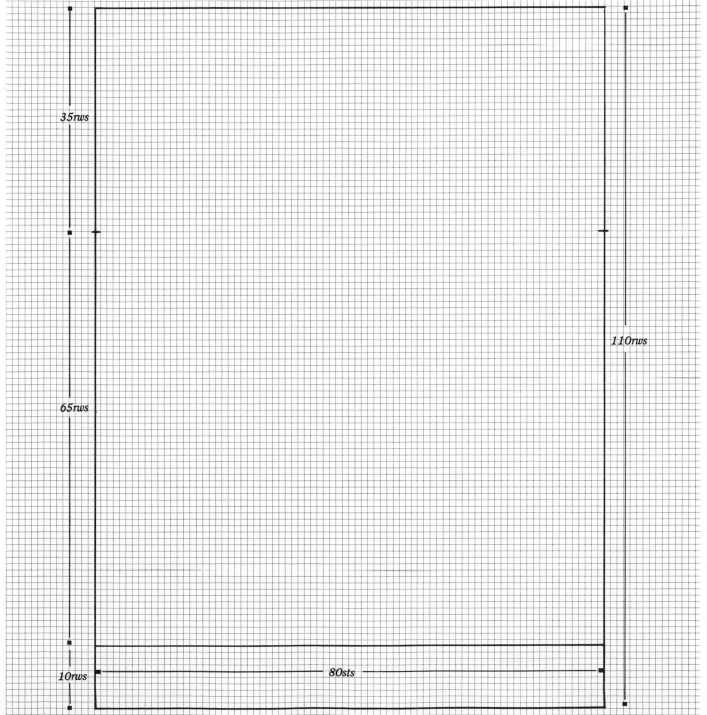

Charted Instructions for Sample Pattern

THUMBNAIL SKETCH

Now that you have an idea of the steps involved in creating your own sweater designs, you are ready to begin designing. Any creative process starts with ideas, dreams, thoughts, images. What you must do is harness some of these ideas and put them down on paper. Start with an "idea" sketch or "thumbnail" sketch, a small drawing of the basic styles you like. Ideally, you should try to include important details such as necklines, sleeve style and length, body length, and any special closures, pockets, buttons, and so on.

Previously, we encouraged you to begin your process with a small sketch of the sweater that you are copying. The process of visually defining the garment is important to the whole concept of being your own designer. Drawing is a method of note taking and will help define your sense of style. If you're afraid to draw, consider this: take a soft pencil, a good eraser, and begin slowly. Remember that practice makes perfect. If you persist, you'll be amazed at your progress.

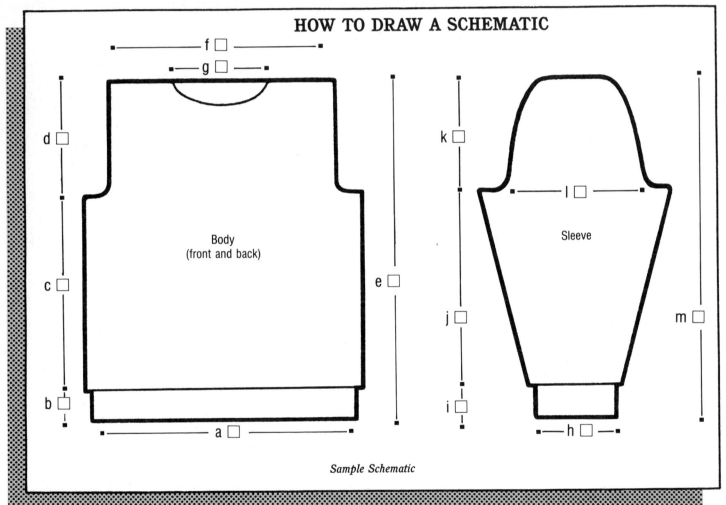

HOW TO DRAW A SCHEMATIC

Body
(front and back)

Sleeve

Sample Schematic

From thumbnail sketches you now graduate to "schematics." The thumbnail shows the entire garment in sketch form. The schematic is also small, but details the sweater separated into its major pieces. Above is a sample schematic for a sweater.

A schematic diagram should show precisely how a sweater is shaped. All construction details should show, and special attention should be paid to the underarm area and collar. The sample schematic has boxes for measurements. Each horizontal measurement multiplied by the stitch gauge will tell you how many stitches are in each row, and every vertical measurement multiplied by the row gauge will tell you how many rows are in each vertical measure. This is the blueprint for your sweater.

Don't forget to include "ease" in your measurements for proper fit, and remember that the total measurements of the garment at the hip or waist, bust, or shoulder will be divided in half for each front and back section.

LETTERS ON THE SCHEMATIC

BODY

[a] —Baseline: one-half the hip or waist measurement. The length of the sweater will determine where to take this measurement. If it's a short sweater that you want to fit closely and fall at the waist, then measure your waistline. If it's going to be a longer sweater, measure where you want the baseline of the garment to be.

[b] —Ribbing length. Again, this is a very subjective decision. You are the only one who can decide how long you want the ribbing. It's a good idea to examine other sweaters you like to see how the ribbing looks.

[c] —Length from top of ribbing to underarm decrease. This measurement will vary more than any other because sweater lengths change for each size and style.

[d] —Length of armhole to shoulder. Refer to the Knitter's Guide Charts (page 19) for specific dimensions for your size. Be sure to measure straight up from the first armhole decrease to the beginning of the shoulder, not along the curve of the armhole.

[e] —Total length of sweater. Measure from the baseline to the shoulder.

[f] —Shoulder to shoulder width. This will vary dramatically between drop shoulder sweaters and those with fitted armholes and sleeves (see page 18, Measurements).

[g] —Neck width. Refer to the Knitter's Guide Charts to determine how many inches to plan for your size (see page 20).

SLEEVE

[h] —Width of sleeve at cuff. This measurement should be taken above the ribbing. Allow enough ease to wear comfortably over other garments.

[i] —Length of cuff ribbing. Determine whether the cuff will fold or not. If you want to create a large folded cuff, knit twice the length.

[j] —Length from top of sleeve ribbing to underarm. The length of the sleeve will vary with the arm measurement of the individual.

[k] —Length of sleeve cap. Refer to the Knitter's Guide Charts to determine the appropriate measure. It will be proportionate to the depth of the armhole (see page 20).

[l] —Width of upper arm at armhole. Be sure to measure your arm at the same level that you measured your armhole.

[m] —Total sleeve length. Measure from the top of the sleeve to the bottom of the cuff, making sure to bend your elbow to allow for that extra movement.

Now you are ready to put your own measurements onto the schematic. On the Prep Page you will see that box #3 gives you a place to record each measurement. The next step is to write down each measurement in the corresponding box on the schematic. Remember, these measurements should include "ease," which will allow for movement and comfort. After you have determined your gauge, multiply by each measurement to determine the number of stitches per row (horizontal measure) and rows per vertical measure, and enter these figures into box #11 on the Prep Page.

TIPS

• *One more bit of advice: schematics are always shown in the order the garment will be knit. This usually means starting from the lower edge of the garment and working up. If the sweater is knit all in one piece, then it is shown that way. If it's a dolman sweater and knit from cuff to cuff, the sweater would appear to be on its side.*

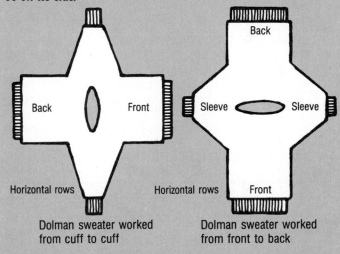

Dolman sweater worked from cuff to cuff

Dolman sweater worked from front to back

• *Applied details such as collar, pockets, or cuffs would be indicated as separate drawings within the schematic box.*

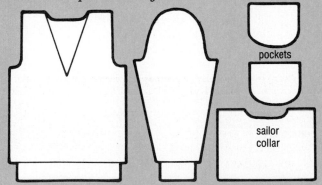

pockets

sailor collar

• *Neck and front openings should all be indicated on the schematic.*

HOW TO CHOOSE A FIGURE-FLATTERING STYLE

Before you begin to design your own garments, it's useful to understand what styles or silhouettes flatter your figure. We all know what styles of clothing do or don't work well on us. The right style will make you look and feel better; the wrong style will end up hanging in your closet. This is especially important with hand-knits, which cling to the body. Depending on the weight and color of the yarn, knits add bulk and may draw attention to problem areas.

The same considerations are important when you're designing gifts for friends and family. You'll want to be sure that the beautiful sweater you've labored on for weeks won't sit at the bottom of your mother's drawer because she thinks it makes her look heavy.

Determine your own body type by standing in front of a full-length mirror, either naked, wearing underwear, or a leotard and tights. Squint your eyes and get a sense of your overall body shape, not just the details. Get a sense of what portions of your figure are dominant. (You will probably already be aware of them because you've been trying to hide them for years!)

Then study the charts on these pages to determine the style that's right for you. You will find answers to each problem that suggest the most flattering silhouette. When you have an idea about what shapes are most flattering for you, it's important to consider what colors flatter you, what yarn weights work best with your figure, and what stitch patterns will make you look the best. All of these points are covered in this chapter.

Armed with these suggestions, you should be ready to begin incorporating new ideas and styles into your own fashion look. Now when you see a wonderful sweater on a mannequin in a store window, or on a woman walking down the street, you will know if it's right for you as well.

And what if that wonderful sweater is a little too body-hugging for your figure? That's one of the great aspects of designing for yourself: you can take the basic elements you like (which might be yarn type, stitch pattern, colors, or shape) and adapt them, making changes in areas where you have problems. It's a perfect way to take the best from the world of fashion and make it work for you.

DO'S AND DON'TS FOR STYLE COMBINATIONS

Do Combine	Crew neck and all collar types; and all sleeve types	Scoop neck and dolman or set-in sleeves; drop shoulder	V-neck and ruffle; all sleeve types	Square neck and set-in sleeves; saddle shoulder; drop shoulder	Boat neck and dolman or set-in sleeve; drop shoulder	Back V and ruffle; all sleeve types	Cardigans and polo collar; ruffle; all sleeve types
Don't Combine		Scoop neck and raglan sleeves; saddle shoulder	V-neck and turtleneck; polo collar; rolled collar	Square neck and turtleneck; polo collar; ruffle; rolled collar; raglan sleeves	Boat neck and raglan sleeve; saddle shoulder	Back V and turtleneck; polo collar; rolled collar	Cardigans and turtleneck; rolled collar

DO'S AND DON'TS FOR FULL-FIGURED WOMEN

If you have determined that what you need to do is add weight, you are the perfect candidate for bulky knits. If you are full-figured, however, keep these tips in mind.

• **Do** choose a soft neckline such as a scoop neck or V-neck, which will draw attention upward from your body to your neck and face.

• **Don't** choose a body-hugging style with small set-in sleeves or puff sleeves. Instead, choose a broadened shoulder, which will offset a wide hip line.

• **Do** choose a stitch which will be slimming, such as a vertical or diagonal stripe or stitch pattern.

• **Don't** choose ribbed stitches, horizontal patterns, and cables, which will add bulk. Do choose smooth and lightly textured stitches such as stockinette, seed, and small basketweave.

• **Do** choose a soft lightweight yarn (preferably a sport or worsted weight) in Shetland or lambswool, rayon or silk, to give the fabric a more supple quality.

• **Don't** choose bulky yarns, which add weight and bulk to one's appearance.

• **Do** choose dark to neutral tones for the most flattering look. If you yearn for color, stay with the pastels, to avoid drawing undo attention to a problem area.

• If you like pictorial designs and jacquard motifs, **do** choose smaller repeat-type patterns. **Don't** choose bold, overall splashy designs.

HOW TO CHOOSE A SHAPE

Now that you understand what types of clothing work best for your figure, you can begin to design with that in mind. Most of the basic sweater shapes are divided into two broad categories: pullover and cardigan. Here we have provided the basic shapes, which are intended to familiarize you with the fundamental options. Whether you lengthen, shorten, make the shoulders wider or the waist narrower is up to you.

PULLOVER AND CARDIGAN SHAPES

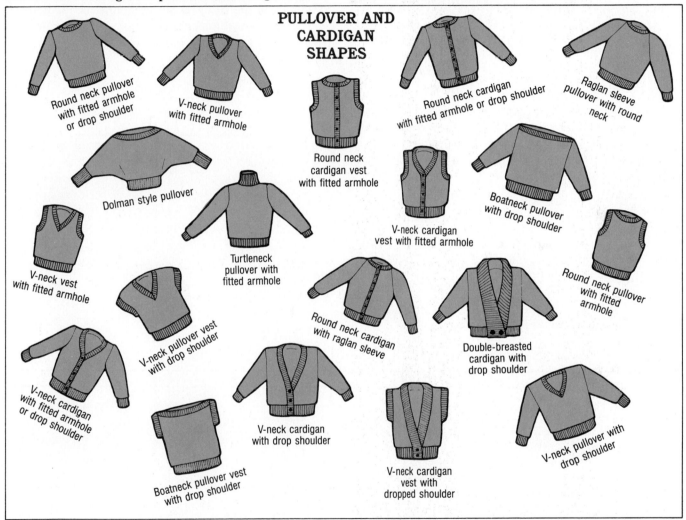

Round neck pullover with fitted armhole or drop shoulder

V-neck pullover with fitted armhole

Round neck cardigan vest with fitted armhole

Round neck cardigan with fitted armhole or drop shoulder

Raglan sleeve pullover with round neck

Dolman style pullover

V-neck cardigan vest with fitted armhole

Boatneck pullover with drop shoulder

V-neck vest with fitted armhole

Turtleneck pullover with fitted armhole

Round neck pullover with fitted armhole

V-neck pullover vest with drop shoulder

Round neck cardigan with raglan sleeve

Double-breasted cardigan with drop shoulder

V-neck cardigan with fitted armhole or drop shoulder

V-neck cardigan with drop shoulder

V-neck pullover with drop shoulder

Boatneck pullover vest with drop shoulder

V-neck cardigan vest with dropped shoulder

PICK AND CHOOSE CHART FOR STYLE COMBINATIONS

The "pick and choose" chart below will show you the various options available for designing sweaters, dresses, and skirts.

Choose one item from each column and make up your own designs.

Collars and Necks		Cardigan styles	Sleeves		Semiclosures	
Necks	**Collars**	Kimono (wrap)	Raglan	Leg o'mutton	Shoulder buttons	Buttons
Crew (round)	Turtleneck	Crew neck	Dolman	Pleated	Polo shirt style	Frogs
Scoop (round)	Polo or Princess	V–neck	Classic set-in	Puff	Zippers	
V–neck	Ruffle	—Double-breasted	Saddle shoulder		**Hemline/Border**	
Square	Rolled	**Closures**	Drop shoulder		1 row reverse stockinette	
Boat		Cords/eyelets	**Cuff Treatments**		Picot (eyelets)	
Back V		Elastic	Turned back cuff		**Trim/Ribbing**	
High-front, back V			Ribbed cuff		Reverse stockinette stitch	Garter stitch
			Rolled cuff		Rib (single and double)	Seed stitch
			Ruffled cuff		Cable rib	

HOW TO CHART A PATTERN

What is charting? A "chart" is simply a visual representation of written instructions. It is an exact representation of your schematic, on either graph paper with one square representing one stitch and one row, or an outline blown up to life-size proportions and executed on butcher paper. Both methods work well. In the beginning it's a good idea to do both if you have the time and inclination. If you don't have the time, the graph paper chart is the essential method for charting.

First, let's explore the full-size outline chart. The purpose of this outline chart is to check the measurements of your knitted piece as you progress. It can also be a big help when you are finished with the garment and are ready to block the pieces. Measure each piece against your outline and stretch a little if necessary, then iron.

FULL-SIZE OUTLINE

To make your outline, you will need heavy paper (butcher paper works well), a measuring tape, a pencil or marker, and scissors. You will be drawing an exact duplication of each garment section with all shaping information included.

Ready?

Step 1 —Using sturdy paper, draw a straight line equal to the widest dimension of the body of the garment (usually the hip or bust measure).

Step 2 —Draw the center line of the garment at a 90-degree angle to the first line.

Step 3 —Using measurements a-m from the schematic, measure all other dimensions from these major axes.

Step 4 —Draw the outline for the sleeve(s) in the same way, starting with the horizontal line of the widest dimension and the perpendicular center line, measuring all other dimensions from there.

Any other major pieces (such as a large collar treatment or pockets) would be outlined in the same way. Ribbing and finishing details are omitted.

Step 5 —You may either leave the drawings on the sheet and roll it up for storage or cut out the pieces. Folding is not recommended because the folded crease will make it difficult to get a true measurement. Always roll the paper and fasten with a rubber band or paper clips.

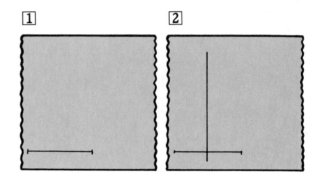

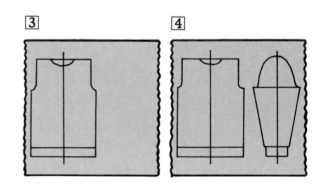

TIPS
• *Generally you can use the same outlined piece for the front and back unless they are very different in styling. Make a notation on the paper where the neckline might vary from front to back.*

• *If you want to make a more complex garment such as a dress or jacket, sewing patterns can be very helpful in making your full-size outline. Remember that you won't need to add seam allowances.*

FULL-SIZE GRID

The most accurate method for charting is a combination of the full-size outline and the graph paper technique: create your own full-size grid from your gauge swatch.

The advantage of this method is that the pictorial designs you chart will be full size, as will all other shaping and body measurements. It is much easier to check your knitting as you progress to be sure the piece fits correctly.

Step 1 —Measure your swatch. Find out how many stitches and rows there are per inch.

Step 2 —Make a grid that duplicates this measurement. For example, if your gauge is 4sts = 1″, 5rws = 1″, rule out a grid on paper that has four squares horizontally in one inch and five squares vertically in one inch. Extend these lines out in all directions to create a very large grid that has many squares of this size. You have to have a grid that is large enough to accommodate the actual dimensions of your sweater. A sheet of 19″ × 24″ paper should work well.

Step 3 —Create the actual dimensions of your garment pieces on tracing paper, over the full-size grid. Use a clear sheet of tracing paper, and follow the method for charting an outline on page 38.

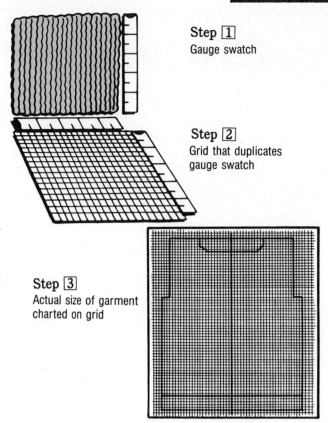

Step 1
Gauge swatch

Step 2
Grid that duplicates gauge swatch

Step 3
Actual size of garment charted on grid

Full-Size Grid

USING KNITTER'S GRAPH PAPER

Knitted stitches don't always conform exactly into a square; sometimes they're wider, sometimes taller. If this is the case when you plot out a garment on regular graph paper you may get a slight distortion of proportion, even though the actual knitted garment will be accurate. This distortion is created by the square representation of the stitch instead of the wider horizontal or taller vertical rectangle, which is a closer representation of the actual stitch. In the Workbook chapter are several different sizes of knitter's graph paper, which will give you a more accurate picture of the real dimensions of your garment.

When you knit your gauge swatch, examine the stitches to see their proportion. You can also tell from your stitch and row gauge whether the stitch format is square, vertical, or horizontal. If the gauge is 4sts = 1″, 5rws = 1″, you know the stitches are more horizontal. If the gauge is 4sts = 1″, 4rws = 1″, they are square. If the gauge is 4sts = 1″, 3rws = 1″, they are vertical.

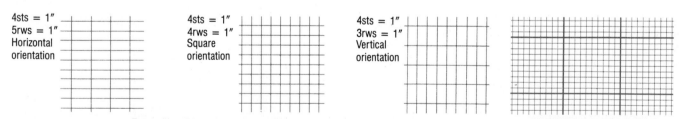

4sts = 1″
5rws = 1″
Horizontal orientation

4sts = 1″
4rws = 1″
Square orientation

4sts = 1″
3rws = 1″
Vertical orientation

Examples of how the gauge affects the orientation of the stitch.

Example of graph paper highlighted with larger grid.

USING GRAPH PAPER

The third method for charting is executed on commercially made graph paper. A local art or stationery store probably has the largest selection of graph paper to choose from. The styles range from small pads with large squares to large pads with small squares. Some grids are highlighted by a larger grid which includes 6 × 6 squares, 8 × 8 squares, or 10 × 10 squares. This type of graph paper works best for designing because it makes it easier to count. Tracing vellum, a transparent sheet with the grid printed on it, is very useful for charting a pattern. If you make a mistake, simply trace your old drawing onto a new sheet of paper.

To save yourself time and frustration, purchase several different sizes of pads and grids. This will allow you more flexibility for scaling your images onto the garment shape.

HOW TO CHART A VISUAL PATTERN

Let's apply these charting techniques to create a chart for your own sweater (see pages 65–78 to learn how to chart skirts and dresses). As a quick review, this chart can either be full size or plotted out on smaller graph paper. If you use your schematic as a blueprint, drawing the chart is really quite simple: all you have to do is multiply your measurements by the stitch gauge and the row gauge to find out how many stitches and rows you'll be plotting. The steps that follow correspond directly to each of the numbered segments on the schematic. (We have provided the illustration of a basic schematic again for you to use as reference.) It would also be helpful to have your Prep Page handy at this time for easy reference.

For example,

Step 1 —Baseline is the hip or waist measure, which coordinates with letter a. This is the first measurement you'll need to record on the schematic. Begin by taking your measurements, adding the ease you want for comfort and dividing in half to get the width of the front or back.

Step 2 —Ribbing length refers to the height of the ribbing, corresponding to letter b on the schematic. This system of working from the schematic directly to the chart should make the charting process simple. For each letter on the schematic, there will be a corresponding step to draw your own chart.
So let's begin.

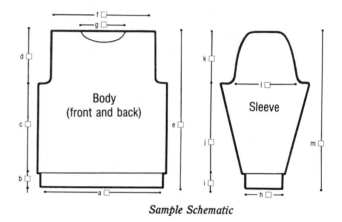

Sample Schematic

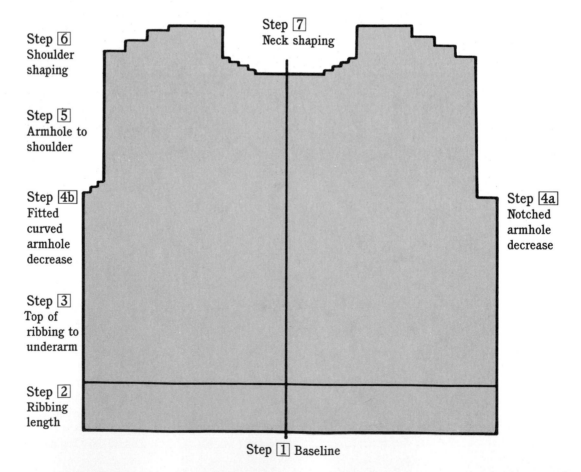

Step 6
Shoulder shaping

Step 7
Neck shaping

Step 5
Armhole to shoulder

Step 4b
Fitted curved armhole decrease

Step 4a
Notched armhole decrease

Step 3
Top of ribbing to underarm

Step 2
Ribbing length

Step 1 Baseline

STEP-BY-STEP INSTRUCTIONS

Our examples will appear in this column. Gauge: 4sts = 1"

5rws = 1"

Step 1

Hips = 36"

36 ÷ 2 = 18"

Ease per side = 2"

18"
+ 2
20"

Stitches per inch
(stitch gauge): 4sts = 1"

20"
×4sts
80sts

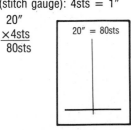

20" = 80sts

Draw a horizontal line 80 squares long, which will represent the baseline.

Step 2

Rows per inch (row gauge): 5rws = 1"
Length of ribbing = 2"

2"
×5rws
10rws

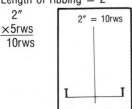

2" = 10rws

Draw a vertical line that is 10 squares high on each side to represent the ribbing.

Step 3

Top of ribbing to underarm measurement = 13"
Row gauge: 5rws = 1"

13"
×5rws
65rws

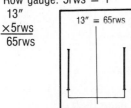

13" = 65rws

Draw a vertical line that proceeds upward for 65 squares, to represent the hip to underarm measurement.

Plot each section of the sweater from the bottom up and in the order each piece will be knit.

Step 1 —Baseline—Take your hip or waist measurement and divide in half. Be sure to add ease for fit (see page 19, ease chart). This total will now be translated into stitches per inch. Multiply this amount by the hip plus ease (or waist-plus-ease measurement. You now have the number of stitches which equal the width of your sweater front or back. Using the graph paper, and counting one square as one stitch, draw a solid line across the bottom of row 1.
Find the center of the line and draw a vertical line up the center of the entire chart.

TIPS
• *Key* In the margin of your pattern include needle sizes, gauge (stitches per inch, rows per inch), yarn color chart and yarn brands, symbolcraft chart of stitch patterns.

• *Checkpoints* In the margin of your pattern, make note of needle-size changes, increases/decreases, color or stitch pattern changes, casting on or binding off.

• *Numbering the chart* If a row begins on the right side of the pattern, you are knitting on the right side. If a row begins on the left side of the pattern, you are knitting on the wrong side of the sweater. Keep track of the right side of your garment by numbering all odd-numbered rows.

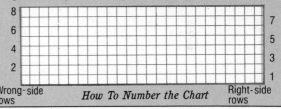

Wrong-side rows   *How To Number the Chart*   Right-side rows

Step 2 —Length of ribbing—Most sweaters begin with ribbing, so decide on the length of ribbing you desire. Measure your gauge swatch vertically to determine the number of rows per inch. Multiply this number by the desired length of ribbing. Since one square equals one row, draw a vertical line from the baseline to the end of the ribbing on each side.

TIP
• *It's a good idea to start your gauge swatch with a few inches of ribbing, using smaller needles in order to determine the gauge for the ribbing as well. Make a note on the Prep Page in box #8, and use this row gauge (for the ribbing only) if it's different from your regular row gauge.*

Step 3 —Top ribbing to underarm measurement—Take your hip to underarm measurement (or your waist to underarm measurement, depending on the length of the sweater), and multiply by the rows per inch. Count up from the end of the ribbing and continue the vertical line to the desired length on each side.

Step 4

Shoulder width = 15″

15″	Baseline = 80sts
×4sts	Shoulder = 60sts
60sts	80sts
	−60sts
	20sts total to be decreased

20 ÷ 2 = 10sts each side

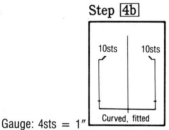

Notched armhole   Curved, fitted

Draw a horizontal line (toward the inside of the sweater) that equals 10 squares, to represent the total underarm decrease.

Step 4a

10sts   10sts

Notched armhole

Step 4b

10sts   10sts

Curved, fitted

Gauge: 4sts = 1″
Row 1 and 2: decrease 4sts
Row 3 and 4: decrease 3sts
Row 5 and 6: decrease 2sts
Row 7 and 8: decrease 1 st

On your chart, draw the lines which represent each of the decreases shown above.

Step 5

Row gauge: 5sts = 1″
Underarm to shoulder measurement = 8″

8″
×5rws
40rws

8″ = 40rws

Draw a vertical line from the armhole decrease to the shoulder which is 40 squares long.

Step 6

Neck measurement = 8″
Stitch gauge: 4sts = 1″

8″
×4sts
32sts

Step 4 —Armhole decrease—

The main purpose of the armhole decrease is to remove excess fabric under the arms and to allow the sleeve to fit snugly into the garment. (No decrease gives you a "drop shoulder" sweater, which is full under the arms.) To do this, you need to reduce the total number of stitches on the needle to that of the shoulder measure.

This can be done in two ways: the curved, fitted armhole, or the notched, "geometric" look. The fitted armhole is created by decreasing in several small steps, the notched armhole in one step.

The first thing to determine is the number of stitches in the shoulder measure. Multiply the number of inches in the shoulder width by the stitch gauge to determine this. Now subtract the number of stitches at the shoulder from the number of stitches at the baseline to determine how many stitches have to be decreased.

Divide in half to determine how many stitches should be decreased from each side.

If you're making a notched armhole (4a), draw a horizontal line straight across, counting the number of stitches you've determined to decrease. If you're making a curved, fitted armhole (4b), a good rule of thumb is to decrease your stitch gauge at the beginning of the next two rows. For example, if your gauge is 4sts = 1″, you would decrease 4 stitches at the beginning of the next two rows. You then want to create a gentle curve by decreasing progressively fewer stitches each row until the stitches on the needle equal the number of stitches at the shoulder.

Step 5 —Underarm to shoulder measurement—

See page 19 for the Knitter's Guide Chart, which will tell you the proper length for your size. Multiply this measurement by the row gauge. Draw a vertical line from the armhole decrease to the shoulder.

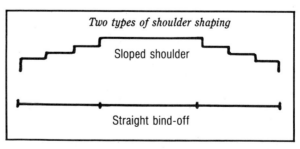

Two types of shoulder shaping

Sloped shoulder

Straight bind-off

Step 6 —Shoulder shaping—

There are two ways to shape a shoulder: straight bind-off or sloped shoulder. To create a sloped shoulder, decrease in more than one step. The table below will tell you how to determine how many steps to use, according to your stitch gauge:

Stitches at shoulder = 60sts
Stitches for neck = 32sts

$$\begin{array}{r} 60\text{sts} \\ -32\text{sts} \\ \hline 28\text{sts} \end{array}$$ (remaining stitches for both shoulders)

28 ÷ 2 = 14sts (for each shoulder)
Stitch gauge: 4sts = 1″
Therefore, shape shoulder in 3 steps.
14 ÷ 3 = 4.6 (round up to 5)

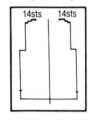

(a) Draw a horizontal line 5 squares long for the first shoulder decrease (on each side).

(b) Draw a vertical line upward for 2 squares to represent the rows in between each decrease.

(c) Draw another horizontal line 5 squares long.

(d) Repeat (b).

(e) You now have decreased 10 stitches. You only want to decrease 14 stitches, so for the last decrease, draw a horizontal line 4 squares long, to represent your final decrease.

Step 7

Draw a horizontal line straight across the shoulder, to represent the bind-off edge.

Base of neckline = 4″ below shoulder

$$\begin{array}{r} 4″ \\ \times 5\text{rws} \\ \hline 20\text{rws below} \\ \text{shoulder} \end{array}$$

Neck measurement = 8″

$$\begin{array}{r} 8″ \\ \times 4\text{sts} \\ \hline 32\text{sts} \end{array}$$

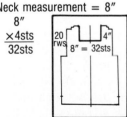

Draw a vertical line from the shoulder downward that equals 20 squares, on each side of the neck. Draw a horizontal line to connect the two neck sides that equals 32 squares, for the base of the neckline.

Shaping shoulders according to gauge
• Stitch gauge of 7 or more stitches per inch = bind off each shoulder in 4 steps
• Stitch gauge of 4–6 stitches per inch = bind off each shoulder in 3 steps
• Stitch gauge of under 4 stitches per inch = bind off each shoulder in 2 steps

The neck measurement is important in shoulder shaping. See page 20 for the Knitter's Guide Chart, which will tell you the proper measurement for your size.

Multiply the neck measurement by the stitch gauge to find out how many stitches to reserve for the neck. Subtract the neck stitches from the stitches remaining at the shoulder. This total is divided in half to equal the number of stitches for each shoulder.

Choose in how many steps you will be decreasing by using the table above. Divide stitches for each shoulder by the number of times you decrease.

TIP
• *When you have a fraction, round off.*

NECKLINE VARIATIONS

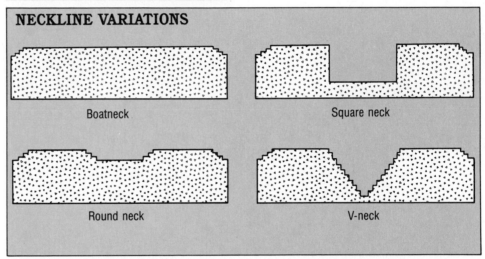

Boatneck

Square neck

Round neck

V-neck

Step 7 —Shaping for neckline variations—After calculating the shoulder decrease, consider the neckline shaping. There are four basic types of necklines: boatneck, square neck, round neck, and V-neck.

Boatneck—By using a straight bind-off for the front and back of the sweater, you create a boatneck. This is the simplest neck shaping as the front and back of the sweater will be the same.

Square neck—To chart this neckline, pick a point 4–6″ below the shoulder, and multiply this number by the row gauge to determine how many squares down to plot the first line of decrease. Since this neckline is square, it will be the same width as the neck, so multiply the neck measurement by the stitch gauge to determine how wide to draw the line. Extend a vertical line from the shoulder straight down to the first neckline decrease on each side.

Depth of neckline = 2"
Row gauge: 5rws = 1"
2" × 5rws = 10rws = first neck decrease

Width of neckline
base = 6"
Stitch gauge: 4sts = 1"

6"
×4sts
24sts

Count downward from the shoulder for 10 squares and make a mark on each side. Draw a horizontal line that is centered and equals 24 stitches. Draw a vertical dotted line straight down from the shoulders at each neck edge to the base of the neckline. By drawing small steps, create a curve on each corner of the neckline.

Depth of neckline = 6"
Row gauge: 5rws = 1"

6"
×5rws
30rws

Count down from the shoulder 30 squares and draw a line.

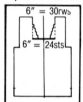

Width of neckline = 6"
Stitch gauge: 4sts = 1"

6"
×4sts
24sts

By counting outward from the center, make the line at the base of the neckline 24 squares wide.
Draw a dotted line straight down from the neck edge to the base of the neckline on each side.
By drawing small steps, create a curve on each corner of the neckline.

Neck measurement = 8"
Stitch gauge: 4sts = 1"

8"
×4sts
32sts

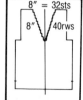

Depth of V = 8"
Row gauge: 5rws = 1"

8"
×5rws
40rws

Draw a point that is 40 squares down from the shoulder on the center line for the base of the V.
32 ÷ 2 = 16sts to decrease each side
40 ÷ 32 = 1.2rws (round down)
Beginning at the base of the V, draw the steps which will show that one stitch will be decreased on each side, every row, until 16 stitches (squares) have been removed.

High round neckline (crew neck)—See page 20 for the Knitter's Guide Chart, which will tell you the proper depth for your size. Take this measurement and multiply by the row gauge to determine the number of squares down to begin the neck decreases. Choose how wide you want the base of the curve to be and multiply that measurement by the stitch gauge to determine how many squares wide to draw the base of the neckline. By drawing a series of small steps, create a curve to the border of the neck edge. (You already determined the width of the neck, which will act as your neckline edge.) Draw a vertical line upward to the shoulder from the last decrease to create the curve.

Low round neckline (scoop neck)—Determine how low you want the scoop to be and multiply by the row gauge. Draw a horizontal line at that point that represents the base of the neckline. Determine how wide you want the base of the neckline to be and multiply by the stitch gauge. Center that number of squares on the line that you just made for the base of the neck. (The more stitches you bind off at this point, the wider the scoop will be. Less stitches bound off will give you a narrower scoop.) Draw a dotted line straight down from the shoulder at the neck edge to the line which represents the base of the neck. Create a gentle curve upward by drawing small steps from the base of the neck to the sides.

Turtleneck—Use shaping instructions for a high round neckline. The turtleneck would be created through the ribbing. All the stitches would be picked up on a circular needle and worked in a rib stitch to the desired length.

TIP
• *Remember that neck shaping and shoulder shaping will occur at the same time.*

V-neck—The V-neck is usually begun on the same row as the armhole decrease. The total number of stitches for the neckline are divided at the center and decreased evenly on each side. The number of stitches to be decreased is your neck measurement (see page 18 to get your proper measurement from the Knitter's Guide Chart), multiplied by the stitch gauge.

First determine the depth of the V and multiply by the row gauge. Count down from the shoulder that many squares for the beginning of the V. This is also the number of rows over which the neck decreases will occur.

Divide the number of neck stitches in half, because there are two sides to the neck shaping. Then divide that number into the total number of rows in the neck shaping to find out how often to decrease on each side.

You may end up with fractions when you divide the number of stitches to decrease into the number of rows. If this occurs, either round up or down, depending on the neckline slope you want. Remember, to decrease 1 stitch on each side of the neck every row would give you a much wider neckline than to decrease 1 stitch on each side of every other row. The latter would create a much steeper angle.

Back V-neck—This is executed exactly as a front V-neck, except back V-necks can be much deeper, which means you begin to decrease earlier. All you have to do is decide how deep you want to make the V. This is an excellent design if you don't have a lot of yarn, as a deep V-back sweater uses much less yarn than other pullovers.

COLLAR VARIATIONS

SEWN-DOWN ROLLED COLLAR

Pick up stitches around the neck edge with circular needle and knit a reverse stockinette stitch for 1" to 4", depending on the size of the roll you want.

Sewn-Down Rolled Collar

Bind off loosely. With an invisible stitch (see page 148) sew the rolled edge down to the sweater on the inside. If you want the roll to be fuller, make the piece a little longer than 4" and roll the extra fabric under.

ROLLED COLLAR (LOOSE)

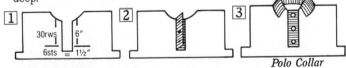

Rolled Collar (Loose)   *Cowl Neck with Ribbing Stitch*

This collar treatment is more akin to the wide turtleneck, but instead of using ribbing, knit garter or stockinette stitch. Pick up the stitches around the neck edge with a circular needle. Choose the stitch you like and work to the desired length. A stockinette or reverse stockinette stitch will give you a full, relaxed roll which naturally curls under. If you use a ribbed stitch, you will get a "cowl neck."

POLO (OR PRINCESS) COLLAR

Decide how deep you want the semiclosure opening for the polo collar. For example, say you want the opening to be 6" deep.

 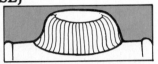

Polo Collar

Step 1 —Draw a line on your chart that equals 6". (Multiply the number of inches by the row gauge to determine the number of rows. 6" × 5rws = 30rws.) Be sure to draw the line from the lowest point of the neckline curve. Decide how wide you want the opening to be. If you want it to be 1½", multiply by the stitch gauge to determine the number of stitches to bind off for the base of the opening (1.5" × 4 = 6sts). Draw this horizontal line and then the two vertical parallel lines to the neck edge. When knitting, bind off the stitches for the width of the opening and knit each side separately.

Step 2 —Pick up the stitches on each side of the opening and work in K1, P1 ribbing for the width you have chosen, making sure to include buttonholes on one side of the opening.

Step 3 —Pick up the neck stitches with a circular needle and work in K1, P1 ribbing, increasing one stitch just inside each outside edge. Work to the desired length.

RUFFLED COLLAR

High Round Neck with Ruffled Collar   *Scoop Neck with Ruffled Collar*

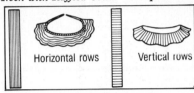

Horizontal rows   Vertical rows

This will work on any type of round neckline. You will knit a piece which is 1½ to 2 times as long as the circumference of the neckline. You can knit this piece on a circular needle, which will give you horizontal rows, or as a long vertical strip, which will give you vertical rows.

Measure the circumference of your neckline.

If you want to knit the collar on a circular needle, multiply the length of the piece by the gauge to determine how many stitches to cast on. For instance, if your neckline was 20" around and you wanted to make the ruffle 1½ times that measurement, you would need a 30" piece. If your stitch gauge is 4sts = 1", 30 × 4 = 120sts. You would cast on 120 stitches for the collar. The ruffle could range from 1½" to 6" in depth. The choice is yours.

If you were going to make one long strip, first you would determine how deep you want the ruffle to be. Let's say you want it to be 4" deep. Multiply your stitch gauge (4sts = 1") by 4 to get 16 stitches to cast on. If the circumference of your neck is 20" and you want to make the collar 1½ times the length of the size of your neck (30"), you would knit the piece 16 stitches wide until you reached 30".

Ruffles are sewn on by taking a strand of yarn and, with a tapestry needle, weaving in and out of one edge of the ruffle piece. Pull together to create a gathered effect. Place the right side of the ruffle on the wrong side of the garment. You may need to tack the piece down with pins and adjust the ruffles so they are evenly distributed. Sew the collar on using a backstitch (see page 147, Finishing Techniques).

SEMICLOSURE SHOULDER BUTTONS

This type of design is quite simple and is an attractive alternative to a regular pullover. Instead of sewing up both shoulder seams, leave one open. Pick up the stitches on one side and work in K1, P1 ribbing, making sure to include

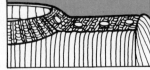

Semiclosure Shoulder Buttons

buttonholes (see page 152, Finishing Techniques). The ribbing should not be longer than 1½". Sew a piece of twill tape to the underside of the other piece to act as a support for the buttons.

SLEEVE VARIATIONS

There are many different styles of sleeves, although the classic, set-in sleeve is the most common. Here we show you basic charting techniques for some popular sleeve styles.

CLASSIC, SET-IN SLEEVE

Covered in basic sleeve charting (see page 51).

RAGLAN SLEEVE

The top of the raglan sleeve joins with the top of the front and back piece to create the neck edge. A good rule of thumb is to allow a 2″ width at the top of the sleeve cap. Chart the sleeve in the same manner as the set-in sleeve to the point of the armhole decrease. Decrease the gauge on the first two rows. Count the number of stitches remaining on the row, and subtract the number of stitches at the cap to determine how many stitches should be decreased from each side.

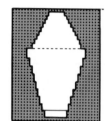
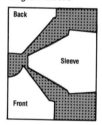

Raglan sleeve

> **TIP**
> • *The rate of decrease of the sleeve cap has to equal the rate of decrease of the front and back so that the angles join properly.*

SADDLE SHOULDER

The top of this sleeve cap is a "yoke," and it becomes part of the neckline and should be between 2″ and 3″ wide, but no wider. The sleeve cap is shaped the same as for a classic, set-in sleeve (see page 51) except it is 1″–1½″ shorter to accommodate the yoke. The length of the yoke is the same as the shoulder width. Chart the sleeve cap in the same manner as the set-in, remembering to make it slightly shorter, and rather than bind off, chart the yoke straight up the length of the shoulder.

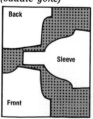

Saddle shoulder (saddle yoke)

SEMI-RAGLAN

This is a combination of the set-in armhole and the raglan armhole. The bottom imitates the raglan, the top is like the set-in. For the front and back in a curve, rather than decreasing the armhole shaping, decrease the same number of stitches on a diagonal, as with a raglan. At the halfway point, knit straight up. For the sleeve, decrease symmetrically on a diagonal, mirroring the front and back, and then bind off straight across.

Semi-raglan sleeve

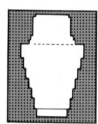

PLEATED SLEEVE

This sleeve can be charted the same as the set-in sleeve to the point just after the armhole shaping. Rather than creating a curved cap, draw a line straight up to the top of the cap, and bind off all in one row. To determine the length of the cap, subtract 1½″ from the length of the armhole to shoulder measure on the front or back. (Front and back measurements are identical.) To create the pleat, bring the two sides of the sleeve cap together as shown in the diagram, and baste with contrasting yarn. After the sleeve has been sewn into the sweater, remove the basting thread.

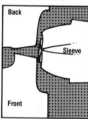

Pleated sleeve

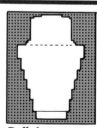

PUFF SLEEVE

This sleeve is charted identically to the pleated sleeve, except the cap is 2″ less than the length of the armhole to shoulder measure on the front or back. When the cap reaches this measure, decrease the width by half over the next four rows as follows: knit every two stitches together across the row, purl the back of the next row. Again, knit every two stitches together across the row, and purl the next row. Bind off. This creates a gathered effect, which gives you a "puff."

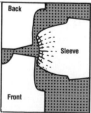

Puff sleeve

DROP SHOULDER

Since the drop shoulder sweater doesn't have an armhole shaping, neither does the sleeve. The body of the drop shoulder style also falls much lower on the arm and has a much wider shoulder measure. Therefore, the sleeve is shorter than a standard sleeve. To ensure a perfect fit, knit the front and back first and sew together at the shoulder seams. Try on the body of the sweater and see where the shoulder falls. Measure from that point to the wrist bone, making sure to bend your elbow for ease. Multiply the number of inches by the row gauge to determine how many rows long the sleeve is. You also have to determine how wide you want the sleeve to be at the shoulder. Measure and multiply by the stitch gauge to determine the number of stitches there are at the top of the sleeve. Subtract the wrist stitches from the shoulder stitches to determine how many stitches to increase. Divide in half to see how many stitches should be added to each side. Finally, divide this number into the number of rows over which the increases will occur to determine how often to increase. Chart the sleeve using the diagram for shape and your figures for the exact measurements.

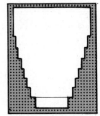

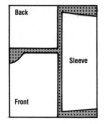

Drop shoulder

LEG O' MUTTON SLEEVE

The design of this sleeve is a combination of several styles. Important measurements are the wrist and upper arm (just below the elbow, where the large increase occurs). The lower part of the sleeve is done in ribbing, switching to larger needles and stockinette stitch at the point of increase.

To determine the lower arm shaping: Multiply each measure (the wrist and the upper arm) by the stitch gauge to determine how many stitches are at each point. Subtract the wrist from the upper arm to find out how many stitches to increase, and divide in half for each side. Measure the length from the wrist to the elbow. Multiply this by the row gauge to determine over how many rows the increases will occur. Divide the number of stitches to be increased (for one side) into the number of rows to find out the rate of increase.

At the elbow, increase 5–15 stitches (depending on ease) evenly across the row. Work straight up until the sleeve reaches the point of armhole decrease. Armhole shaping is the same as for the classic, set-in sleeve. Once the shaping is finished, knit straight up until the cap measures 1½″ less than the measurement from the underarm to the shoulder for the front and back. Create the same type of gathering recommended for the puff sleeve and bind off.

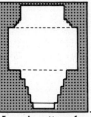

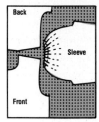

Leg o' mutton sleeve

Ribbed Cuff

Sewn-Down Rolled Cuff

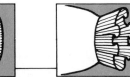

Ruffled Cuff

CUFF VARIATIONS

Traditional cuffs are made with a ribbing stitch. The most common variations are either K1, P1, repeat, or K2, P2, repeat. The length of the cuff is a personal choice. If you like a rolled back cuff, knit it twice the length.

RUFFLED CUFFS

Follow directions for ruffle collar (see page 45). You may have to substitute double-pointed needles for a circular needle, depending on the circumference of the cuff.

SEWN-DOWN ROLLED CUFF

This is made similarly to the sewn-down rolled collar. Pick up the stitches around the cuff edge with a circular needle or three double-pointed needles. Work in a reverse stockinette stitch or garter stitch for 1″–4″, depending on the size of the roll you want. (If you created a rolled neckline, it's appropriate to make matching rolled cuffs.) Bind off loosely. With an invisible stitch, sew the rolled edge down to the inside of the sleeve (see page 148, finishing for seams).

CLASSIC CARDIGANS

Charting the outside shape and armhole shaping for a cardigan is basically the same as for a pullover. The difference occurs in the front opening and neckline shaping. You also have to consider how to handle front border treatments, buttonholes, and collars. We suggest that those who are new at designing use simple ribbed borders and stay away from complicated collar treatments. You can either knit the borders into the garment as you go or knit a long strip of border and sew it on after you've sewn up the sweater. You will find lots of good ideas for buttonholes and border treatments in Chapter Five, Finishing Techniques.

ROUND NECK CARDIGAN

This is the simplest neckline for a cardigan, as the front panels are worked straight up. The inside edges meet to form the front opening. The curve of the neck is created in exactly the same way as for a pullover, except you are working the neckline in two separate pieces (the right and left fronts).

You should determine how deep you want the curve of the neckline to be. Try drawing several different depths on your chart in pencil, once you've established your outside shape. When you decide how deep you want it, multiply the number of inches by your row gauge to determine how many rows down to begin your decrease. Plot the neckline on your chart, as in all previous charting examples.

When you are ready to do your ribbing, consider the simple approach: pick up the neck stitches with a circular needle and work in K1, P1 ribbing to desired depth. Bind off. Pick up the stitches along each front edge, with straight needles (including the neck stitches that border the front edge) and work in K1, P1 ribbing to the same depth as the ribbing on the neck edge. Bind off.

In all of the diagrams of cardigans shown here, we have first drawn a thumbnail sketch of the sweater and then shown what the shape would look like in the schematic.

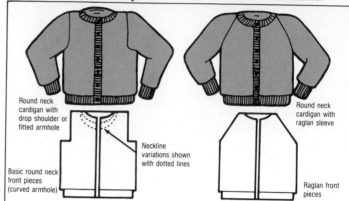

Round neck cardigan with drop shoulder or fitted armhole

Round neck cardigan with raglan sleeve

Basic round neck front pieces (curved armhole)

Neckline variations shown with dotted lines

Raglan front pieces

Step 1 —Pick up stitches along front. Knit to desired width. Bind off.

TIP
• *Knit both sides of the front at the same time to be sure the pieces will be the same length.*

Step 2 —With circular needle, pick up neck stitches (including the front ribbed bands), and work to same width as front bands.

TIP
• *You could also do this process in reverse order: (1) Pick up neck stitches with circular needle and work to desired width. (2) Pick up stitches along front opening (including neck stitches) and work to same depth.*

CARDIGAN BORDERS

These can either be knit into the design or added on after sewing up. If you want to create the border as a part of the design, determine what kind of stitch you would like to use. Garter, seed, and ribbing stitches are the most common, and widths range from ¼″ to 1½″. You may want to use needles of a smaller size for the border to make the gauge match. This is not a problem for a border treatment at the bottom of the sweater. If you want to do a front border treatment for the opening for a cardigan and use a smaller needle size, you will have to come back and do it after the front pieces have been completed. Then sew it on.

If you like, when you cast on, figure in the number of stitches for the front border. When you begin to knit the body of the sweater, put that number of stitches (for the front borders) onto a holder. When you have finished the front

pieces, you can come back, pick up those stitches, knit the border upward to the desired length, and sew it on. This helps to create an integrated look at the bottom edge of the garment.

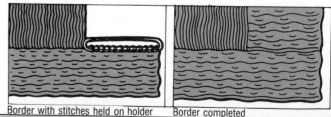

Border with stitches held on holder | Border completed

TIP
• *Don't forget to include the buttonholes on one side of the ribbing on the front opening.*

V-NECK CARDIGAN

Again, the principle is the same as for the pullover version. Determine how deep you want the V to be. Multiply this measurement by the row gauge to see how many rows down to begin your decrease for the V. How wide do you want the V to be? Are you interested in a wide or narrow shoulder? (The wider the V, the narrower the shoulder.) To figure the rate of decrease for the V, determine how many stitches are on the needle at the point of the first decrease (usually the same number that you have cast on) and subtract the number of stitches in the shoulder. (You figure the number of stitches in the shoulder by multiplying the number of inches by the stitch gauge.) Once you know the number of stitches to be decreased, divide into the number of rows over which the decrease will occur to find out how often to decrease. Draw your new information on your chart.

For instance, if you wanted the V to be 10″ deep and the row gauge is 5sts = 1″, you would multiply the two (10″ x 5rws = 50rws) to determine that the first decrease for the V will be 50 rows down from the shoulder. You should make a mark on your chart to tell you where to begin. If you wanted the shoulder to be 4″ wide and your stitch gauge is 4sts = 1″, multiply the two to get 16 stitches at the shoulder. If each front of your sweater is 10″ wide, multiply by the stitch gauge to get 40 stitches to cast on.

To know how many stitches to decrease, subtract the shoulder stitches from the cast-on stitches (40 − 16 = 24). If the V begins 50 rows down from the shoulder, you know that's the number of rows the decrease will occur over, so divide 24 into 50 to get 2. You will decrease one stitch, at the neck edge, every second row, 24 times.

An easy way to do the ribbing on a V-neck cardigan is to pick up the stitches with a circular needle all the way around the front opening, the neckline, and the other front opening. Make the ribbing all one piece to the desired width. It's nice not to have to sew up any extra seams, and having the ribbing all in one piece helps to pull the sweater together.

V-neck cardigan with high neck

Basic pieces for high V-neck cardigan

V-neck cardigan drop shoulder with lower neck

Basic pieces for low V-neck cardigan

Pick up the stitches on the entire neck and front opening with a long circular needle, and knit ribbing to desired width.

DOUBLE-BREASTED CARDIGAN

There are several different ways to design a double-breasted cardigan, but the most common buttons either at the lower edge or within the lower third of the sweater. This style of cardigan usually has a V-neckline, and the front pieces are knit identically, although one buttons on the inside, one on the outside of the sweater.

Many variations of this style have neck ribbing. If the ribbing is wide, it can be the overlapping section, which works well with buttonholes and buttons. If the ribbing is narrow, design the crossover into the body of the sweater.

These illustrations show the relationship between the amount of ribbing and the size of the body of the garment. Less ribbing means more stitches are required for the front of the sweater. More ribbing means fewer stitches for the front of the sweater.

Less ribbing means more stitches to cast on for each front section.

Double-breasted cardigan with narrow ribbing

Front pieces for wide-ribbed double-breasted style.

Double-breasted cardigan with wide ribbing

This variation wraps much farther across and buttons within the body of the garment.

Kimono-style double-breasted cardigan

KIMONO WRAP CARDIGAN

This is an extreme version of a double-breasted style, although it usually has a self-belt or applied belt to keep it closed rather than buttons. The width of the two front panels should be wider than your average cardigan, because one side needs to wrap over the other.

Kimono cardigan with wide ribbing

Front pieces for kimono wrap

Kimonos vary widely:

How much wrap do you want? You will need to add more width across the front of the sweater for a wider wrap.
How long do you want it to be?
How deep do you want the front ribbing?
The deeper the ribbing, the less you will need to knit for each front section.

HOW TO WRITE YOUR OWN PATTERN

Fill in the boxes with the calculations from the schematic.

If you have a basic understanding of how to chart a pattern and how to write a pattern, you can design anything. No more confusion over not being able to decipher a pattern from a book—when you make up your own, you get it just the way *you* want it.

To create a written record of your pattern instruction, here is a step-by-step format to learn on. The instructions appearing in boldface may be extracted and used over again simply by working up new figures for each new garment. With experience, you may improvise and create your own style of written instructions.

Begin the pattern-writing process with a thumbnail sketch of your sweater and a schematic diagram with the measurements included (see page 34 for

instructions). We have provided these drawings at the beginning of the pattern in a separate column, where you will also see a breakdown of what should be filled in to each box for our example.

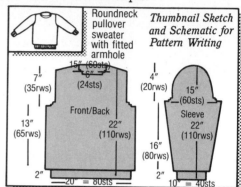

Roundneck pullover sweater with fitted armhole

Thumbnail Sketch and Schematic for Pattern Writing

15" (60sts)
7" (35rws)
6" (24sts)
4" (20rws)
15" (60sts)
Sleeve
22" (110rws)
Front/Back
13" (65rws)
22" (110rws)
16" (80rws)
2"
20" = 80sts
2"
10" = 40sts

Gauge: 4sts = 1"
5rws = 1"

Our Examples

80sts

2"

Back:—Cast on ■ stitches (using needles two to three sizes smaller than needles used to make your gauge swatch) for ribbing. K1, P1 (or K2, P2, K3, P3, depending on your preference) for ■ inches. (The average rib is about 2½ inches.) Change to larger needles.

(Have you chosen your stitch? For example, we'll use stockinette stitch, which is one of the most basic.)

Depending on the style of sweater you've chosen, you may want to increase on the first row. One stitch added on each end will add fullness. To create a blousy effect, you can increase two stitches or more, divided evenly across the row.

Most sweater patterns "work even" to the armhole, meaning no increases or decreases will occur *(optional)*.

0   80sts

15"

(optional)
We aren't increasing for this design.

Add ■ stitches across the first row, making ■ stitches in total. Work even until piece measures ■ inches to armhole.

How long do you want your sweater to be? The length of the sweater is always figured from the armhole downward. (If you were knitting a drop shoulder sweater there would be no armhole, therefore you would "work even" until you reached the shoulder measure.)

15"
shoulder width = 15" × 4sts
                      60sts

80sts   60sts

80 sts
−60sts
20sts total to decrease
20 ÷ 2 = 10sts each side

Now we will plot the armhole decrease. What we need to do is reduce the body of the garment to the width of the shoulders. So take the number of inches at the shoulder, and multiply it by the gauge, to get the number of stitches at the shoulder. We know we have ■ stitches on the needle, which should be reduced to ■, so subtract the shoulder stitches from the chest stitches to discover the total number of stitches to be decreased. Divide this in half to determine how many stitches to decrease on each side.

These stitches cannot all be decreased at once if you desire a curved, fitted armhole. (If you want a notched armhole, they can. In that case, the sleeves would also have to be notched in the same manner to fit correctly.) So, for a curved, fitted armhole, begin by binding off your stitch gauge on the first two rows. Now you want to create a gradual curve for the armhole shaping. Decrease progressively fewer stitches on every other row, until you've decreased the total number required. The instructions would read:

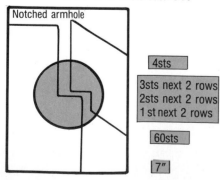

Notched armhole

4sts

3sts next 2 rows
2sts next 2 rows
1 st next 2 rows

60sts

7"

Bind off ■ stitches at the beginning of next 2 rows. Now decrease ■st each end every ■ row ■ times.

Armhole completed.

The number of stitches left on the needle should now correspond to the number of stitches you need at the shoulder: ■. (See page 19 for the Knitter's Guide Chart, which will give you the proper armhole length for your size.)

Work even until armhole measures ■ inches.

Now you have reached the shoulder. You have several options, depending on the style you have chosen. If you choose a boatneck or drop shoulder sweater, your instructions would read Bind off all stitches.

If you choose a more fitted garment, you should decrease in steps to create a sloped shoulder. The following table will be helpful in determining how many steps you should take in binding off.

> Stitch gauge of 7sts or more per inch = bind off each shoulder in 4 steps.
> Stitch gauge of 4–6sts per inch = bind off each shoulder in 3 steps.
> Stitch gauge of under 4sts per inch = bind off each shoulder in 2 steps.

Now turn to page 20 for the Knitter's Guide Chart, which will tell you how many inches to leave for the neck. Multiply the number of inches times your stitch gauge to get the number of stitches at the neck. To determine how many stitches you will bind off on each side, subtract the number of neck stitches from the number of shoulder stitches and divide in half. You know from the chart in how many steps you should bind off. We now need to know how many stitches should be decreased in each step. So, divide the number of steps into the number of stitches in each shoulder.

Bind off ▥ stitches at beginning of next ▥ rows. (Two rows at right and two at left.)

Now we are left with the neck stitches, which can either be bound off or put on a holder and picked up later for the neck ribbing. The instructions would read:

Either bind off or put the remaining neck stitches on a holder.

Front

If you are knitting a pullover sweater, the instructions for the front will be identical to the back until you get to the neck opening. Therefore, to write the instructions, refer to those for the back and duplicate to that point.

To choose your neck style, see page 44 for neckline variations. There you will find instructions for basic neckline styles.

Sleeve

We are going to show you how to record these instructions in two ways: a verbal description and a visual description (charting), using graph paper.

Get a piece of graph paper, and as you read these instructions, plot out your own sleeve.

There are many types of sleeves, and the instructions will depend on the style you have chosen. Let's assume, for now, that you're going to make a classic, set-in sleeve with a cuff at the wrist. Here's how you would proceed.

Step 1 —Having determined your wrist measurement, multiply the number of inches times the gauge to get the number of stitches to cast on.

Cast on ▥ sts on smaller needles.

(We like to make both sleeves at once, so they're identical, which means you cast on for one sleeve, then take another ball of yarn and cast on again for second sleeve.)

Assuming each box on the graph paper equals one stitch, draw a line on paper that equals the number of stitches at wrist. Find the center line and draw a dotted line up to the top of the page.

Step 2 —Take your upper arm measurement and multiply by the stitch gauge to get the number of stitches. Using your own judgment, choose an area 2/3 of the way up the page, and plot out this number of stitches using the center line to create symmetry.

Step 3 —Now we'll figure out the length of the sleeve from armhole to wrist and the number of stitches we should increase. We have already done the ribbing. Your final increase should be 3″ below the armhole bind off. To determine how many inches over which to increase, subtract these two figures from the total length from wrist to armhole.

Multiply the number of inches by the row gauge to determine how many rows to plot on the graph.

Draw a dotted line straight down (counting out the number of rows) to make a rectangle, between the wrist and armhole.

Gauge: 4sts = 1″
Bind off in 3 steps

Neck = 6″   6″   60sts = shoulder
        ×5sts   −30sts = neck
       ─────   ──────
        30sts   30sts

30 ÷ 2 = 15sts each shoulder

15 ÷ 3 = 5sts each step

5sts   6rws

Step 1

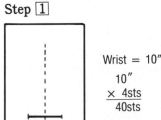

Wrist = 10″

10″
× 4sts
─────
40sts

40

Step 2

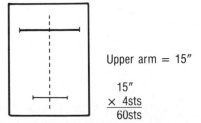

Upper arm = 15″

15″
× 4sts
─────
60sts

Step 3

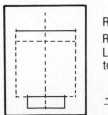

Ribbing = 2″
Row gauge: 5rws = 1″
Length from wrist
to armhole = 18″

2″   18″   13″
+3″   − 5″   × 5rws
───   ───   ─────
5″   13″   65rws

Stitches at wrist = 40sts
Stitches at upper arm = 60sts

$$60\text{sts}$$
$$\underline{-40\text{sts}}$$
$$20\text{sts} \quad 20 \div 2 = 10\text{sts each side}$$

$65 \div 10 = 6.5$ (round up)

Increase 1 st each side every 7th rw.

Step 4

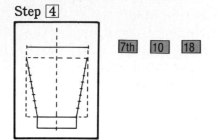

7th   10   18

Step 5

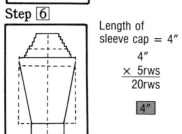

4sts

3sts next 2rws
2sts next 2rws
1st next 2rws

Step 6

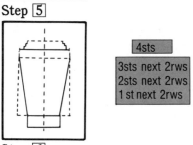

Length of
sleeve cap = 4″

$$4''$$
$$\underline{\times \ 5\text{rws}}$$
$$20\text{rws}$$

4″

Step 4 —Subtract the number of stitches at the wrist from the number of stitches at the upper arm to determine the number of stitches you should increase.

Divide this figure in half to see how many stitches will be increased on each side.

Take this last figure and divide it into the number of rows over which you'll be increasing. This figure tells you to increase one stitch on each side this many times.

On your graph paper, begin with the first row after changing to larger needles and draw your first increase here. Count up to the next increase and draw one more stitch each side, and so on, all the way up to the final increase. Your instructions would now read:

Increase 1 stitch each end every ■ row ■ times until piece measures ■ inches to armhole.

Step 5 —The sleeve cap has to fit successfully into the front and back. Therefore repeat the armhole shaping that you did on the front and back.

Bind off ■ stitches at the beginning of next 2 rows. Now decrease ■ stitches each end every ■ row ■ times.

Step 6 —See page 20 for the Knitter's Guide Chart to determine how many inches the sleeve cap should be for your size. Multiply this figure by the row gauge to determine how many total rows are in the cap.

Decrease 1 stitch each end every other row until cap measures ■ inches. Bind off remaining stitches.

Please, be assured that as complicated as this may seem at first reading, you will soon catch on and be creating your own sweaters in no time! Have patience!

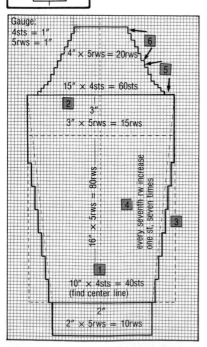

Gauge:
4sts = 1″
5rws = 1″

6

4″ × 5rws = 20rws

5

15″ × 4sts = 60sts

2
3″
3″ × 5rws = 15rws

16″ × 5rws = 80rws

every seventh rw increase
one st. seven times

4

3

1

10″ × 4sts = 40sts
(find center line)

2″
2″ × 5rws = 10rws

Finishing

We have provided an entire chapter on finishing techniques, which you may use as a guide.

At left is your finished sleeve chart. We have numbered each step on the chart so you can see the progression.

*Completed Diagram for a
Classic, Set-In Sleeve*

CREATE YOUR OWN PICTORIAL SWEATERS

At this point you should have a good grasp of what shape is, how to choose a shape that is flattering to your figure, and how to create a pattern for your garment. Now the fun begins: creating your own pictorial sweaters.

The words "pictorial," "jacquard," and "intarsia" all refer to multicolored knitting. There are many different ways of creating these "jacquard" effects, and we will go into much more detail about them later in this section. The major types of designs that are covered are:

- Stripes, checks, and plaids
- Argyles
- Fabric motifs, including floral patterns
- Pictorial landscapes (or realistic imagery)
- Two-color stitches (also called "bicolor" and "mosaic")
- Scandinavian, Fair Isle, and Icelandic motifs
- Free-form, free-hand painting, abstract, and geometrics

Now that you have a good supply of graph paper, you are ready to begin.

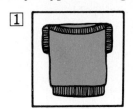

Step 1 —<u>Choose a shape for your sweater.</u> Remember to start with something simple.

Step 2 —<u>Using the principle of one square equals one stitch and one row, plot the outside shape of the sweater</u> (see page 34). Remember that the gauge will help you determine how many stitches are in each row. Follow the schematic for all these important measurements.

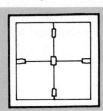

TIP
- *Depending on the size of the grid you have chosen, you may not be able to fit the entire garment on one sheet of paper. If you need more space, tape four sheets together to allow plenty of room. Be sure to keep the grid properly aligned from sheet to sheet.*

Step 3 —<u>Put number across the bottom and up the side of the outline to help keep track of stitches while knitting</u> (see page 22).

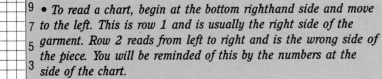

TIP
- *To read a chart, begin at the bottom righthand side and move to the left. This is row 1 and is usually the right side of the garment. Row 2 reads from left to right and is the wrong side of the piece. You will be reminded of this by the numbers at the side of the chart.*
  For circular needle, always read from right to left.

Step 4 —<u>Choose an image, motif, or pattern that you want to put on the sweater.</u> We have used simple geometric shapes to illustrate how to plot curves and angles.

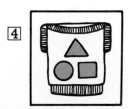

Step 5 —<u>Using a pencil, sketch the image onto the graph paper.</u> (If you want to trace an image to create a more realistic appearance, see page 60 for instructions.)

Step 6 —<u>Still using the pencil, go over the sketch, making it contour to the stepped lines of the grid.</u> You will see in this figure how to determine where to draw the steps. If the diagonal or curved pencil line is less than half of the square, do not include the square in the step. If it is more than half, do include it. Remember that for any object that is symmetrical, such as a circle or triangle, both sides must correspond.

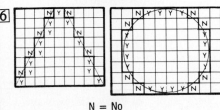

N = No
Y = Yes

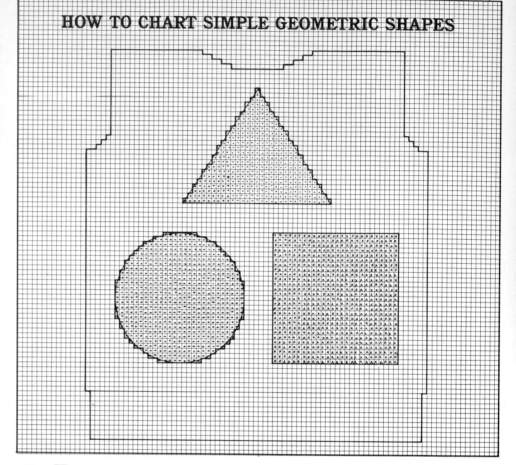

HOW TO CHART SIMPLE GEOMETRIC SHAPES

Blue	•
Red	+
Yellow	x
White	

Step 7 —<u>Choose your colors</u>. The easiest way is to use colored pencils or markers. This way you can see how the colors and shapes work together. This will also help you to see if the shapes have been correctly charted. When you fill an outline with color, the form becomes clearer, and you see where the shape needs refinement. If you've realized that you don't like your drawing at this stage, it is easy to erase and change.

Another way to assign color to shapes is through symbols. This works well if you have to translate a pattern into black and white (i.e., if you want to photocopy it to give to a friend or keep for your files). Either make up your own symbols or choose from the ones we've provided at left. A good way to keep track of which symbol relates to each color is to make a box on the side of the chart with either a swatch of the yarn, colored pencil, or colored paper next to the symbol.

Step 8 —<u>Outline your design with pen for permanence</u> once you know it's the way you want it. You're now ready to knit.

HOW TO SCALE IMAGES AND MOTIFS

To "scale" an image means either to enlarge or to reduce it, in order to fit an assigned space. This is an important skill to learn for designing your own pictorial sweaters. Let's say you have a favorite skirt that has a flying duck motif. To make a matching outfit, you would like to use that duck as a large image on the front of a sweater. The duck is obviously too small in its present form. How do you enlarge it to fit your charted pattern?

First consider what size graph paper to use. If the graph paper has a small grid structure, your sweater outline will be relatively small also. In this case, depending on how large you want the duck to be, you may not need to enlarge it at all. If, however, you are making a full-size outline of the garment, using the second method described (see page 38), you will have to enlarge the duck considerably.

The easiest method of reducing and enlarging is the new copy machine. For little time and money, you can have an instant copy of your image transformed to the size you want.

Original size   Same size   Motif slightly larger   Motif larger yet   Motif very large

Enlarging and Reducing Motifs

HOW TO PREPARE YOUR IMAGE FOR PHOTOSTATING

Step 1 —Mount your image on a piece of cardboard by taping the corners.

Step 2 —Place a tissue over the top and write your sizing instructions on the tissue. Be sure to specify how large you want the finished image to be. For example, if you have a 3½″ × 5″ snapshot and you want to enlarge it to 16″ × 20″, write in bold letters, Enlarge entire photograph to 16″ × 20″.

Step 3 —*(optional)* Include any cropping instructions. Cropping is a way of retrimming an image to include only what you want. For instance, you have an instamatic print of a friend in a large crowd of people but only want to enlarge the image of your friend. You should draw a rectangle around the figure that you want to keep and enlarge, and be sure to specify how large you want the finished image to be. (Do any drawing or writing on the tissue overlay.)

How To Prepare Your Image for Photostating

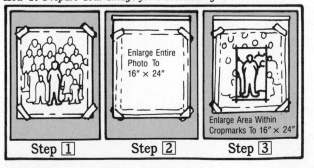

Step 1   Step 2   Step 3

HOW TO ENLARGE BY USING A GRID

Step 1 —Begin by putting a piece of tracing paper over the image and drawing a grid over it.

Step 2 —Decide how large you want the image to be and draw a grid with the same number of squares on a larger sheet of paper.

Step 3 —Go through each square and copy the configuration of lines that exist in the smaller version. This is a tedious method and is only recommended for simple graphic images.

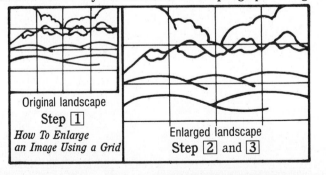

Original landscape
Step 1
How To Enlarge an Image Using a Grid

Enlarged landscape
Step 2 and 3

TIP

• *In the knitted piece, the degree of complexity of an image is in direct relation to the gauge you choose. If you decide that you want to use knitting worsted and your gauge is 4sts = 1″, realize that you can better depict a complex image than if you use a bulkier yarn with 2sts = 1″. Conversely, you will have less detail with the worsted than if you choose a sport weight yarn with a gauge of 6sts or 8sts = 1″. The more stitches per inch, the more possibility for color and detail complexity.*

PROGRESSIVE EXAMPLES OF CHARTING MOTIFS

Following are a series of examples of charting for different kinds of pictorial images and motifs. These are grouped according to styles and progress from the simplest level to the more complex.

If you are a beginner, start with example A, chart it yourself, and begin multicolor knitting. As you gain confidence about using more than one color at a time, move on to example B, perhaps in a different category. Always practice charting each design on graph paper, with your own sweater shape and a gauge swatch. Your choice of shape, yarn weight, and color will make the sweater your own original.

If you are a beginner, choose a simple outline shape such as a drop shoulder sweater (see page 37), which is a simple rectangle with no armhole shaping. It's also a good idea to begin with a 4-ply or knitting worsted yarn; the smooth texture will make it easier to check the tension and gauge.

TIPS

• When knitting a sweater, a good way to keep track of your place is to mark your chart with a pencil at the end of each row you finish. If the design is especially complicated, you may want to make a few marks throughout the row. That way, if you are suddenly called to the phone you won't lose your place. When you're finished with the garment, simply erase all of the marks and the pattern is ready to be used again.

A ruler or straight edge also works well to remind you which row you are working on. Move the ruler up as you finish each row.

• If you're new to charting, it's a good idea to measure your "work in progress" frequently, to be sure that the gauge and tension are correct. Because of the elasticity of the ribbing, stretch it a bit to measure the base of the garment. Pin it down if necessary to your ironing board. Remember to check the gauge at all times. If it appears that the garment is too small or too large, you know that you either didn't figure properly or you're not knitting the original gauge. Rip it out before you get too far along and make the corrections needed. You may recheck your math on the Prep Page or remeasure your original gauge swatch.

STRIPES, CHECKS, AND PLAIDS

Stripes are one of the most basic motifs and can be combined in many creative color combinations. If you combine both horizontal and vertical stripes, you create checks. If you go one step further and introduce a simple line pattern, a plaid pattern is created. More complex plaids can be created by simply overlapping more lines in each direction and by varying the colors.

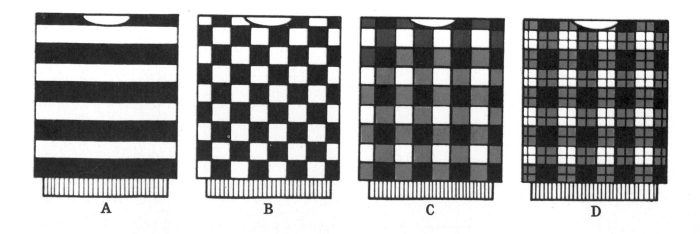

A   B   C   D

ARGYLES

Argyles were originally inspired by the Scottish clan Campbell of Argyll, and are a relative of the plaid family. These are basically checks that have been placed on a diagonal with colored lines crossing in each section. Because of constant color changes, we recommend using bobbins. This helps to avoid excessive tangling (see page 62).

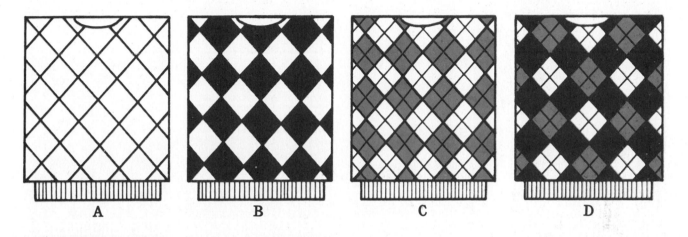

A   B   C   D

FABRIC MOTIFS

Fabric motifs are a wonderful source of creative ideas for the knitwear designer. Pick up even the simplest motif, using just one or two colors, or duplicate the swatch in its entirety.

A   B   C

BICOLOR DESIGNS

Bicolor designs are a great way to learn about handling more than one color at the same time. These can be as easy or as difficult as you like. Play with the possibilities and see what you can invent yourself.

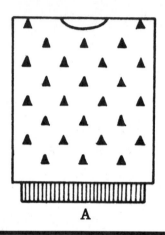

A

B

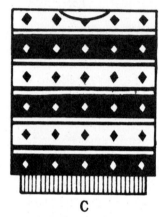

C

D

FREE-FORM, ABSTRACT, AND GEOMETRIC

Free-form, abstract, and geometric designs are great ways to play with shape and color. Have you ever wondered what your favorite painting would look like on a sweater? Get a print of it, blow it up, and chart it onto a sweater. Do you have a great matchbook cover from your favorite restaurant? Blow up a corner of it and knit an unusual piece of Pop Art. Other inspirations could be your own handwriting, maps, magazine clippings, numbers, graffiti, greeting cards, comics, and so on.

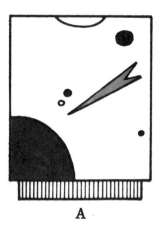

A

B

C

D

SCANDINAVIAN, FAIR ISLE, AND ICELANDIC

The islands off the coasts of England, Ireland, and Scotland as well as the Scandinavian countries were among the first to develop knitting motifs. These are our knitting heritage, and the lineage of charted designs from this region is impressive. There are many similarities between the motifs of these countries because their basic approach is the same. The coloration is what is most different. The Scandinavian sweaters traditionally used only two colors, the backgrounds being dark for men and light for women.

Fair Isles traditionally are worked in natural shades derived from vegetable dyes created from the surrounding landscape: lavender and mauve, heather tones, mossy greens, the colors of sea and soil. Fair Isle motifs are similar to Scandinavian but are repeated in such frequency that a dense patterning is created.

Because of the complexity of Fair Isle designs, many people shy away from making them.

There is a simple way of achieving the same Fair Isle look using the same design motifs without having to go through the complex process of color changes.

Find a variegated yarn that has a lot of color changes within each strand, and is in a general color range that would appear on a Fair Isle. Choose a background color that coordinates, remembering that Fair Isles have very subtle color changes. Use the solid color as the background, the variegated yarn as the color which picks up the design: the variegation will create an effect of color change without all the work.

Icelandic motifs are similar to Fair Isle designs, but the colors are strictly limited to those that occur naturally. These use the thick furry yarn called "lopi," and in its natural state its colors are rich blacks, whites, grays, and beiges. Due to the thickness of the yarn, the designs are simple and bold and appear as simplified Scandinavian motifs.

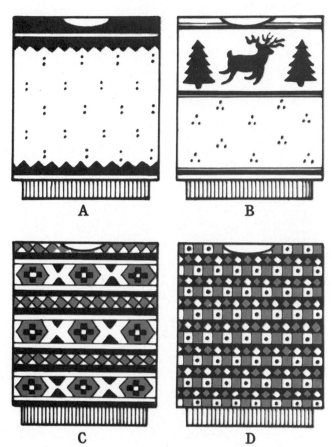

A

B

C

D

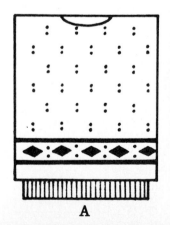

A

B

C

D

TIP
• *For bicolor knitting: If you're working with an overall jacquard repeat motif that is small in size (three or four stitches per repeat), be sure that the number of stitches on the needle is divisible by that number; otherwise you will begin or end a row in the middle of the pattern. If it's a larger repeat motif, be sure to center the pattern so that each side is symmetrical.*

CHARTING A LANDSCAPE OR REALISTIC IMAGE

As you start thinking about pictorial sweaters, you'll realize that the possibilities are endless and exciting. Have you ever seen a beautiful painting or photograph and thought it would be great for a sweater? Well, you can do it! This is a perfect gift idea: for example, take a photograph of your best friend's country home and knit the image on a sweater. It'll make a comfy Christmas present. Do the front as a "painting in yarn," and knit the back in a single color. If you want to get more elaborate, make the entire sweater into a painting by coordinating the design across the sleeves and even onto the back.

However, this type of sweater requires a lot more concentration than your average "jacquard" motif. In order to make the process clearer, we've provided step-by-step illustrations.

light brown	= ⊟	light green	= ⊿	sky blue	= ⊡	dark brown = ⊠
pink	= ⟑	dark green	= ◿	turquoise	= ⊞	white = ☐

Step 1 —Start by choosing a simple shape for the sweater. (Pictorial sweaters work best on simple shapes.) Draw a thumbnail sketch.

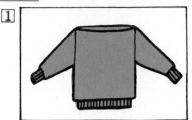

Step 2 —Draw a schematic with all the important measurements included. Don't forget to include "ease."

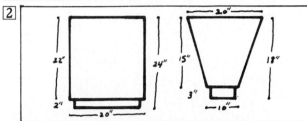

Step 3 —Choose the yarn, realizing that the thickness of the strand (the weight) is directly related to the gauge. The gauge will determine the amount of detail which can be achieved in images and color shadings. (For example, six to eight stitches per inch will achieve much more detail than two stitches per inch.)

TIP
• *Worsted weight and sport weight yarns work best for complex pictorials because these have a smooth texture when knit up, and the color selection is larger than other varieties. Usually worsted yarns have a gauge of 4–5sts = 1" and sports have a gauge of 6–8sts = 1" The smaller gauge will also take more time to knit.*

More advanced knitters might enjoy playing with different yarns and textures for different effects within the landscape. Clouds look ethereal when knitted with angora or mohair; trees, bushes, and grasses with shaggy textural yarns or any of the new novelty yarns; water with shiny lurex; rocks, pebbles, and dirt with bouclés; birds with feather yarn; animals with furry yarn.

Step 4 —Knit a swatch using stockinette stitch and several of the colors that make up the bulk of the sweater and determine the gauge.

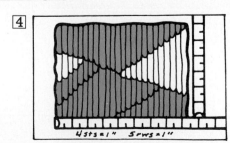

Step 5 —Select the image you want to use (if you're not drawing it free-hand). You can select an image from a magazine, postcard, calendar, photograph, or illustration. The main thing to be concerned with is the complexity of the image and how it will translate onto the sweater grid. (For your first attempt choose something simple.)

Step 6 —Select the size of tracing paper that will accommodate the image size. If it is either too big or too small, adjust the size using scaling methods (see page 55).

Step 7 —Draw the outline of the sweater front on the graph paper, using the dimensions from the schematic.

Step 8 —Trace the image with pencil through the graph paper, positioning the image on the center of the front. (Remember, the side and underarm areas won't be visible, so the main focus should be center front.)

Step 9 —Translate the rough pencil lines into the stepped lines of the grid. You may have to eliminate some of the detail of the image to create a clear, sharp image.

Step 10 —Choose colors for each area and indicate them with colored pencils or markers. This is a great way to use up remnants of yarns from other projects.

TIP
• *When you are finished and have added color, study the piece to see whether you have included all the detail you want. Remember, you can always embroider detail on top of the finished sweater.*

Step 11 —Make a chart at the side of the graph which assigns a color to each color choice. You can put symbols in each square, if you wish, for permanence. For the actual first "knit-through," it's easier with colors on the grid.

Step 12 —Take your chart to the yarn store and select the yarn. Generally, you will need one skein per color except for the background color(s). If in doubt, ask the salesperson.

Step 13 —Start knitting!

HOW TO KNIT WITH MORE THAN ONE COLOR

There are two methods used in knitting with two or more colors to help keep order: using bobbins to create separate "balls" of yarn for each color section, and carrying the yarn across the back of the work.

When your sweater pattern calls for 2 or more colors, there are 2 methods to help keep order. You can knit with bobbins when you don't want to use as much yarn, and when you don't want a double-thickness. You can carry yarn across the back when there are distinct color sections or when the color change is frequent.

BOBBINS

Bobbins were created to help the knitter avoid tangled yarn when working with many different colors. If a color is used once in an isolated shape and not later in that row, wind a special bobbin for it.

Argyle and plaid patterns, which may use the same color many times in one row, are exceptions. Because there are so many color changes, it is most efficient to wind a bobbin for each colored shape or line in the pattern. It is possible to have up to fifteen or twenty bobbins dangling off the back of the needle.

Remember to twist the strands together when changing colors to avoid holes in the knitted fabric. While twisting, pay attention to the stitch tension: the stitches should be neither too loose nor too tight.

Bobbins can either be purchased at a yarn store or made by hand.

HOW TO MAKE YOUR OWN BOBBINS

Step 1 Take a piece of cardboard or heavy poster board and cut rectangles approximately 1½″ × 3″.

Step 2 Either make a simple slit from each end halfway to the center, or cut a small window at each end.

Step 3 Wind as much yarn around the bobbin as will comfortably fit.

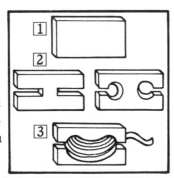

TIPS

• *When you run out of yarn on a bobbin, either tie on a new piece and weave the ends in after the garment is finished, or splice it in as you go.*

• *Knitting in the round? Do not use bobbins. Carry the yarn across the back for color changes. Bobbins are used to carry colored yarns from one point to another on a row and must be held at the beginning of a color change. On a knit row, use the bobbin to knit from point A to point B; on a purl row use the bobbin to purl from point B to point A. This back and forth "weaving" of colors creates the pattern. In circular knitting, which is always worked in the same direction, there is no way to get the color back to its point of origin.*

CARRYING YARN ACROSS THE BACK

If the color is used repeatedly across the row, as in bicolor knitting or Fair Isle patterns, carry the yarn across the back of the piece. Be sure to twist the yarn that isn't being used into the yarn that is being used every fourth or fifth stitch to avoid looped strands dangling off the inside of the garment. Done properly, this "carrying" creates a woven quality across the back of the work.

This method will add thickness to the garment, also warmth. It's a good idea to consider what kind of a garment it is: if it's a ski sweater that will be worn for warmth and bulk, then this technique would be appropriate. If you want to minimize your figure, it would be inappropriate. Knitted fabric created with bobbins gives a single-thickness, smoother fabric, which is more appropriate for those who need to minimize bulk.

TIPS

• *"Carrying" may not work with certain types of yarn, mohairs, for example. Due to the fluffy quality of mohair, the fibers become integrated with each other and show through to the front of the garment. Bobbins are recommended.*

Also, darker yarns don't work well when carried across the back of lighter yarns. They'll create a shadow effect that makes the garment look slightly dingy. Use bobbins.

• *When carrying yarn, be sure to check the gauge often. The process of working and twisting several strands together creates a tighter tension. If you find the gauge is getting tighter, switch to larger needles. Also, try to keep stitches spaced evenly across the needle and not bunched up at the tips. This will help to keep the knitted fabric from puckering.*

HOW TO DESIGN AN ARAN SWEATER

The Aran sweater tradition comes from a small cluster of islands off the western coast of Ireland where the women make rugged, waterproof, and beautifully crafted sweaters for their husbands and sons who are fishermen. Originally each fisherman's family had its own design, and many of the stitch patterns symbolized married life and the fisherman's trade. The hallmark of these sweaters is the highly textured surfaces with many unique stitches and cables.

One of the reasons many people shy away from knitting Aran sweaters is their complex appearance. One look at a typical pattern for an Aran and even those who love to read stitch patterns could get confused. Don't despair, it's actually easier and more fun to design your own Aran than to try to follow someone else's pattern.

We'll take you through a description of what elements make up an Aran, help you to start a section in your Workbook devoted to Aran swatches, and teach you how to chart your own Aran designs. Just start with a simple shape and several stitches that you feel comfortable with and you'll be ready to knit one in no time.

A typical Aran is made from four-ply worsted weight yarn. If you choose a yarn with lanolin in it, you'll have an authentic waterproof outdoor wrap. You'll need between 28 and 40 ounces of yarn for a large sweater, which is more yarn than called for in an average large because the complex cables and stitches pull the strands tighter together, using more wool.

All Arans have a wide central panel flanked by narrower bands repeated on both sides. There are usually three to four different motifs involved, and the background is a reverse stockinette stitch, which acts as a "ground" for all the stitches to stand out against. Cables are an absolute *must*. The sleeves generally repeat two or three of the same motifs, but the panels are more condensed and of equal widths.

A great way to familiarize yourself with some of the various stitch patterns is to buy a skein of worsted yarn and begin to knit gauge swatches. Start a section in your Workbook devoted to Arans. As you create a swatch of a new stitch pattern, lightly press it with a steam iron and staple it onto a piece of paper. You will want to record the gauge, needle size, written instructions for the stitch, and a symbolcraft graph for the stitch. It's a good idea to practice using symbols for stitch patterns because they are easier to read and understand *at a glance*. If you get in the habit of making a graph of each stitch that you learn, you may never go back to written instructions. What you will eventually create is a catalog of the stitches and cables that you know how to knit and an instant reference for gauge and texture. When you begin to design your own Arans, take your Workbook to the copy center and photocopy each swatch. This will make the designing process a simple matter of cut and paste to see which combination you like best.

True Arans are very complex, but it's possible to create an Aran effect using stitch patterns that are quite simple. Below you will find a description of each of the major elements in an Aran and the most basic patterns that can be used for each stitch section. (See pages 23–25 for instructions.)

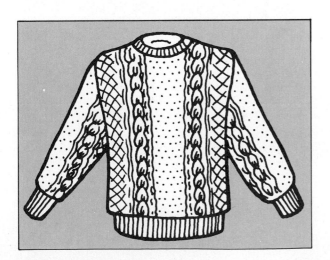

TIPS
• *If a design looks too plain and you want to spice it up, add bobbles at regular intervals. Popcorn and bobble stitches add wonderful dimensionality to a sweater.*

• *Cables tighten gauge. To offset this, add several stitches to either side of the cable. A good way to observe this is to knit a swatch of stockinette stitch then directly above it begin a cable stitch. You will see how the cables pull and contract the horizontal measure of the swatch.*

• *Use pencil to mark the end of each finished row.*

• *Use markers to divide stitch patterns from each other.*

• *If you want the ribbing to be much tighter than the body of the sweater, subtract 10–20 percent of the stitches needed to cast on. When you change needles and begin to knit the first row of the sweater, add those stitches on by increasing them, evenly spaced, across the first row.*

CENTRAL PANEL

The central panel is the major focus of the sweater and usually shouldn't exceed the width of the neck. (Refer to Knitter's Guide Charts for your proper neck measurement, p. 20). The width of this panel determines how many stitches remain on either side for other stitches. Fancy cables often go here, but equally popular are highly textured stitches. The basic stitches that would work well are moss, sand, Irish moss, double moss, and wasp's nest, also called honeycomb.

SIDE PANELS

It's important to create a good balance of stitches, cables, and background. The side panels have different pattern stitches from those on the central panel. They are arranged symmetrically and equally spaced from the central panel, and are narrower as well.

DIVIDERS

Generally each panel is framed by a vertical line of divider stitches. Ideas for basic dividers are changing rib, tweed stitch rib, pearl twisted rib, knotted cord, and crossed stitches. (Remember, the possibilities are endless. These are some simple suggestions.)

CABLES

An integral part of an Aran, cables can be placed anywhere. They can act as divider stitches or can be the central focus of attention. We have provided some interesting cables in the stitch section.

STEP-BY-STEP INSTRUCTIONS FOR ARAN SWEATERS

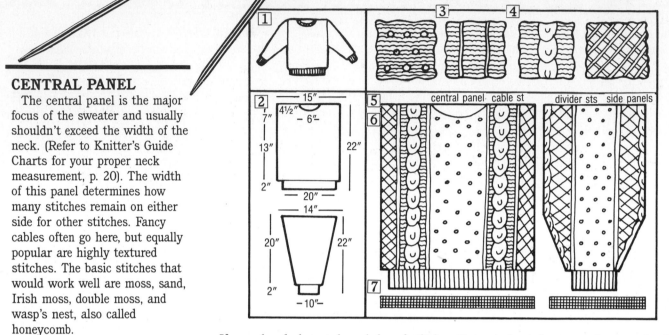

If you already have a knowledge of stitch patterns or have done some homework with swatching, you are ready to actually chart your own Aran design. Follow along step by step with your own graph paper and our illustrated instructions to begin:

Step 1 —Choose a sweater shape and draw a thumbnail sketch. If you're a beginner, start with a simple rectangular drop shoulder shape; you don't even need to do a neck shaping if you really want to simplify. Also, no sleeve cap shaping will be required, which works well with the pattern stitches.

Step 2 —Draw a schematic of major pattern pieces, including the measurements plus ease.

Step 3 —Choose your stitch patterns. Choose one for the central panel, side panels, divider stitches, and cables.

Step 4 —Measure each stitch pattern for gauge. Don't stretch the fabric.

Step 5 —Using graph paper, plot out the shape of the sweater (front/back) first and then sleeve using 1st = 1 square, 1rw = 1 square.

Step 6 —Experiment with the placement of the stitches. Start with the center panel and work outward to the side panels, remembering to keep a symmetrical design.

Step 7 —Using symbolcraft, convert the written pattern instructions into visual symbols and place at the bottom of the chart. Make sure to position each symbol directly under the stitch to which it corresponds.

Step 8 —Sleeves: Go through Steps 3 – 7 , keeping in mind that the panels will be more compact and of equal width. If you would prefer to avoid increasing within a stitch pattern or cable, you might consider positioning small stitch cables or border stitches along either side of the sleeve edge. You can increase on the inside edge of the cable or add more border stitches.

SKIRTS

Today, hand-knit skirts are as fashionable as hand-knit sweaters. The same principles apply to skirt design as to sweaters. Begin by considering the shape of a skirt as contained within a basic rectangle: the longest measure being the length of the rectangle, the widest measure being the width. Shaping is achieved through increasing to create a gradual slope from the narrowest points to the widest points, or vice versa.

There are several ways to make a skirt: either in two flat pieces on straight needles, or in one piece on circular needles. Generally flat pieces are worked from the bottom (hemline or "baseline") up to the waistline, and shaping occurs along the outside edge of the garment piece. In circular knitting you can knit from the bottom up or from the top down, and all shaping is achieved within the garment through increasing and decreasing. (See page 15 for increasing and decreasing.)

TIPS
• *Generally the shape for the front and back of a skirt will be the same. All increases and decreases are made as gradually as possible, with the exception of a "gathered" look, which is made by concentrated increases or decreases within one row.*

• *Check your measurements from a garment that fits you well. Proper measurements are especially important for skirts and dresses because you want to allow plenty of room at the hemline for a good walking step. Other points to pay attention to for ease are the waist and hips.*

SIMPLE SKIRT IN TWO FLAT PIECES

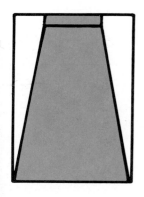

Here are diagrams for each step of the charting process, which show how to chart the example of a simple skirt in two flat pieces. Steps ⑤ and ⑥ specifically tell you how to draw the first lines of your chart. The steps thereafter assume you will continue to do this. Simply follow the diagrams to see where to draw each new line on your chart.

Step ①

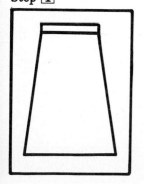

Body measurements for our example:
Shoulder = 15″
Bust = 34″
Waist = 32″
Hips = 36″
Waist + ease = 34″
Hips + ease = 40″
Gauge: 4sts = 1″
5rws = 1″

Step ① —Draw a thumbnail sketch.

Steps 2 and 3

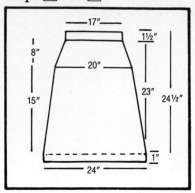

Step 2 —Draw schematic of the pieces.

Step 3 —Take your measurements, adding ease for waist, hips, and hemline and write them on the schematic.

Step 4 —Choose a charting technique, either full-size or small-scale graph paper.

Step 5

24″ = baseline width
× 4sts
96sts

Step 5 —Baseline. Multiply the number of inches at the baseline by the stitch gauge to get the number of stitches. Draw a horizontal line for the baseline. If it's a full, gathered skirt, the waistline could be as wide as the hemline.

Step 6

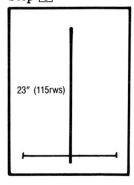

23″ = total length
× 5rws
115rws

Step 6 —Total length. Multiply the total length of the skirt by the row gauge to get the total number of rows in the skirt. Draw center line at a 90-degree angle to the baseline, to equal the number of rows.

Step 7

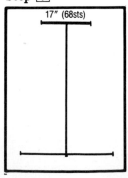

Waist = 34″
34 ÷ 2 = 17″
   17″ width of waistline
× 4sts
68sts

Step 7 —Waistline. Multiply half the width of the waist measurement by the stitch gauge to determine the number of stitches at the waist.

Step **8**

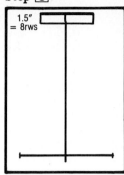

Waistband = 1½"
1.5"
× 5rws
7.5rws (round up to 8)

Step 8 —<u>Depth of waistband.</u> How deep do you want your waistband to be? Multiply that figure by the row gauge to determine how many rows to chart.

Step **9**

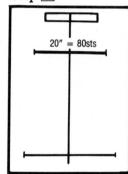

Hipline = 40"
40 ÷ 2 = 20" = width of hipline
× 4sts
80sts

Step 9 —<u>Hipline.</u> Multiply half the width of the hip measurement by the stitch gauge to determine how many stitches are at the hipline.

80sts = hip
−68sts = waist
12sts to be decreased

Step 10 —<u>Hip shaping.</u> Subtract the waist stitches from the hip stitches to get the number of stitches to decrease for hip shaping.

12 ÷ 2 = 6sts to decrease each side

Step 11 —<u>Stitches to decrease each side.</u> Divide the number of stitches determined in Step **10** in half to determine how many stitches to decrease on each side.

8" = waist to hip
×5rws
40rws

Step 12 —<u>Waist to hip measure.</u> Measure the distance between the waist and hip and multiply by the row gauge to determine the number of rows over which the decrease will occur.

Step **13**

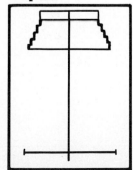

40 ÷ 6 = 6.6 (round up to 7)

Decrease 1 st each side every 7th rw (6 times)

Step 13 —<u>Rate of decrease for hip shaping.</u> Divide the number of stitches to be decreased (from one side) (Step **11** into the number of rows over which the decrease will occur (Step **12**) to determine how often to decrease.

96sts = baseline
−80sts = hip
16sts

Step 14 —<u>Hip to baseline shaping.</u> Subtract the number of hip stitches from the number of stitches at the baseline to determine how many stitches to decrease in the body of the skirt.

16 ÷ 2 = 8sts each side

Step 15 —Stitches to decrease on each side. Divide the total from Step 14 in half to determine how many stitches to decrease on each side.

23″ = total skirt length
– 8 = waist to hip
15″
× 5rws
75 rws

Step 16 —Total length of skirt shaping. Subtract the waist to hip measure from the total skirt length and multiply by the row gauge to determine the number of rows over which the skirt shaping will occur.

Step 17

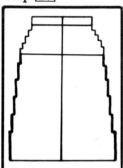

75 ÷ 8 = 9.3 (round down)

Decrease 1st each side every 9th rw (8 times)

Step 17 —Rate of decrease for skirt shaping. Divide the total from Step 15 into the total from Step 16 to determine how often to decrease.

SIMPLE SKIRT ON CIRCULAR NEEDLES FROM THE TOP DOWN

There are diagrams for each step of the charting process, which show how to chart the example of a simple skirt on circular needles. Step 5 specifically tells you how to draw the first line of your chart. The steps thereafter assume you will continue to do this. Simply follow the diagrams to see where to draw each new line on your chart.

Step 1

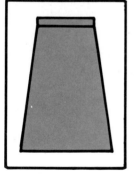

Step 1 —Draw a thumbnail sketch.

Step 2 and 3

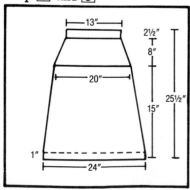

Body measurements for our example:
Shoulder = 15″
Bust = 34″
Waist = 32″
Hips = 36″

Waist + ease = 34″
Hips + ease = 40″
Gauge: 4sts = 1″
5rws = 1″

Step 2 —Draw a schematic.

Step 3 —Take your measurements. Pay special attention to add ease at the waist, hips, and baseline. Write them on the schematic.

Step 4 —Choose your charting technique, either full-size or small-scale graph paper.

Step 5

17" = width of waistband

17"
× 4sts
68sts

Step 5 —Waistline. Multiply the number of inches at the waist by the stitch gauge to determine how many stitches to cast on. Draw a horizontal line equal to this on your chart.

Step 6

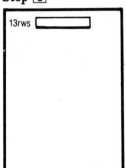

2.5" = depth of waistband
× 5rws
12.5rws (round up to 13)

Step 6 —Depth of waistband. What kind of waistband do you want? On page 79 we have shown you two sample waistbands, one using elastic and one with cord and eyelits. Decide on the depth of the waistband and multiply by the row gauge to determine the number of rows for the waistband.

Step 7

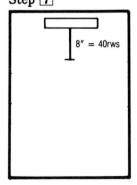

8" = waist to hip
×5rws length
40rws

Step 7 —Waist to hip measure. Measure the distance from waist to hips. Multiply this figure by the row gauge to determine over how many rows the increases will occur.

Step 8

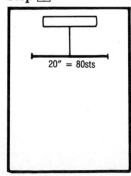

20" = width of hipline
× 4sts
80sts

80sts = hip
−68sts = waist
12sts total to increase

12 ÷ 2 = 6sts each side

Step 8 —Hipline. Measure the hipline plus ease, divide in half, and multiply by the stitch gauge to determine how many stitches are at the hipline.

Step 9 —Hip shaping. Subtract the waist stitches from the hip stitches to determine how many stitches to increase.

Step 10 —Stitches to increase on each side. Divide the total from Step 9 in half to determine how many stitches to increase on each side.

Step 11

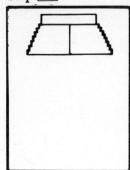

40 ÷ 6 = 6.6 (round up to 7)

Increase 1 st each side every 7th rw (6 times)

Step 11 —<u>Rate of increase for hip shaping.</u> Divide the number of stitches to be increased (from one side) (Step 10) into the number of rows over which the increases will occur (Step 7) to see how often to increase. For double increases, the increments would be done half as often.

Step 12

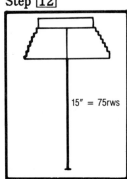

15″ = hip to baseline
× 5rws
75rws

Step 12 —<u>Hip to baseline length.</u> Measure the length from the hip to the baseline and multiply this measurement by the row gauge to determine how many rows long to draw the center line.

One advantage to this method is that you can try on your skirt as you knit it to make sure it fits properly.

Step 13

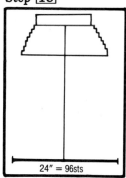

48″ = width of baseline
48 ÷ 2 = 24″

24″
× 4sts
96sts

96sts = baseline
−80sts = hip
16sts total to increase

16 ÷ 2 = 8sts each side

Step 13 —<u>Width of the baseline.</u> Determine the width of the skirt at the baseline and divide in half. Multiply this measure by the stitch gauge to determine how many stitches to chart at the baseline.

Step 14 —<u>Hip to baseline shaping.</u> Subtract the number of stitches at the baseline from the number of stitches at the hip to determine how many stitches to increase in the body of the skirt.

Step 15 —<u>Stitches to increase on each side.</u> Divide the total from Step 14 in half to see how many stitches to increase on each side.

Step 16

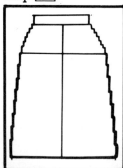

75 ÷ 8 = 9.3 (round down to 9)
Increase 1 st each side every 9th rw (8 times)

Step 16 —<u>Rate of increase for hip to baseline shaping.</u> Divide the number of stitches to be increased (for one side) (Step 15) into the number of rows over which the increases will occur (Step 12) to determine how often to increase.

Once the chart for the skirt is finished, get two sets of circular needles, one two sizes smaller than the other. After completing the waistband on the smaller needle, switch to the larger needle to knit the body of the skirt.

Remember to keep track of your place on the skirt by putting a pencil mark on the chart at the end of each finished row, or by using a row counter.

DRESSES

The same principles apply to dress designing as to sweaters. Consider the shape of the dress as contained within a rectangle, the longest measure being the length of the rectangle, the widest measure being the width. Shaping is achieved through gradually increasing from the narrowest points to the widest points, or vice versa.

There are two basic dress shapes: the chemise, which is a straight tube-type garment like an elongated sweater, and the fitted waist or shirtwaist. The chemise can be worn with a belt for shape or worn straight. The shirtwaist is tapered at the waist for a shapelier appearance.

As with all basic shapes, many variations can be added for interest. The variations can occur in any of the major areas: sleeves, necklines, waistlines, hiplines, and hemlines. At the end of this chapter is a chart of the different variations, and a do's and don'ts section to guide you in making your choices.

Here you will find charting techniques for the two basic styles. Remember to start simply and add to your repertoire as you feel comfortable.

> **TIP**
> • *Sewing patterns are a good source for more complex shapes and designs.*

Here are diagrams for each step of the charting process, which show how to chart the example. Steps 5 and 6 specifically tell you how to draw the first lines of your chart. The steps thereafter assume you will continue to do this. Simply follow the diagrams to see where to draw each new line on your chart.

SIMPLE DRESS

The chemise dress can be worked with a drop shoulder or fitted armhole. Since the drop shoulder is a simple rectangle, we'll show you how to plot the armhole decrease for a fitted armhole.

Step 1

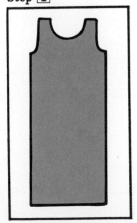

Body measurements for our example:
Shoulder = 15″
Bust = 34″
Waist = 32″
Hips = 36″

Waist + ease = 34″
Hips + ease = 40″

Gauge: 4sts = 1″
        5rws = 1″

Step 1 —Draw a thumbnail sketch.

Steps 2 and 3

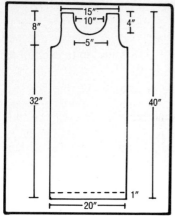

Step 2 —Draw a schematic of major pieces.

Step 3 —Take your measurements. Add ease to hip and hemline. (You want to be sure you can take a walking step.) Write them on the schematic.

Step 4 —Choose a charting technique, either full-size or small-scale graph paper.

Step 5

20″ = baseline width
× 4sts
80sts

Step 5 —Baseline. Multiply the number of inches at the baseline by the stitch gauge to determine the number of stitches to chart. Draw a horizontal line for the baseline.

Step 6

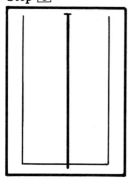

40″ = total length
× 5rws
200rws

Step 6 —Total length. Multiply the measurement for the total length of the dress by the row gauge to determine how many rows in length to draw your line. Draw the center line at a 90-degree angle to the baseline. Also draw the lines to show the sides of the dress.

Step 7

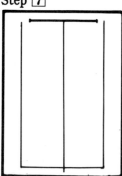

15″ = shoulder width
× 4sts
60sts

Step 7 —Shoulder width. Measure the width of the shoulder and multiply by the stitch gauge to determine how many stitches wide to make your line.

Step 8

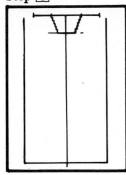

a) 10" = neck width at shoulder

$$\begin{array}{r} 10'' \\ \times\ 4\text{sts} \\ \hline 40\text{sts} \end{array}$$

b) 4" = neck depth

$$\begin{array}{r} 4'' \\ \times\ 5\text{rws} \\ \hline 20\text{rws} \end{array}$$

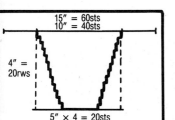

c) 5" = width at base of neckline

$$\begin{array}{r} 5'' \\ \times\ 4\text{sts} \\ \hline 20\text{sts} \end{array}$$

d)
$$\begin{array}{r} 40\text{sts} = \text{shoulder} \\ -20\text{sts} = \text{base} \\ \hline 20\text{sts total to decrease} \end{array}$$

20 ÷ 2 = 10sts each side

20 ÷ 10 = 2

Decrease 1 st each side neck edge every 2 rws (10 times)

Step 8 —Neck shaping

a) See page 20, the Knitter's Guide Chart, for the proper neck measurement for your size. (Or, if you want a wider neckline, decide the total neck width you prefer.) Multiply this measurement by the stitch gauge to determine the number of stitches in the neck width. (This is the width of the neckline at the shoulder.)

b) Decide on the depth of the neckline and multiply by the row gauge to determine how many rows down to start the first bind-off. Draw a vertical dotted line to that point on each neck edge.

c) Decide on the width of the base of the neckline and multiply by the stitch gauge to determine how wide to draw the horizontal line.

d) Subtract the number of stitches at the base of the neckline (Step 8c) from the number of neck stitches at the shoulder (Step 8a) to determine how many stitches to decrease for the neck shaping. Divide this figure in half to see how many stitches to decrease from each side. Divide this number into the number of rows over which the decreasing will occur to see how often to decrease.

Step 9

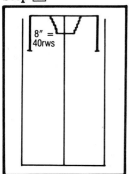

$$\begin{array}{r} 8'' = \text{length of armhole} \\ \times\ 5\text{rws} \\ \hline 40\text{rws} \end{array}$$

Step 9 —Length of the armhole. See page 19, the Knitter's Guide Chart, to determine the length of the armhole for your size. Multiply this measurement by the row gauge to determine how many rows long to draw the line for the armhole shaping.

$$\begin{array}{r} 80\text{sts} = \text{baseline} \\ -60\text{sts} = \text{shoulder} \\ \hline 20\text{sts total to decrease} \end{array}$$

Step 10 —Armhole shaping. Subtract the number of stitches at the baseline (Step 5) (same as the number at the bust in a chemise) from the number of stitches at the shoulder (Step 7) to determine how many stitches to decrease for the armhole shaping.

20 ÷ 2 = 10sts to decrease each armhole

Step 11 —Stitches to decrease for each armhole. Divide the number of stitches from Step 10 in half for each armhole.

Step 12

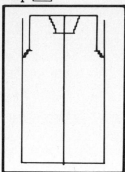

Gauge: 4sts = 1″

So decrease 4sts each side
Decrease 3sts next 2 rws
Decrease 2sts next 2 rws
Decrease 1 st next 2 rws

Step 12 —Armhole shaping. Subtract the stitch gauge on each side for the first decrease for the armhole shaping. For the rest of the decreases, create a gentle curve by decreasing fewer stitches every other row.

> **TIP**
> • *A good rule of thumb for the first decrease in the armhole shaping is to bind off the number of stitches that are in the stitch gauge. If the gauge is 4sts =1″, bind off 4 stitches in the first two rows of the shaping.*

FITTED DRESS

Step 1

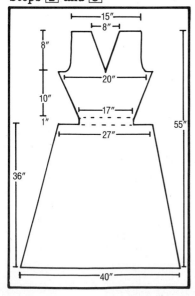

Here are diagrams for each step of the charting process, which show how to chart the example. Steps 5 and 6 specifically tell you how to draw the first lines of your chart. The steps thereafter assume you will continue to do this. Simply follow the diagrams to see where to draw each new line on your chart.

Step 1 —Draw thumbnail sketch.

Steps 2 and 3

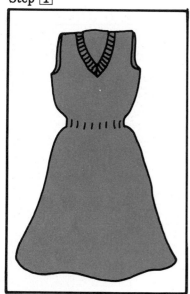

Body measurements
for our example:
Shoulder = 15″
Bust = 34″
Waist = 32″
Hips = 36″

Waist + ease = 34″
Hips + ease = 40″

Gauge: 4sts = 1″
        5rws = 1″

Step 2 —Draw a schematic of the major pieces.

Step 3 —Take your measurements. Add ease for bust, waist, and hips. Write them on the schematic.

Step 4 —Choose charting technique, either full-size or small-scale graph paper.

Step 5

40″ = width of baseline
× 4sts
160sts

Step 5 —Baseline. Multiply the number of inches at the baseline by the stitch gauge to get the number of stitches to chart. Draw a horizontal line equal to the baseline.

Step 6

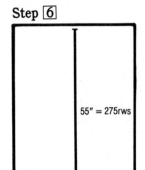

55″ = total length of dress
× 5rws
275rws

Step 6 —Total length. Multiply the total length of the dress by the row gauge to get the total number of rows to chart. Draw a center line at a 90-degree angle to the baseline to equal the length of the garment.

Step 7

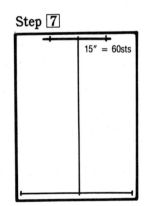

15″ = shoulder width
× 4sts
60sts

Step 7 —Shoulder width. Multiply the width of the shoulders by the stitch gauge to get the number of stitches in the shoulder measure.

Step 8

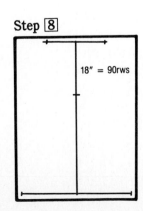

18″ = shoulder to waist
× 5rws
90rws

Step 8 —Shoulder to waist measurement. Measure the length from the shoulder to the waist and multiply by the row gauge to determine how many rows to count down for the waistline. Make a mark at that point on the chart to indicate the position of the waistline.

SKIRT SHAPING

Step ⑨

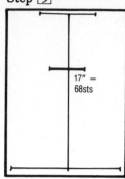

34″ = waist width
34 ÷ 2 = 17″

$$\begin{array}{r} 17″ \\ \times\ \ 4sts \\ \hline 68sts \end{array}$$

Step ⑨ —<u>Waistline.</u> Measure the waist, add ease, and divide in half. Multiply by the stitch gauge to determine the number of stitches at the waistline.

Step ⑩

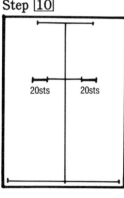

a) $\begin{array}{r} 17″\ =\ \text{waist} \\ +10″\ =\ \text{added fullness} \\ \hline 27″\ =\ \text{top of skirt} \end{array}$

b) $\begin{array}{r} 27″ \\ \times\ \ 4 \\ \hline 108sts\ =\ \text{total number of stitches in} \\ \text{top of skirt} \end{array}$

c) $\begin{array}{r} 108sts\ =\ \text{top of skirt} \\ -\ \ 68sts\ =\ \text{waist} \\ \hline 40sts\ \text{to decrease} \end{array}$

d) 40 ÷ 2 = 20sts each side

Step ⑩ —<u>Fullness at the top of the skirt.</u> Decide how much fullness you want to add to the top of the skirt (the row just below the waistline). If you want a full skirt, you might want to add 5″–10″ across the row for a gathered effect. If you want a more tapered look, don't add the stitches here, rather add them gradually to give the skirt an A-line look.

a) Add the number of inches you want for fullness (for either the front or back, this is half the total number of inches you're adding) with the number of inches at the waist to determine the total number of inches in the top of the skirt.

b) Multiply by the stitch gauge to see how many stitches this equals.

c) Subtract the number of waist stitches from the total number of stitches at the top of the skirt. This is the amount you'll decrease in one row.

d) Divide this amount in half to see how many stitches to draw on each side of the waist on the chart. (In actuality, you won't decrease all these stitches at the beginning and ending of this row. You would space them out evenly across the whole row.)

Step ⑪

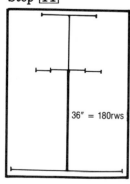

$$\begin{array}{r} 36″\ =\ \text{waist to baseline length} \\ \times\ \ 5rws \\ \hline 180rws \end{array}$$

$$\begin{array}{r} 160sts\ =\ \text{baseline} \\ -108sts\ =\ \text{top of skirt} \\ \hline 52sts\ \text{to decrease} \end{array}$$

52 ÷ 2 = 26sts each side

Step ⑪ —<u>Waist to baseline length.</u> Measure the length from the waist to the baseline. Multiply this figure by the row gauge to determine how many rows are in the skirt.

Step ⑫ —<u>Top of skirt to baseline shaping.</u> Subtract the number of stitches at the top of the skirt (Step ⑩b) from the total stitches at the baseline (Step ⑤), to determine how many stitches to decrease.

Step ⑬ —<u>Shaping each side.</u> Divide Step ⑫ in half to know how many stitches to decrease on each side.

Step 14

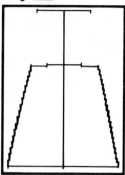

180 ÷ 26 = 7.1 (round down to 7)

Decrease 1 st each side every 7th rw (26 times)

Step 14 —<u>Rate of decrease.</u> Divide this number (Step 13) into the total rows over which the decreases will occur (Step 11), to see how often to decrease.

BODICE SHAPING

Step 15

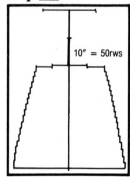

$$\begin{array}{r} 10'' = \text{waist to underarm length} \\ \times\ 5\text{rws} \\ \hline 50\text{rws} \end{array}$$

Step 15 —<u>Waist to underarm length.</u> Measure the length from the waist to the underarm and multiply by the row gauge to determine the number of rows for this measure.

Step 16

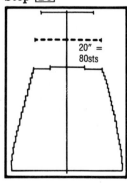

$$\begin{array}{l} 40'' = \text{bust width} \\ 40 \div 2 = 20'' \\ \quad\ 20'' \\ \times\ 4\text{sts} \\ \hline \ \ 80\text{sts} \end{array}$$

$$\begin{array}{r} 80\text{sts} = \text{bust} \\ -\ 68\text{sts} = \text{waist} \\ \hline 12\text{sts total to increase} \end{array}$$

12 ÷ 2 = 6sts each side to be increased

Step 16 —<u>Width of the bust at the underarm.</u> Measure the width of the bust at the underarm, including ease, and divide in half. Multiply this figure by the stitch gauge to determine the number of stitches.

Step 17 —<u>Waist to underarm shaping.</u> Subtract the waist stitches (Step 9) from the bust stitches (Step 16), to determine how many stitches to increase.

Step 18 —<u>Shaping each side.</u> Divide the number arrived at in Step 17 in half to determine how many stitches to increase on each side.

Step 19

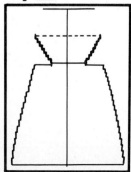

50 ÷ 6 = 8.3 (round down to 8)
Increase 1 st each side every 8th rw (6 times)

$$\begin{array}{r} 80\text{sts} = \text{bust} \\ -60\text{sts} = \text{shoulder} \\ \hline 20\text{sts to decrease} \end{array}$$

20 ÷ 2 = 10sts each side

Step 19 —<u>Rate of increase.</u> Divide the figure from Step 18 into Step 15 to determine the rate of increase.

Step 20 —<u>Armhole shaping.</u> Determine the type of armhole shaping you want. Subtract the shoulder stitches (Step 7) from the bust stitches (Step 16) to determine how many stitches to decrease at the armhole.

Step 21 —<u>Shaping each side.</u> Divide the figure from Step 20 in half to equal the number of stitches to decrease from each side.

Step 22

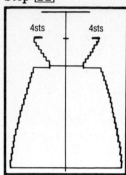

Gauge: 4sts = 1"
So decrease 4sts each side

3sts next 2 rws
2sts next 2 rws
1 st next 2 rws

Step 22 —Armhole shaping. Subtract the stitch gauge on each side for the first decrease. For the rest of the decreases, create a gentle curve by decreasing fewer stitches every other row.

Step 23a

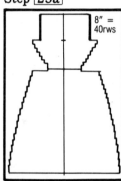

8" = depth of armhole
× 5rws
40rws

Step 23 —Neck shaping. Decide which neck style you would like. Here we will chart a V-neck. The first decrease on a V-neck is usually on the same row as the armhole decrease.
  a) Place a dot at that point on the center line.

Step 23b

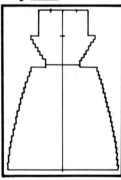

8" = neck width
×4sts
32sts

32 ÷ 2 = 16sts each side

b) See page 20 for the Knitter's Guide Chart which provides the right neck measurement for your size. Multiply by the stitch gauge to determine how many stitches to chart for the neckline (at the shoulder). This is the number of stitches to decrease for the neck shaping.

Step 24 —Shaping each side. Divide the number of neck stitches (Step 23b) in half to determine how many stitches to decrease on each neck edge.

Step 25

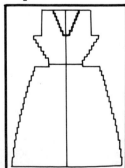

40 ÷ 16 = 2.4 (round down to 2)

Decrease 1 st each side every 2nd rw
(16 times)

Step 25 —Rate of decrease. Divide the number of stitches to be decreased (from one side) (Step 24) into the number of rows over which the decreases will occur (Step 23) to determine how often to decrease.

WAISTBANDS, PLEATS, AND HEMS

Elastic thread waistbands can be worked in several ways. Simply knit in elastic thread in a color that matches the yarn. This will also work with stockinette stitch, rib stitch, or garter stitch.

ELASTIC BAND

Elastic bands come in different widths and weights. A good one for waistbands is ½" wide. Knit the waistband twice the desired length for the finished garment, turn the band to the inside of the skirt, and slipstitch in place. If the skirt is made in two pieces, sew up one side seam first. Cut the elastic to 2" less than your waist measurement, and attach a safety pin to one end. Push the safety pin through the sewn-up band until it comes out the other end. Sew the two ends of the elastic together, and then sew the skirt side seam and waistband seam together for a finished garment.

PLEATS

Pleats are a good way to add movement to a skirt. Be aware that they do add fullness at the waist, are most suited to slender figures, and work best in lightweight yarns. Two types of pleats are knife pleats and mock pleats; the latter don't have true folds but give the appearance of a pleat without the added work. Pleat tops should be sewn together at the waistline and the top row of stitches picked up for a knitted-in waistband. Here are several pattern stitches which work well for pleats, but you can make up your own by changing the width of the pleats.

Knife pleats

Knife pleats have three sides: a face, turnback, and underside. Pleats that face the same direction are called "knife" pleats, and the three faces are all the same width. You will use a multiple of 26 for this pattern. Right side: *K16, s1 1, K8, P1*. Wrong side: *K1, P25*.

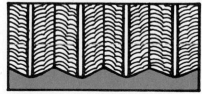

Mock pleats

Mock pleats give the impression of folds but are made by knitting in one purl stitch at regular intervals to create a ridge (or turning edge) across the face of all garter stitches. You will be knitting a multiple of 8. Right side: *K7, P1*. Wrong side: K3, *P1, K7*, P1, K4.

EYELET WAISTBAND

If you want to work a lacy effect into the waistband of a skirt or dress, try this: to make holes for the cord to pass through, work a series of eyelets across the center row of the waistband. (An eyelet is made by making a yarnover, then knitting two stitches together (yo, K2tog). If the waistband is double ribbed stitches, then yo, K2tog, yo, P2tog.

To make a cord to pass through the eyelets and act as a belt, take a long strand of yarn and double it (the length is up to you). Attach one end to a doorknob and twist until it's as tight as possible. Remove from doorknob, double it again and twist in the other direction until it reaches a point where it doesn't kink or untwist itself. Tie the ends in a knot and it's ready to be used as a belt.

HEMS

A hem works well on any garment that doesn't have ribbing (mainly skirts and dresses), and it keeps the edge from curling. The main thing to do is create a turning edge like the purl edge (the simplest), and slipped stitch edge, or a lacy picot edge, which looks scalloped.

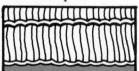

A Purl Edge (as the Turning Edge) on a Knit Stitch

Purl edge (on a knit stitch). Cast on with needles one or two sizes smaller than those used for the garment. This is to help pull in the hem so it won't be bulky. Work to the desired length, usually no more than two inches, in stockinette stitch. Create the turning row by purling if you're on a knit row, or knitting if you're on a purl row. Change to larger needles and continue in stockinette stitch to the desired length of the garment. Sew up the hem after sewing up the side seams.

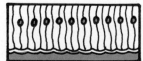

A Picot Edge (as the Turning Edge) on a Knit Stitch

Slipped stitch or picot edge. Cast on a multiple of two stitches and with smaller needles work in stockinette stitch to desired length of hem, ending on a wrong side row. On right side row, K2tog, K1, repeat across the row. Change to larger needles and knit to the desired length for the garment. Sew up the hemline after the side seams.

CHAPTER THREE
OUR PATTERNS

Here's a sampling of sweaters, skirts, and dresses we've designed with you in mind. In the next sixteen pages, you'll find a wide range of styles, stitches, and techniques that echo much of what has been discussed elsewhere in the book. We've included cotton, wool, silk, blended, and novelty yarns to express the varieties of the seasons. Whether you're a beginner, intermediate, or advanced knitter you'll be able to find styles of interest and excitement. A special section on page 97 will also show you how to adapt patterns to make them simple or complex. And many of the sweaters can be made for either men or women.

The patterns are coded for their level of difficulty: *Beginner, **Intermediate, and ***Advanced. Choose the level that feels most comfortable to you for an enjoyable knitting experience.

2

3

4

5

6

7

8

11

12

13

14

15

16

17

18

19

20

21

22

23

24

26

25

27

29

28

OUR PATTERNS

31

32

30

Pattern Editing and Grading: Charlotte Bir
Photography: Tim Geaney
Photographer's Assistant: Francine Fleisch
Stylist: Pam Choy
Models: Nancy De Weir
        Lori Schumacher
        Corey Dorson
        Laura Altman
Hair: Lindy King
Antiques/Vases: Malmaison

HOW TO MODIFY OUR PATTERNS

On the following pages, you'll find the instructions for our sweater, skirt, and dress designs. At the beginning of each, we have graded them according to difficulty, with explanations on how to simplify them if you're a beginner. Many of our sweaters have charted multi-colored designs which add to their difficulty. To make it easier, choose a single color you like and follow the written instructions only.

Another way to modify a pattern to make it suit your needs is shown in the following generic patterns. Here you see how a basic pullover can be made as a vest, a short- or long-sleeved sweater with either V-neck, round neck, or turtleneck. Refer to this page if you need a model for altering one of our patterns.

For example, a men's V-neck vest found in this section has colored geometric shapes on the front. Here are some of the ways you can change that sweater to make it different:

- Knit it in a solid color.
- Knit it with short sleeves.
- Knit it with long sleeves.
- Knit it as a round neck or turtleneck with short or long sleeves.
- Make it either shorter or longer in length.
- Knit it for either a man or a woman.

Basic V-neck vest with fitted armhole

V-neck pullover with fitted armhole and short sleeves

Round neck pullover with fitted armhole and short sleeves

V-neck pullover with fitted armhole and long sleeves

Turtleneck with fitted armhole and long sleeves

Extra long turtleneck with fitted armhole and long sleeves

✳✳✳

1 **Blue Plaid Mohair Pullover (for advanced knitters)**

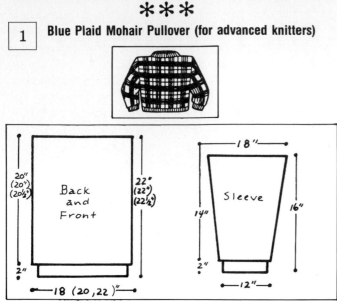

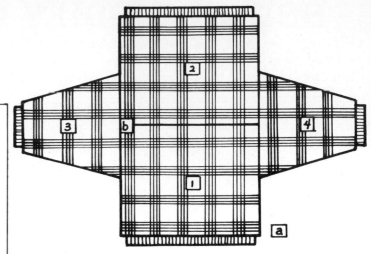

Finished Garment Measurements			
Women's	Small	Medium	Large
Bust	36"	40"	43"

Drop shoulder, stand-up collar, and roomy fit. A five-color traditional plaid worked with bobbins. Shown in a women's size 36" bust (small). Directions are for 8–10. Changes for 12–14 and 16–18 are in parentheses.

MATERIALS

Yarn: 7(8,9) 100 gr/3.5 oz (approx 109 yds) balls 100% wool Zamart's Bulky Weight Mohair, navy blue (MC), 2 balls each same yarn green (A) and maroon (B), 1 ball same yarn yellow (C).

Needles: One pair each #7, #8, and #9 (or size to obtain gauge), 1 16" #7 circular needle, 16 bobbins, 1 crochet hook or tapestry needle.

GAUGE

5sts and 5rws = 1" (in St st on #8 needles).
17sts = 4"; 5rws = 1" (in St st on #9 needles).
CHECK GAUGE TO ASSURE PROPER FIT.

STITCH PATTERN

Ribbing Stitch: Rw 1: *K2, P2*. Rep between *'s to end of rw.
Rw 2: Knit the K sts, purl the P sts. Rep rw 2 for patt.
Stockinette Stitch: *K1 rw (RS), P1 rw, (WS). Rep between *'s for patt.

NOTES

When changing colors, be sure to twist new yarn around dropped yarn in back of work.

Prepare bobbins: 5 of MC, 4 each of A and B, 3 of C.

When sewing seams match plaid.

INSTRUCTIONS

Back: Cast 75(83,93)sts on #7 needles in MC. Work in ribbing for 11rws. Change to #9 needles. Using bobbins, work even in St st rep rws 1–19 of chart 1 for color changes until piece measures 11".

Armhole Shaping: Bind off 3(4,6)sts at beg of next 2rws. There are 69(76,81)sts rem on needle. Work even in color and stitch patt until armholes measure 9(9,9½)" from beg. Bind off.

Front: Work as for back. Sew shoulders, leaving a 9" neck opening.

Sleeves: From RS with #8 needles and MC, pick up and K94sts along entire armhole edge. Work in St st rep rws 1–25 of chart 2 for color changes once, then rws 7–25 3 times, then rws 7–17 once more, and at same time dec 1 st at each end of every 3rd rw 17 times until 60sts rem on needle. Change to #7 needles. Work in ribbing for 11rws. Bind off. Sew side seams and sleeve seams.

Neckband: From RS with circular needle and MC, pick up and K60sts around entire neck edge. Work in rnds of ribbing for 11 rnds. Bind off.

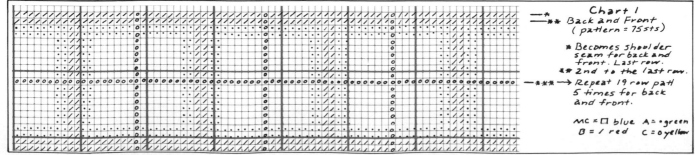

Chart 1
Back and Front
(pattern = 75sts)

* Becomes shoulder seam for back and front. Last row.
** 2nd to the last row.
*** Repeat 19 row patt 5 times for back and front.

MC = □ blue A = • green
B = / red C = ○ yellow

2 ✱✱
Pastel Mohair Pullover (for intermediate knitters)

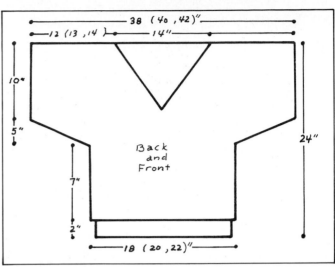

Finished Garment Measurements			
Women's	Small	Medium	Large
Bust	36"	40"	44"

Dolman or "kimono" style sweater, knit in two pieces. For beginners, choose one color and follow the written instructions only. Shown in women's size 36" bust (medium). Directions are for 8-10. Changes for 12-14 and 16-18 are in parentheses.

MATERIALS

Yarn: 4(5,6) 40 gr/1⅜ oz (approx 135 yds) balls Welcomme Le Super Mohair, pink (MC), 3 balls same yarn, yellow (CC).
Needles: One pair each #6 and #8 (or size to obtain gauge), 1 29" #8 circular needle, 1 24" #6 circular needle, 4 large bobbins.

GAUGE

4sts and 5rws = 1" (in St st on larger needles).
CHECK GAUGE TO ASSURE PROPER FIT.

STITCH PATTERN

Ribbing Stitch: Rw 1: *K1, P1*. Rep between *'s to end of rw. Rw 2: Knit the K sts, purl the P sts. Rep rw 2 for patt.
Stockinette Stitch: *K1 rw (RS), P1 rw (WS)*. Rep between *'s for patt.

NOTES

When changing colors be sure to twist new yarn around dropped yarn in back of work to avoid holes. Prepare 2 large bobbins of each color.

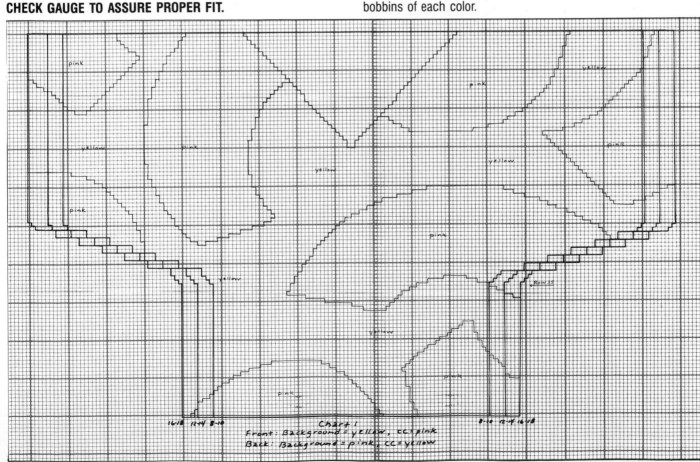

Chart 1
Front: Background = yellow, cc = pink
Back: Background = pink, cc = yellow

INSTRUCTIONS

Back: Cast 72(80,88)sts on smaller needles in MC. Work in ribbing for 2″. Change to larger needles. Work even in St st foll chart for color changes until piece measures 9″, end on rw 35.
Underarm Shaping: Cont to foll chart, changing to #8 circular needle to accommodate number of sts, and inc 1 st at each end of the next 3rws; cast on 6sts at the end of next 10rws, then cast on 5sts at end of next 2rws. Inc 1 st at each end of foll 2rws. There are now 152(160,168)sts on needle. Cont color changes and work even in St st until piece measures 24″. Bind off.
Front: Work same as for back, foll chart for color changes until piece measures 18″, end on rw 70.
V-Neck Shaping: Next rw: K75(79,83)sts, join another ball of yarn, and bind off center 2sts, complete rw. There are now 75(79,83)sts on each side. Working both sides **at the same**

time, with sleeve edges even, cont color changes and *dec 1 st at neck edge on 3rd rw once each side, then dec 1 st every rw 10 times*, rep between *'s once more, then dec 1 st every rw 5 times more each side. There are 48(52,56)sts on each side. Bind off.
Finishing: Block all pieces. Mohair is delicate, so only a gentle blocking is necessary. Sew shoulders.
Neckband: From RS with 24″ circular needle and MC, pick up 56sts across back neck edge and 80sts evenly spaced across front neck edge. There are 136sts on needle. Work in ribbing until neckband measures 9″. Bind off loosely.
Cuffs: From RS with smaller needles and MC, pick up and K100sts across sleeve edge. Work in ribbing for 1″. Next rw: cont in ribbing, dec 1 st every 3rd st across. Cont in ribbing for 1″. Next rw: cont in ribbing, dec 1 st every 7th st across. Cont in ribbing until cuff measures 7″. Bind off loosely. Sew side and underarm seams, including cuffs.

✳✳✳

3 **Aztec Tunic for Women (for advanced knitters)**

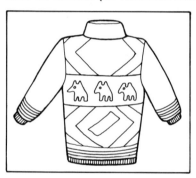

Finished Garment Measurements	
Women's	Small / Medium / Large
Bust	53″
Sleeve/Upper Arm	17½″

Knee-length mohair tunic with charted geometric and primitive animal motif. Drop shoulders, cowl neck collar with stripe pattern lining. Ribbed collar and cuffs. One-size oversized garment, small-medium-large, 53″ width at chest.

MATERIALS

Yarn: 11 50 gr (approx 165 yds) balls Ironstone Yarns English Mohair, purple (MC), 6 balls same yarn gold (D), 6 25 gr (approx 86 yds) balls each Patricia Roberts Woollybear Yarns Mohair, rust (A) and magenta (B), 3 balls same yarn turquoise (C), 1 cone copper metallic lurex. **Needles:** One pair #9 (or size to obtain gauge), 1 16″ #9 circular needle, 44 bobbins, 2 stitch holders, 1 tapestry needle or crochet hook.

GAUGE

18sts = 5″; 5rws = 1″ (in St st on larger needles).
CHECK GAUGE TO ASSURE PROPER FIT.

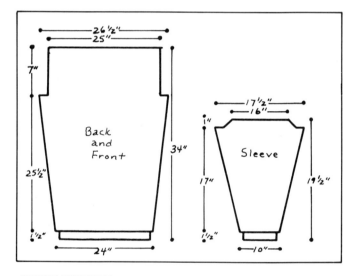

STITCH PATTERN

Ribbing Stitch: Rw1: *K1, P1*. Rep between *'s to end of rw. Rw 2: Knit the K sts, purl the P sts. Rep rw 2 for patt.
Stockinette Stitch: *K1 rw (RS), P1 rw (WS)*. Rep between *'s for patt.

NOTES

When changing colors, be sure to twist new yarn around dropped yarn in back of work.
Prepare bobbins as follows: For chart 1, 4 of MC, 1 each of A, B, and C; for chart 2, 9 of MC, 10 of A with 1 strand D and 1 strand lurex tog, 12 of B, 6 of C. For chart 3, use bobbins from chart 1. On chart 2, work color changes very loosely.

Back: Cast 84sts on straight needles in MC. Work in ribbing for 1½″. Change to D and lurex. Next rw (WS): P across, inc 7sts evenly spaced. There are now 91sts. Cont in St st working in stripe patt as foll: *3rws more with D and lurex, 4rws with MC,

3rws with C, then 2rws each with MC, A, MC, B, MC, A, MC; then 3rws with C, 4rws with MC, and 4rws with D and lurex*. Work in St st foll chart 1 (with appropriate bobbins) to top for color changes and inc 1 st at each end of rw 21 and every 10th rw thereafter twice more. There are 97sts on needle. Then cont in St st and foll chart 2 (with bobbins) for color changes to rw 37.

Armhole Shaping: Bind off 3sts at beg of next 2rws until 91sts rem. Complete chart. Cont in patt and foll chart 3 for color changes to top.

Shoulder Shaping: Bind off 25sts at beg of next 2rws. Place rem 41sts on holder for neck.

Front: Work same as for back using appropriate colors.

Sleeves: Cast on 35sts in D and lurex. Work in ribbing for 1½″. Next rw (WS): P across, inc 15sts evenly spaced. There are now 50sts. Cont in St st and rep between *'s of stripe patt at beg of back. Change to MC. Work in patt, inc 1 st at each end of every 4th rw 7 times. There are now 64sts on needle. Work even until piece measures 18½″.

Cap Shaping: Bind off 3sts at beg of next 2rws. There are 60sts rem on needle. Work even for 1″. Bind off loosely. Block pieces. Sew shoulders, leaving an 11″ neck opening.

Collar: From RS with circular needle and MC, pick up and K82sts evenly spaced around entire neck opening. Work in rnds of St st for 5″. Then work in stripe patt as foll: 4rws with D and lurex, 4rws with MC, 3rws with C, then work 2rws each with MC, A, MC, B, MC, A, and MC; then work 3rws with C and 6rws with MC.

Finishing: Fold collar to inside along D and lurex stripe. Sew in place. Sew side and sleeve seams. Sew in sleeves.

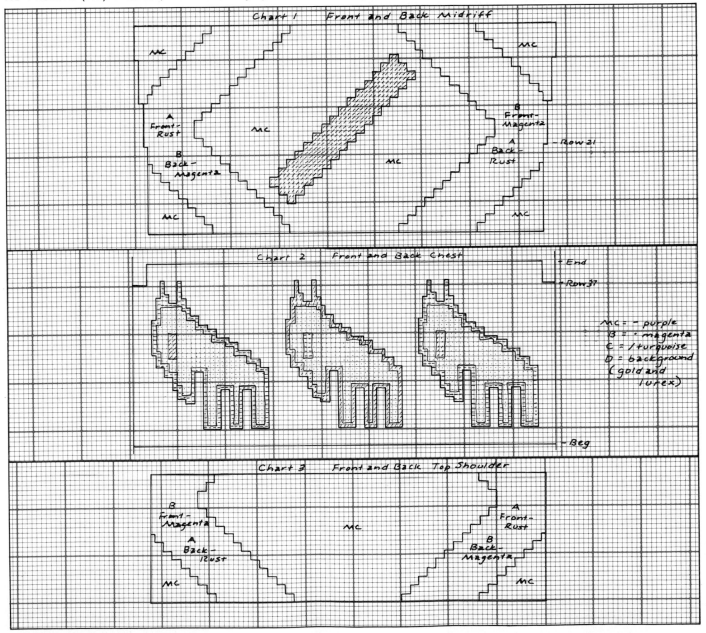

*

4   Black and White Tweed Suit (for beginning knitters)

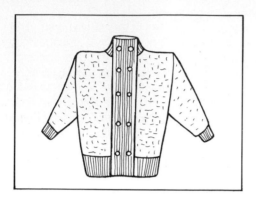

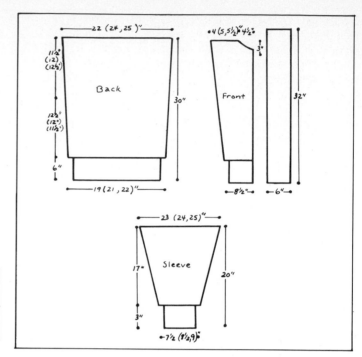

Finished Garment Measurements			
Women's	Small	Medium	Large
Bust	44"	48"	50"
Sleeve/Upper Arm	23"	24"	25"

Double-breasted suit jacket with drop shoulder. Shown in women's size 36" bust (medium). Directions are for 8–10. Changes for 12–14 and 16–18 are in parentheses.

MATERIALS

Yarn: 13(14,15) 50 gr (approx 38 yds) balls Welcomme Le Tweed Soft, white (MC), 4(4,5) 3.5 oz (approx 109 yds) balls 100% wool Reynolds Lopi, black (CC).
Needles: One pair each #9 and #11 (or size to obtain gauge), 2 stitch holders, markers, 10 1" buttons.

GAUGE

2sts and 3rws = 1" (in patt st on larger needles).
4½sts and 5rws = 1" (in ribbing on smaller needles).
CHECK GAUGE TO ASSURE PROPER FIT.

STITCH PATTERN

Ribbing Stitch: Rw 1: *K2, P2*. Rep between *'s to end of rw.
Rw 2: Knit the K sts, purl the P sts. Rep rw 2 for patt.

Irish Moss Stitch:
Rws 1 and 2: *K1, P1*, rep between *'s to end of rw.
Rws 3 and 4: *P1, K1*, rep between *'s to end of rw.
Rep rws 1–4 for patt.

INSTRUCTIONS

Back: Cast 76(84,88)sts on smaller needles with CC. Work in ribbing for 6". Change to larger needles and MC. K2tog across next rw until 38(42,44)sts rem on needle. Work in Irish moss st inc 1 st at each end every 10th rw 3 times. There are now 44(48,50)sts on needle. Work even until piece measures 30". Bind off.

Left Front: Cast on 49(53,55)sts with smaller needles in CC. Work in ribbing for 6". Next rw: Work in ribbing 27sts, change to larger needles and place these sts on holder for front panel ribbing, then change to larger needles and MC and K2tog across rem sts, leaving 11(13,14)sts on needle. Work in patt st and inc at side edge same as for back, until there are 17(19,20)sts and piece measures 27"; end at front edge.
Neck Shaping: Dec 1 st at beg of next rw (neck) and at same edge every rw 9 times until 8(10,11)sts rem. Bind off.
Right Front: Work same as left front, reversing panel ribbing and shapings.

Sleeves: Cast on 40sts with smaller needles in CC. Work in ribbing for 3". Change to larger needles and MC and K2tog across next rw to leave 20sts rem on needle. Work in patt st, inc 1 st each side every 3rd rw 13(14,15) times. There are now 46(48,50)sts on needle. When piece measures 20", bind off.
Finishing: Block all pieces.
Left Front Ribbed Panel: With smaller needles, pick up sts from front holder and work in ribbing until piece measures 32". Bind off in ribbing. Mark positions of 10 buttons on panel.
Right Front Ribbed Panel: Work same as left front making eyelet buttonholes at markers with *yo, K2tog*.
Sew shoulders.
Neck Rib: From RS with CC and smaller needles, pick up 84sts around neck edge. Work 1 rw in ribbing, placing a marker at each shoulder seam. Cont in ribbing, dec 1 st at each marker on back section of neck, every rw until neck rib measures 5". Bind off.
Finishing: Sew front panels in place.

Mark sides of front and back 11½(12,12½)" from shoulder. Sew sleeves to sides between markers. Sew side and sleeve seams.

✳

5 | Black Skirt for Suit (for beginning knitters)

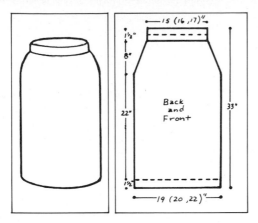

Finished Garments Measurements			
Women's	Small	Medium	Large
Waist	30"	32"	35"
Hip	38"	40"	44"

Knit from the top down on a circular needle, the waist is elasticized and the hip shaping is minimal. Shown in women's size 36" hip (medium). Directions are for 8–10. Changes for 12 and 16 are in parentheses.

MATERIALS

Yarn: 6(7,9) 50 gr (approx 135 yds) balls 50% silk/50% wool Crystal Palace Creme.

Needles: 1 29" #6 circular needle (or size to obtain gauge), 1 row marker, 1 yd ½" elastic.

GAUGE

5sts and 6rws = 1" (in St st on larger needles). **CHECK GAUGE TO ASSURE PROPER FIT.**

STITCH PATTERN

Stockinette Stitch: *K1 rw (RS), P1 rw, (WS). Rep between *'s for patt.

INSTRUCTIONS

Waistband: Cast 150(160,176)sts on circular needle. Join to work in ends, being careful not to twist sts. Mark end of rnd. Work even in St st for 1½", P 1 rnd for turning ridge. Work even in St st for 1½". P 1 rnd.

Hip Shaping: Next rnd: K75(80,88)sts, place marker, complete rnd. Inc 1 st at each marker side on next and every other rnd 20(20,22) times, alternating the side of the marker on which the inc occurs. There are now 190(200,220)sts. Work even until skirt measures 30", or length desired. P 1 rnd for turning edge of hem. Cont in St st for 1½". Bind off.

Finishing: Block Skirt. Sew hem. Fold waistband on turning ridge and sew in place, leaving a 3" opening. Cut a 27(30,37)" (or desired length for waist) piece of ½" elastic and attach a large safety pin to one end. Thread the elastic through the waistband and sew ends together. Finish sewing up seam.

✳✳

6 | Women's Block Plaid Cardigan (for intermediate knitters)

Finished Garment Measurements			
Women's	Small	Medium	Large
Bust	36"	40"	44"
Sleeve/Upper Arm	20"	20"	20"

Roomy V-neck cardigan in overall block plaid design with ribbed polo collar and cuffs and front button closure. Front and back are knit in one piece. Sleeves are knit from sides and form drop shoulder. Shown in women's size 36" bust (medium). Directions are for 8–10. Changes for 12–14 and 16–18 are in parentheses.

MATERIALS

Yarn: 8(9,10) 100 gr (yardage varies, sold by weight) balls Charity Hill Farms Wool Tweed, brown (MC), 2 balls same yarn beige (A), and vermilion (B).

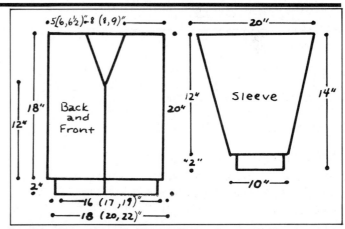

Needles: One pair each #7 and #9 (or size to obtain gauge), 1 crochet hook (for vertical stripes), 1 16" #7 circular needle, 7 ¾" red buttons.

GAUGE

3sts and 4rws = 1" (in St st on larger needles). **CHECK GAUGE TO ASSURE PROPER FIT.**

NOTES

Body is worked in one piece. Horizontal stripes are knit in garment. Vertical stripes are crocheted on after pieces are complete. Sleeves are knit from side of front/back.

STITCH PATTERN

Ribbing Stitch: *K1, P1*. Rep between *'s to end of rw. Rw 2: Knit the K sts, purl the P sts. Rep rw 2 for patt.

Stockinette Stitch: *K1 rw (RS), P1 rw (WS)*. Rep between *'s for patt.

INSTRUCTIONS

Back: Cast 48(52,58)sts on smaller needles with MC. Work in ribbing for 2", inc 6(8,8)sts evenly spaced across last rw. There are 54(60,66)sts on needle. Change to larger needles. Work even in St st with stripe patt as foll: *8rws with MC, 2rws with A, 4rws with MC, and 2rws with B*. Cont to rep stripe patt as set until piece measures 20", end with 7th rw of MC on WS. Now divide for fronts. Next rw (RS): With MC, work across first 15(18,20)sts (right shoulder), join another ball of yarn and bind off center 24(24,26)sts (neck), work across rem sts (left shoulder). There are 15(18,20)sts on each side.

Front Neck Shaping: Working both sides at once, work 2rws with A, inc 1 st at neck edge, once each side. Then cont to inc 1 st at neck edge every 3rd rw 8(8,9) times until there are 24(27,30)sts on needle, and **at same time** rep 16rws of color stripes foll color sequence, inc 1 st each neck edge every 3rd rw until there are 27sts each side, as foll: 2rws with B, 4rws with MC, 2rws with A, and 8rws with MC. Then work even in stripe patt until piece measures 18" from back neck. Change to smaller needles. With MC, work in ribbing for 2". Bind off. Mark side edges 10" from bottom ribs for armholes.

Sleeves: From RS with larger needles and MC, pick up and K60sts evenly spaced between markers. Work in stripe patt same as for back of body until piece measures 14", and **at same time** dec 1 st at each end of every 4th rw 12 times until there are 36sts rem on needle. Change to smaller needles. With MC, work in ribbing for 2". Change to A and work 2rws more. Bind off.

Collar: From WS with smaller needles and with MC, beg at base of neck V and pick up and K92sts along neck edge to opposite front. Work in ribbing for 4". Change to A and work 2rws more. Bind off. Fold down collar and blind stitch points to cardigan fronts.

Front Buttonbands: From RS with smaller needles and MC, pick up and K45sts along right front edge. Work in ribbing for 2rws. Next rw: K1 (bind off 2sts for buttonhole, rib over next 6sts) 5 times; bind off 2sts, P1. Next rw: Work in ribbing and cast on 2sts over each buttonhole. Work in ribbing for 2 more rws. Bind off. With smaller needles and MC, pick up and K45sts along left front edge and work in ribbing for 6rws. Bind off. Sew buttons on left band.

Finishing: Block body and sleeves. Holding yarn below piece and pulling through to top with crochet hook, work 2rws each color in chain stitch, following diagram for placement. Sew sleeve and side seams.

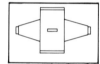

| 7 | **Men's Bulky Gray Cardigan (for beginning knitters)** |

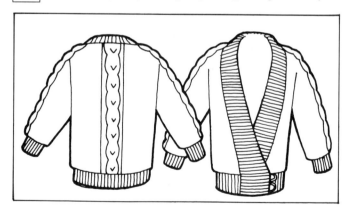

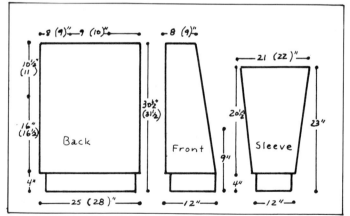

Finished Garment Measurements		
Men's	Small/Medium	Medium/Large
Chest	50"	56"
Sleeve/UpperArm	21"	22"

Drop shoulder, low-slung, double-breasted cardigan made with bulky rug weight yarn. Make in one solid color for a simpler design. Shown in men's size 44" chest (medium-large). Directions are for small-medium. Changes for medium-large are in parentheses.

MATERIALS

Yarn: 3(4) 4 oz (yardage varies, sold by weight) balls rug weight yarn, light gray (A), 3(4) balls same yarn, dark gray (B).

Needles: One pair each #15 and #17 (or size to obtain gauge), 1 29" #15 circular needle, 1 cable needle, crochet hook, 2 markers, 3 1" buttons.

GAUGE

5sts = 3"; 2rws = 1" (in St st on larger needles).
CHECK GAUGE TO ASSURE PROPER FIT.

STITCH PATTERN

Ribbing Stitch: Rw 1: *K1, P1*. Rep between *'s to end of rw.
Rw 2: Knit the K sts, purl the P sts. Rep rw 2 for patt.

NOTE

When changing colors, be sure to twist new yarn around dropped yarn in back of work to avoid holes.

INSTRUCTIONS

Back: Cast 21(24)sts on smaller needles in A, cont to cast on 21(24) more sts in B. There are now 42(48)sts. Work in ribbing for 4", end on WS. Change to larger needles.
Rws 1, 3, 5, and 7: Join A to B and K15(18)sts, P2, K4, change to B and K4sts, P2, K15(18).
Rws 2 and alt rws: K the K sts, P the P sts.
Rw 9: With A K15(18)sts, P2, place next 4sts on cn and hold in back; with B K the next 4sts, with A K the 4sts from cn, with B P2, K15(18).
Rws 11, 13, and 15: With A K15(18), P2, with B K4, with A K4, with B P2, K15(18).
Rw 17: With A K15(18), P2, place next 4sts on cn and hold in back, K next 4sts, with B K the sts from cn, P2, K15(18).
This cable interweaves the two colors on the back. Rep rws 3-17 for patt until piece measures 31". Bind off.
Left Front: Cast 21(24)sts on smaller needles in A. Work in ribbing for 4". Change to larger needles and B. Work even foll rws 1-17 until piece measures 9", end on WS.
Neck Shaping: Dec 1 st at beg of next rw (neck) and at same edge every 3rd(4th) rw 6 times. There are now 16(18)sts rem

on needle. Work even until piece measures 31". Bind off.
Right Front: Work same as for left front using B for ribbing, A for body, and reversing shapings.
Sleeves: (Work one sleeve each in A and B): Cast 24sts on smaller needles in A. Work in ribbing for 2½", end on WS. Change to larger needles and B.
Rws 1, 3, 5, and 7: K7, place marker, *P1, K8, P1*, place marker, K7.
Rws 2 and alt rws: Inc 1 st at each end, K the K sts, P the P sts.
Rw 9: K to marker, *P1, place next 4sts on cn and hold in back, K next 4sts, K 4sts from cn, P1*, K to end of rw.
Rep rws 1-9 for patt and cont to inc 1 st at each end of every other rw 9(10) times in all until there are 42(44)sts on needle. Work even until piece measures 23". Bind off.
Finishing: Block all pieces. Sew shoulders.
Neckband: From RS with circular needle and B pick up 80sts along entire right front and neck edge to center back. Work in ribbing for 4". Bind off. With A, rep ribbing in same way along left front to center back of neck. Sew center back seam. Mark side edges of front and back 10½"(11") from shoulders. Sew sleeves between markers.
Shoulder Cable: From RS with smaller needles and sleeve color, pick up 10sts across top of sleeve cable. Rep between *'s of sleeve cable patt for 9". Bind off. Slipstitch cable in place over shoulder seam and to neck edge.
Buttonholes: Using crochet hook, make a simple chain st (see page 149) and secure both ends to the ribbed area at the bottom of the sweater. Make another loop directly above the first. Make a third loop and secure to inside edge of rib. Sew buttons on ribbing near side seams and on inside of front.

---

*

8 **Gray Checkerboard Vest (for beginning knitters)**

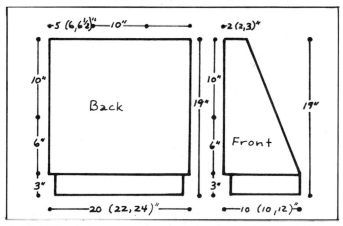

Finished Garment Measurements			
Women's	Small	Medium	Large
Bust	40"	44"	48"
Armhole	20"	20"	20"

Bulky double-breasted sweater with drop shoulder shape. Neckline can be rolled back or buttoned across neckline. Shown in women's size 36" bust (medium). Directions are for 8-10. Changes for 12-14 and 16-18 are in parentheses.

MATERIALS

Yarn: 3(3,4) 4 oz (yardage varies, sold by weight) balls bulky rug weight yarn, dark gray (MC), 2(2,3) balls same yarn, light gray (CC).
Needles: One pair each #15 and #17, 1 29" #5 circular needle, 1 crochet hook, 12 bobbins, markers, 2 1" buttons.

GAUGE

2sts and 2rws = 1" (in St st on larger needles).
CHECK GAUGE TO ASSURE PROPER FIT.

STITCH PATTERN

Ribbing Stitch: Rw 1: *K1, P1*. Rep between *'s to end of rw.
Rw 2: Knit the K sts, purl the P sts. Rep rw 2 for patt.

Colorwork:
Rws 1 and 3: *K4sts in MC, K4sts in CC*, rep between *'s,
end rw with K4sts in MC(CC,CC).
Rws 2 and 4: *P4sts in MC, P4sts in CC*, rep between *'s,
end rw with P4sts in MC(CC,CC).
Rws 5 and 7: *K4sts in CC, K4sts in MC*, rep between *'s,
end rw with K4sts in CC(MC,MC).
Rws 6 and 8: *P4sts in CC, P4sts in MC*, rep between *'s,
end rw with P4sts in CC(MC,MC).
Rep rws 1–8 for patt.

NOTES

When changing colors, be sure to twist new yarn around
dropped yarn in back of work to avoid holes.

Prepare bobbins: 6 each of MC and CC. Large bobbins work
better for bulky yarn.

INSTRUCTIONS

Back: Cast 40(44,48)sts on smaller needles in MC. Work in K1,
P1 ribbing for 3″. Change to larger needles. Using bobbins for
color changes, work even in patt st until piece measures 19″.
Bind off.

Front: Cast 20(20,24)sts on smaller needles in MC. Work in K1,
P1 ribbing for 3″. Change to larger needles. Using bobbins for
color changes, work in patt st dec 1 st at neck edge every
other row until 4(4,6)sts rem on needle and piece measures
19″. Bind off rem sts.

Neck Ribbing: From RS with smaller needles and MC, pick up
38sts along front neckline diagonal. Work in K1, P1 ribbing dec
1 st at bottom edge every other row until 26(25,25)sts rem on
needle. Bind off. Rep ribbing on other front piece.

Finishing: Block both pieces. Mark each end of back neck.

Neck Ribbing: From RS with smaller needles and MC, pick up
20(20,22)sts across back neck edge and work in ribbing for
4½(4,4½)″. Bind off.

Sew shoulders, including neck ribs.

Mark sides of fronts and back 10″ from shoulders.

Armbands: With circular needle of smaller size and MC, pick up
40sts between armhole markers. Work in ribbing for 8rws or
2½″. Bind off loosely in ribbing. Sew side seams, including
armbands.

Buttonloops: Using crochet hook, make a simple chain stitch
(see page 149) large enough to accommodate button, and
secure it to the bottom edge of the ribbing. Make another loop
directly above the first on the ribbing. Sew buttons on ribbing.
(Button at neck edge is optional.)

| 9 | **Women's Striped Pullover (for beginning knitters)** |

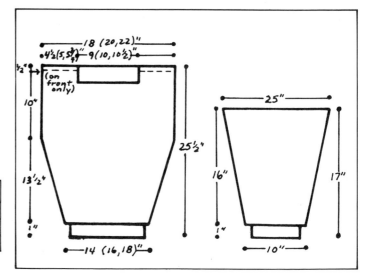

Finished Garment Measurements			
Women's	Small	Medium	Large
Bust	36″	40″	44″
Sleeve/Upper Arm	25″	25″	25″

Women's striped pullover with button shoulders, square
neck. Knit on circular needles, sleeves are worked from sides
of garment (also on circular needles). Shown in women's 40″
bust (medium). (This is an oversized garment.) Directions are
for 8–10. Changes for 12–14 and 16–18 are in parentheses.

MATERIALS

Yarn: 6(6,7) 100 gr/3.5 oz (approx 180-200 yds) balls each Neveda
100% Worsted Weight Wool, cream (A) and gray (B).
Needles: One 16″ #6 circular needle (or size to obtain gauge),
1 29″ #6 circular needle, 1 pair #6 straight needles, 1 crochet
hook or tapestry needle, 4 1″ buttons, 2 stitch holders.

GAUGE

4sts = 1″; 11rws = 2″
CHECK GAUGE TO ASSURE PROPER FIT.

NOTES

Increases are worked evenly spaced around the last rw or rnd
of a striped patt. Body is knit on circular needle in rnds to
armhole, where work is divided for front and back. Sleeves are
worked in rnds, changing needle lengths to accommodate sts.

STITCH PATTERN

Ribbing in rws: Rw 1: *K2, P2*. Rep between *'s to end of rw. Rw 2: Knit the K sts, purl the P sts. Rep rw 2 for patt.
Ribbing in rnds: Rnd 1: *K2, P2*. Rep between * around. Rep rnd 1 for patt.
Stockinette Stitch in rws: *K1 rw, (RW), P1 rw (WS)*. Rep between *'s for patt.
Stockinette Stitch in rnds: K every rnd.
Stripe Pattern: *5rws or rnds with A, 5rws or rnds with B*. Rep between *'s for patt.

INSTRUCTIONS

Body: Cast 112(128,144)sts on longer circular needle in A. Join sts to work in rnds. Mark beg of rnd. Work in ribbing for 6 rnds. Work in rnds of St st following stripe patt and inc 2sts evenly spaced around the last rnd of every stripe (the 5th rnd) 4(5,4) times. There are now 120(138,152)sts on needle. Continue in stripe patt and work even until piece measures 13½". Divide in half to work back and front.
Back: Next rnd: With straight needles, work in patt across first 60(69,76)sts for back; place rem 60(69,76)sts on holder for front. Now work in rws of stripe patt, inc 4sts evenly spaced across the last rw of every stripe 3 times. There are now 72(81,88)sts on needle. Work even until piece measures 24". Bind off.

Front: Place sts from front holder on straight needles and work same as for back until there are 72(81,88)sts on needle. Work even for 5" more, end on last rw of a color stripe.
Neck Shaping: Next rw: Work in patt across first 18(20,23)sts, join another ball of color in progress, and bind off center 36(41,42)sts; complete rw. Working both sides at once, work even in St st for 1½" (or until next color change). Change to A.
Shoulder Mock Buttonbands: Working both sides at once, work in ribbing for 6 rws. Bind off.

Finishing: Block piece. Overlap mock buttonbands on back shoulders. Sew 2 buttons on each band through both thicknesses.

Neckband: From RS with shorter circular needle and A, pick up and K90(98,98)sts around entire neck opening, working through both thicknesses at mock buttonbands. Work in ribbing for 6 rnds. Bind off tightly.

Sleeves: From RS with longer circular needle and A, pick up and K100sts around entire armhole edge, working through both thicknesses at buttonbands. Work in rnds of St st and stripe patt, dec 10sts evenly spaced around the last rnd of every stripe 6 times and changing sleeve for 15½", or until last rw of color; change to shorter circular needle to accommodate smaller number of sts. Work even in patt on 40sts until piece measures 16", end on last rw of stripe. Change to A and work in ribbing for 6 rnds. Bind off. Block sleeves.

✳✳

10 | **Men's Beige Cable V-Neck (for intermediate knitters)**

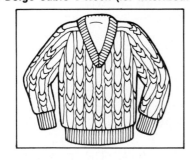

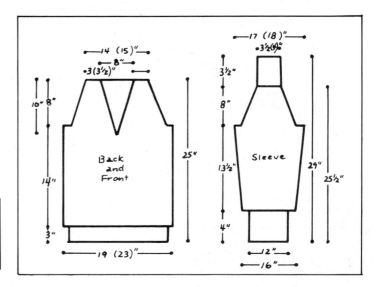

Finished Garment Measurements		
Men's	Small/Medium	Medium/Large
Chest	40"	48"
Sleeve/UpperArm	18"	18"

Men's V-neck pullover with overall cable design and saddle-yoke shoulders. Shown in men's size 40" chest (medium-large). Directions are for small-medium. Changes for medium-large are in parentheses.

MATERIALS

Yarn: 6(7) 100 gr/3.5 oz (approx 200 yds) balls Tahki Chelsea Silk.
Needles: One pair each #6 and #8 (or size to obtain gauge), 1 24" #6 circular needle, 2 stitch holders, 1 cable needle, 1 row counter.

GAUGE

4sts and 5rws = 1" (in St st on larger needles).
Cables will often tighten the overall gauge of a sweater, but in this case they are so spread out that the gauge is not affected. **CHECK GAUGE TO ASSURE PROPER FIT.**

STITCH PATTERN

Ribbing Stitch: Rw 1: *K2, P2*. Rep. between *'s to end of rw. Rw 2: Knit the K sts, purl the P sts. Rep rw 2 for patt.

Cable Stitch (multiple of 20sts, worked over 40rws):
Rws 1, 3, 5, and 7: *P1, K8, P2, K8, P1*; rep between *'s across rw.
Rw 2 and alt rws: Knit the K sts, and purl the P sts.
Rw 9: *P1, place 4sts on cn and hold in back of work, K next 4sts, K4sts from cn—cable twist made, P2, K8, P1*; rep between *'s across rw.
Rws 11, 13, 15, and 17: Rep rw 1.
Rw 19: Rep rw 9.
Rws 21, 23, 25, and 27: Rep rw 1.
Rw 29: *P1, K8, P2, place 4sts on cn and hold in back of work, K next 4sts, K4sts from cn, P1*; rep between *'s across rw.
Rws 31, 33, 35, and 37: Rep rw 1.
Rw 39: Rep rw 29.
Rep rws 1–40 for patt.

NOTE

A row counter is helpful to keep track of your place within the patt st, as is placing a ruler under the rw you're knitting on the symbolcraft chart.

INSTRUCTIONS

Back: Cast 76(92)sts on smaller needles. Work in ribbing for 3", inc 4(8)sts evenly spaced across last rw. There are now 80(100)sts on needle. Change to larger needles. Work in cable st patt until piece measures 17", end on WS.
Raglan Shaping: Keeping in patt, bind off 3(4)sts at beg of next 2rws. Then dec 1 st at each end every other rw 10(14) times (to dec on RS rw: K2, dec 1 st, work to last 3sts, dec 1 st, K2). There are now 54(64)sts on needle. Work even in patt until raglan measures 8". Bind off.
Front: Work same as for back until piece measures 15", end on WS.
Raglan and V-Neck Shaping: Rw 1: Work in patt across first 39(49)sts, join another ball of yarn and bind off 2sts at center of piece; complete rw. There are now 39(49)sts on each side. Keeping in patt and working both sides at once, dec 1 st at neck edge every 3rd rw 13(16) times each side, and **at same time**, when piece measures 17", work raglan shapings same as for back. Work even on neck edges and cont raglan shapings

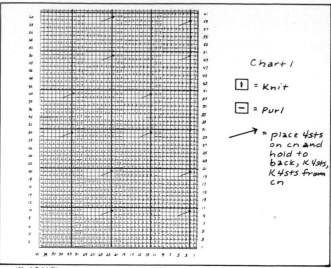

Chart 1

⬆ = Knit

− = Purl

↗ = place 4sts on cn and hold to back, K 4sts, K 4sts from cn

until 13(15)sts rem on each side. (Do not work a cable next to neck shaping.) Work even until raglan measures 8" from beg. Bind off.
Sleeves: Cast 46(48)sts on smaller needles. Work in ribbing for 4", inc 14(12)sts evenly spaced across last rw. Change to larger needles. There are now 60sts on needle. Work in cable patt, inc 1 st at each end of rw every 3½(2½)" 4(6) times. There are now 68(72)sts on needle. Work even until piece measures 17¼", end on WS.
Raglan Shaping: Bind off 3(4)sts at beg of next 2rws. Then *dec 1 st (inside edge same as for back) at each end every rw twice, then work 1 rw even*. Rep between *'s 11 times more. There are now 14(16)sts on needle.
Saddle Shoulders: Work even for 3½". Place sts on holder.
Finishing: Block all pieces. Lay all pieces on a flat surface (as shown on page 147) and sew raglan and saddle shoulders. Sew the underarm and side seams.
Neckband: From RS with circular needle, pick up and K36sts across back of neck, 14(16)sts from sleeve holder, 56sts from left front neck edge, 2sts at center, 56sts from right front neck edge, and 14(16)sts from sleeve holder. You now have 178(182)sts on needle. Work in rnds of ribbing for 2", dec 1 st on each side of the 2 center sts every rnd (to dec before center, sl 1, K1, psso; to dec after center K2tog). Bind off tightly.

✳✳

11 **Shetland V-Neck Men's Vest (for intermediate knitters)**

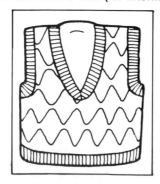

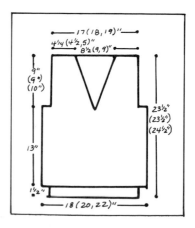

V-neck men's vest with classic curved armhole, solid color back and diamond jacquard front. Ribbing at neck, bottom, and armholes. This pattern can easily be adapted for women. Shown in men's size 38″ chest (medium). Directions are for 34. Changes for 36–38 and 40–42 are in parentheses.

Finished Garment Measurements			
Men's	Small	Medium	Large
Chest	36″	40″	44″
Armhole	9″	9″	10″

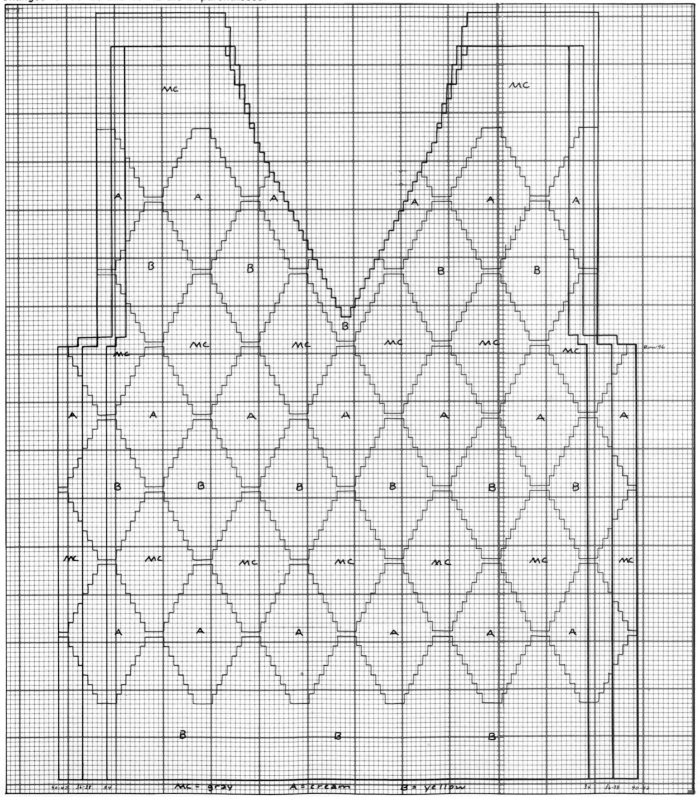

MC = gray   A = cream   B = yellow

MATERIALS

Yarn: 5(5,6) 100 gr (approx 180-200 yds) balls 100% Shetland wool, sportweight, gray (MC), 2 balls each yellow (A) and cream (B).

Needles: One pair #7 (or size to obtain gauge), 1 29" #7 circular needle, 18 bobbins, 1 stitch holder.

GAUGE

11sts = 2"; 7rws = 1" (in St st on larger needles).
CHECK GAUGE TO ASSURE PROPER FIT.

STITCH PATTERN

Ribbing Stitch: Rw 1: *K2, P2*. Rep between *'s to end of rw. Rw 2: Knit the K sts, purl the P sts. Rep rw 2 for patt.
Stockinette Stitch: *K1 rw (RS), P1 rw, (WS)*. Rep between *'s for patt.

NOTES

When changing colors, be sure to twist new yarn around dropped yarn in back of work.

Prepare bobbins: 6 each of MC, A, and B.

INSTRUCTIONS

Back: Cast 86(94,102)sts on smaller needles. Work in ribbing for 1½", inc 14(16,18)sts evenly spaced across last rw. There are now 100(110,120)sts on needle. Work in St st until piece measures 13", end on WS.

Armhole Shaping: Bind off 2(3,4)sts at beg of next 4rws. There are now 92(98,104)sts rem on needle. Work even in St st until armholes measure 9(9,10)".

Shoulder Shaping: Bind off 23(25,27)sts at beg of next 2rws. Place rem 46(48,50)sts on holder for neck.

Front: Work ribbing as for back, end with 100(110,120)sts on needle. Work in St st foll chart for color changes and shaping armholes as for back through rw 96.

V-Neck Shaping: Next rw (RS): Work in patt 45(48,51)sts, join another ball of yarn, and bind off center 2sts; complete rw. There are 45(48,51)sts each side. Working both sides at once, cont to foll chart and dec 1 st at neck edge every other rw 18 times each side; then every 3rd(3rd,4th)rw 4(5,6) times. Work even on 23(25,27)sts until armholes measure 9(9,10)". Bind off. Sew shoulders.

V-Neck Ribbing: From RS with circular needle and MC, beg at base of V and pick up and K124(124,136)sts along entire neck, including sts on holder. Work in rws of ribbing for 5rws. Bind off. Overlap left end of ribbing over right end and sew in place.

Armbands: From RS with smaller needles and MC, pick up and K88(88,100)sts along entire armhole edge. Work in ribbing for 5rws. Bind off. Sew side seams, including armbands.

| 12 | **Diagonal Rib Pullover (for beginning knitters)** |

Finished Garment Measurements			
Women's	Small	Medium	Large
Bust	36"	40"	44"
Sleeve/Upper Arm	17½"	18"	18½"

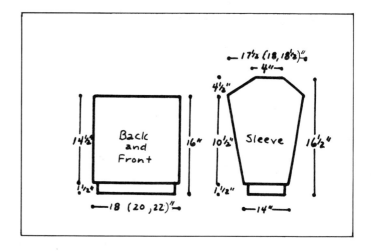

Waist-length, box-shaped pullover sweater in diagonal rib stitch with dropped shoulder line, ¾-length sleeves, and cowl neck. Shown in women's size 36" bust (medium). (This is an oversized garment.) Directions are for 8-10. Changes for 12-14 and 16-18 are in parentheses.

MATERIALS

Yarn: 10(11,12) 100 gr/3.5 oz (approx 150 yds) balls 100% wool Phildar Reine schafwole, cream.
Needles: One pair #11 (or size to obtain gauge), 1 16" #11 circular needle, 2 stitch holders, 1 crochet hook or tapestry needle.

GAUGE

3sts = 1"; 9rws = 2" (in patt st).
CHECK GAUGE TO ASSURE PROPER FIT.

STITCH PATTERN

Ribbing Stitch: Rw 1: *K2sts, P2sts*. Rep between *'s to end of rw. Rw 2: Knit the K sts, purl the P sts. Rep rw 2 for patt.

Pattern Stitch: Rw 1: *K2, P2*, rep between *'s, end with K2. Rw 2: P1, *K2, P2*, rep between *'s, end with K1. Rw 3: *P2, K2*, rep between *'s, end with P2. Rw 4: K1, *P2, K2*, rep between *'s, end with P1. Rep rws 1–4 for patt.

NOTE

When picking up neck sts on circular needle, start at RS front, work right to left. Work patt st making sure that sts in front match.

INSTRUCTIONS

Back: Cast on 54(60,66)sts. Work in ribbing for 8rws. Then work even in patt st until piece measures 16".
Neck Shaping: Bind off 18(20,22)sts at beg of next 2rws. Place rem 18(20,22)sts on holder for neck.
Front: Work as for back until piece measures 15", end on WS.
Neck Shaping: Next rw: Work in patt 21(23,25)sts, place center 12(14,16)sts on holder, join another ball of yarn; complete rw. There are 21(23,25)sts on each side. Working both sides at once, dec 1 st at neck edge every other rw 3 times each side (to dec at beg: sl1, K1, psso; to dec at end:

K2tog). Bind off rem 18(20,22)sts on each side.
Sleeves: Cast on 42sts. Work in ribbing for 8rws. Work in patt st, inc 1 st at each end of every 8th rw 5(6,6) times. There are 52(54,56)sts on needle. Work even until piece measures 12".
Cap Shaping: Bind off 3(3,4)sts at beg of next 2rws. Dec 1 st at each end of every rw 3 times; then every other rw 6 times; then every rw 5(6,6) times. Bind off 3sts at beg of next 4rws. Bind off 12 rem sts.
Finishing: Block all pieces. Sew one shoulder.
Collar: From RS with straight needle, pick up and K44(48,48)sts along entire neck edge, including sts on holders. Next rw: Work in patt st, inc 30sts evenly spaced across. There are now 74(78,78)sts on needle. Cont in patt st until collar measures 2", end on RS. Place sts on circular needle. Sew other shoulder. Cont on collar, working now in rnds of ribbing for 4". Bind off. Sew side and sleeve seams. Sew in sleeves, easing in fullness at shoulders.

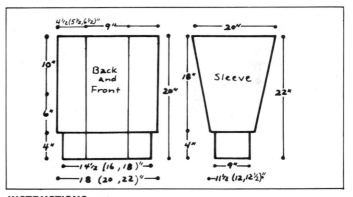

| 13 | **Spumoni Tweed Sweater (for beginning knitters)** |

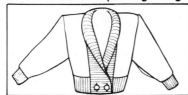

Finished Garment Measurements			
Women's	Small	Medium	Large
Bust	36"	40"	44"
Sleeve/UpperArm	20"	20"	20"

Double-breasted, waist-length, drop shoulder sweater is shown in women's size 36" bust (medium). Directions are for 8–10. Changes for 12–14 and 16–18 are in parentheses.

MATERIALS

Yarn: 19(20,22) 50 gr (approx 45 yds) balls Tahki Spumoni.
Needles: One pair each #8 and #10 (or size to obtain gauge), 1 29" #8 circular needle, 2 1" buttons.

GAUGE

3½sts and 5rws = 1" (in St st on larger needles).
CHECK GAUGE TO ASSURE PROPER FIT.

STITCH PATTERN

Ribbing Stitch: Rw 1: *K2, P2*. Rep. between *'s to end of rw.
Rw 2: Knit the K sts, purl the P sts. Rep rw 2 for patt.
Broad Diagonal Rib:
Rw 1: *K6, P6*, rep between *'s to end of rw.
Rw 2 and alt rws: Knit the K sts, purl the P sts.
Rw 3: P1, *K6, P6*; rep between *'s, end last rep with K5.
Rw 5: P2, *K6, P6*, rep between *'s, end last rep with K4.
Rw 7: P3, *K6, P6*, rep between *'s, end last rep with K3.
Rw 9: P4, *K6, P6*, rep between *'s, end last rep with K2.
Rw 11: P5, *K6, P6*, rep between *'s, end last rep with K1.
Rep rws 1–12 for patt.

INSTRUCTIONS

Back: Cast 50(56,62)sts on smaller needles. Work in ribbing for 4", inc 13(14,15)sts evenly spaced across last rw. There are now 63(70,77)sts on the needle. Change to larger needles. Work even in patt st until piece measures 20". Bind off.
Front: (Make 2): Cast 12(14,16)sts on smaller needles. Work in ribbing for 4", inc 4(6,8)sts evenly spaced across last rw. Change to larger needles. Work even in patt st until piece measures 20". Bind off.
Sleeves: Cast 30(30,32)sts on smaller needles. Work in ribbing for 4", inc 10(12,12)sts evenly spaced across last rw. Change to larger needles. Work in patt st, inc 1 st at each end every 5th(5th,6th)rw 15(14,13) times. There are now 70sts on the needle. Work until piece measures 22". Bind off.
Finishing: Block all pieces. Sew shoulders.
Front Ribbed Band: From RS with circular needle, pick up 80sts along left front, 26sts across back neck, and 80sts on right front. There are now 186sts on the needle. Work in ribbing for 7rws. Rw 8: (RS) work 6sts, bind off 4sts (for buttonholes); complete rw. Rw 9: work in ribbing and cast on 4sts over bound-off sts to complete buttonholes. Work in ribbing until band measures 7", end on WS. Rep rws 8 and 9. Cont in ribbing until band measures 9". Bind off.
Finishing: Mark side edges of front and back 10" from shoulders. Sew sleeves between markers. Sew side and sleeve seams.

✱✱

14 **Aqua Cabled Cardigan (for intermediate knitters)**

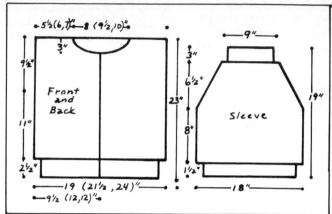

Finished Garment Measurements			
Women's	Small	Medium	Large
Bust	36"	43"	45½"
Sleeve/UpperArm	18"	18"	18"

Cabled cardigan with button-off sleeves, drop shoulder, scalloped cabled front, and buttonholes are created by base of the cable. Shown in women's size 36" bust (medium); the sweater is oversized. Directions are for 8–10. Changes for 12–14 and 16–18 are in parentheses.

MATERIALS

Yarn: (For vest only) 7(8,8) 100 gr / 3.5 oz (approx 110 yds) balls 100% wool Tahki Soho Bulky Tweed aqua, (for complete sweater) 11(12,13) balls same yarn.
Needles: One pair each #8 and #10½ (or size to obtain gauge), 1 cable needle, 1 rw counter, 23 ¾" buttons.

GAUGE

3½sts and 5rws = 1" (in St st on larger needles).
20sts and 20rws = 4" (in cable st on larger needles).
CHECK GAUGE TO ASSURE PROPER FIT.

STITCH PATTERN

Ribbing Stitch: Rw 1: *K1, P1*. Rep between *'s to end of rw.
Rw 2: Knit the K sts, purl the P sts. Rep rw 2 for patt.

Cable Stitch (multiple of 12sts, worked over 8rws):
Rws 1, 3, 5, and 7: K all sts.
Rws 2 and alt rws: P all sts.
Rw 9: *Place 3sts on cn and hold in back of work, K3, K the 3sts from cn. Place next 3sts on cn and hold in front of work, K3, K the 3sts from cn*. Rep between *'s to end of rw.

INSTRUCTIONS

Back: Cast 82(90,98)sts on smaller needles. Work in K1, P1 ribbing for 2½". Change to larger needles and inc 14(18,22)sts evenly spaced across first rw to make 96(108,120)sts. Work even in patt st foll chart 1, until piece measures 23". Bind off.
Front: Cast 42(52,52)sts on smaller needles. Work in K1, P1 ribbing for 2½". Change to larger needles and inc 6(8,8)sts evenly spaced across first rw to make 48(60,60)sts. Work even in patt st until piece measures 20", end at center front.
Neck Shaping: Keeping in cable st, bind off 13(18,18)sts at cardigan front opening once; then at same edge bind off 3sts once and 2sts 1(2,1) time. Dec 1 st at neck edge every rw

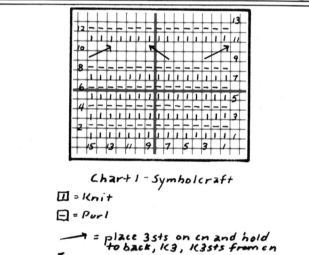

Chart 1 – Symbolcraft
☐ = Knit
☐ = Purl
→ = place 3 sts on cn and hold to back, K3, K3sts from cn
← = place 3 sts on cn and hold to front, K3, K3sts from cn

2(5,5) times. There are now 28(30,35)sts on needle. Work even until piece measures 23". Bind off.
Finishing for Vest: Block front and back pieces. Sew shoulders.
Neckband: From RS with smaller size needles, pick up 108(118,122)sts around neck edge. Work in K1, P1 ribbing for 3rws. Next rw: Work in ribbing across first 4sts, yo, P2tog for buttonhole; complete rw in ribbing. Cont in ribbing for 4 more rws, or until rib measures 1½". Bind off tightly, so edge isn't saggy.
Mark side edges of front and back 9½" from shoulders.
Armbands: From RS with smaller needles, pick up 80sts between armhole markers. Work in ribbing for 3rws. Next rw: Work in ribbing across first 4sts, *yo, K2tog for buttonhole, rib across next 8sts*. Rep between *'s 7 times, end last rep with rib across 4sts to create 8 eyelet buttonholes. Work even in ribbing for 4 more rws. Bind off tightly.
Sleeves: (worked from the top of sleeve to cuff): Cast on 80sts with smaller needles. Work in K1, P1 ribbing for 1½" or 8rws, to match ribbing on vest. Change to larger needles. Inc 10sts evenly spaced across first rw, to make 90sts. Work even in patt st until piece measures 9½", end with a rw 6 of cable st and foll chart 2 for sleeve shaping and instructions for how to dec

on cables. Work until piece measures 16″ and 46sts rem on needle. Change to smaller needles and work in ribbing for 3″. Bind off loosely, so cuff can turn back easily.

Finishing: Block sleeves. Sew side seams, including armbands.

Sew sleeve seams. Pin sleeves in place, and mark positions for buttons on top rib of sleeve by using straight or safety pins guided through buttonholes. Sew buttons on sleeves. Sew buttons on cardigan left front.

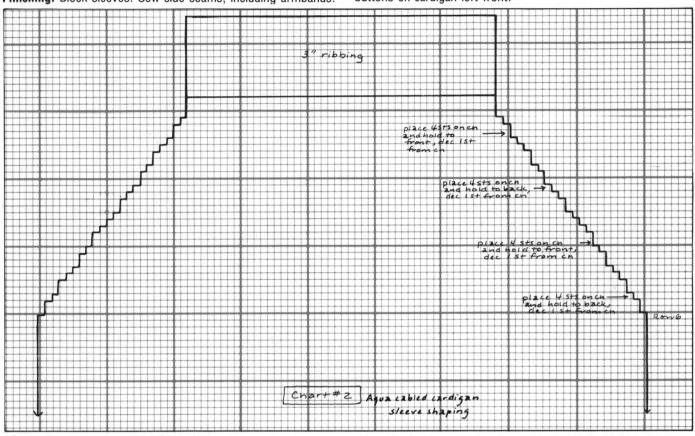

3″ ribbing

place 4 sts on ch and hold to front, dec 1st from ch

place 4 sts on ch and hold to back, dec 1st from ch

place 4 sts on ch and hold to front, dec 1st from ch

place 4 sts on ch and hold to back, dec 1st from ch

Row 6

Chart #2 | Aqua cabled cardigan sleeve shaping

✱✱✱

15 **Ski Sweater and Hat (for advanced knitters)**

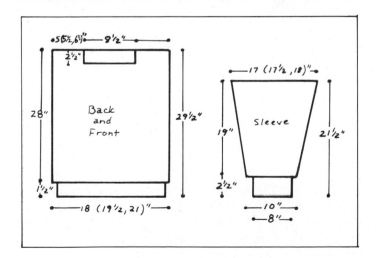

• 5 (5½, 6)″ • — 8½″ —
2½″
Back and Front
28″
29½″
1½″
— 18 (19½, 21)″ —

— 17 (17½, 18)″ —
Sleeve
19″
21½″
2½″
— 10″ —
— 8″ —

Hip-length tweed wool ski sweater with skier and snowflake motif on front and back and snowflake motif on one sleeve. Drop shoulder with high side button collar worn turned down. Cuffs are worn turned back. Collar and cuffs have contrasting stripe. Hat is worked as one panel with seam at side and top. Worked in size 38 (women's medium). (This is an oversized garment.) Directions are for size 8–10. Changes for 12–14 and 16–18 are in parentheses.

Finished Garment Measurements			
Women's	Small	Medium	Large
Bust	36″	39″	42″
Sleeve/UpperArm	17″	17″	17″

MATERIALS

Yarn for Sweater: 13(14,15), 50 gr/1¾ oz (approx 63 yds) balls balls Joseph Galler's Ping Pong Laines Plassard (wool, cotton, alpaca, and poly mix), gray tweed (MC), 10 10 gr/⅓ oz (yardage varies, sold by weight) balls 100% angora ACA Supreme, white, (A), 2 100 gr/3.5 oz (approx 110 yds) balls 100% wool Tahki Soho Bulky Tweed, aqua tweed (B).

Yarn for Hat: 2 50 gr/1¾ oz (approx 63 yds) balls Joseph Galler's Ping Pong Laines Plassard (wool, cotton, alpaca, and poly mix), gray tweed, 1 skein silver metallic lurex (mixed with A).

Needles: One pair #9 (or size to obtain gauge), 1 tapestry needle, 15 bobbins, 3 ½" buttons.

GAUGE

4sts and 4rws = 1" (in St st on larger needles).
CHECK GAUGE TO ASSURE PROPER FIT.

NOTE

Prepare bobbins: 7 of MC, 2 of 1 strand A and 1 strand lurex tog, 6 of B.

STITCH PATTERN

Ribbing Stitch: Rw 1: *K2, P2*. Rep between *'s to end of rw.
Rw 2: Knit the K sts, purl the P sts. Rep rw 2 for patt.
Stockinette Stitch: *K1 rw (RS), P1 rw (WS)*. Rep between *'s for patt.

INSTRUCTIONS

Back: Cast on 72(76,80)sts in MC. Work in ribbing for 1½", inc 2(2,4)sts on last rw. Work even in St st on 74(78,84)sts foll chart 1 for color changes until piece measures 28½", end on WS.

Neck Shaping: Next rw: Work across first 25(27,30)sts, join another ball of yarn, and bind off center 24sts; complete rw. Working both sides at once, bind off 5sts at neck edge once each side until 20(22,25)sts rem on each side. Work even until piece measures 29½". Bind off.

Front: Work same as for back, foll chart 2 for color changes until piece measures 27", end on WS.

Neck Shaping: Next rw: Work across first 28(30,33)sts, join another ball of yarn, and bind off center 16sts; complete rw. Working both sides at once, bind off 4sts at neck edge once each side, then 2sts twice each side. Dec 1 st once each side of neck. Work even on 20(22,25)sts until piece measures same as back. Bind off.

Chart 1 Back
MC = □ gray   A = · white   B = / aqua

Chart 2 Front
MC = □ gray   A = · white   B = / aqua

Left Sleeve: Cast on 32(32,36)sts in MC. Work in ribbing for 2rws. Change to B and work 2rws more. Change to MC and work until ribbing measures 2½", inc 8sts evenly spaced across last rw. There are 40(40,44)sts on needle. Work in St st, inc 1 st at each end of every 3rd rw 7(7,8) times, then every 6th(6th,5th) rw 7(8,8) times. Work even on 68(70,72)sts until piece measures 21½". Bind off.

Right Sleeve: Work same as for left sleeve foll chart 3 for color changes.

Finishing: Block pieces. Sew left shoulder. Mark side edge of front and back 8½(8¾,9)" from shoulders for armholes. Sew sleeve between armhole markers. Sew side and sleeve seams.

Collar: From RS pick up and K68sts along entire neck edge. Work in ribbing for 2rws. Change to B and work 2rws more. Change to MC and work ribbing for 5½" more. Bind off loosely. Block collar. Sew other shoulder to neck edge. Overlap front edge over back edge of collar and sew 3 buttons through both thicknesses, evenly spaced.

Hat: Cast on 72sts in MC. Work even in St st for 14". Bind off. Block. Fold piece in half. Sew top and side seam.

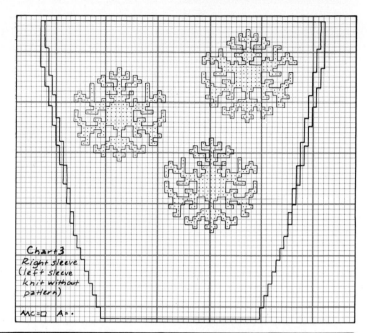

Chart 3
Right sleeve
(left sleeve
knit without
pattern)

MC = ☐   A = ·

*

| 16 | **Mock Wraparound Skirt (for beginning knitters)** |

Wraparound knee-length skirt with elasticized waist and front button closure. Directions are for size 36" hip (medium).

MATERIALS

Yarn: 7(8,9) 50 gr/1¾ (approx 63 yds) oz balls Joseph Galler's Ping Pong Laines Plassard (wool, cotton, alpaca, poly mix), gray tweed.

Needles: One pair #9 needles (or any size to obtain gauge), 5 ½" buttons, 1 yd ¾" waistband elastic, 1 tapestry needle.

GAUGE

4sts and 4rws = 1".
CHECK GAUGE TO ASSURE PROPER FIT.

NOTE

Block piece, stretching slightly in each direction. This will help to reduce bulk where garment is double-thickness.

STITCH PATTERN

Ribbing Stitch: Rw 1: *K2, P2* rep between *'s to end of rw. Rw 2: Knit the K sts, purl the P sts. Rep rw 2 for patt.
Stockinette Stitch: *K1 rw (RS), P1 rw (WS)*. Rep between *'s for patt.

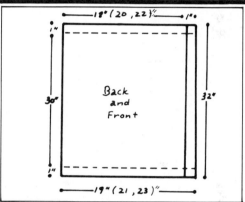

18" (20 ,22)" 1"
1"
Back
and
Front
30"   32"
1"
19" (21 ,23)"

Finished Garment Measurements			
Women's	Small	Medium	Large
Waist	24"–25"	26"–28"	30"–32"
Hips	33"–34"	36"–38"	40"–42"

INSTRUCTIONS

Back: Cast on 76(84,92)sts. Work even until 32", or length desired. Bind off.

Front: Work same as back.

Finishing: Block pieces. Sew seam on one side (center back). Turn up bottom edge 1", and top edge down 1". Hem and press. Wrap skirt around waist loosely, placing seam at center back. Pin inside edge to front of skirt. Cut elastic to waist measurement plus 2". Thread elastic through top casing, beg at inside edge and ending at pin (on front side). Stitch elastic edges together tightly on inside.

Mock Buttonband: From RS with MC, pick up and K120sts along entire outside edge at front overlap. Work in ribbing for 1". Bind off. Sew top of front overlap to waistband. Sew 1 button at waistband through all thicknesses. Sew 4 more buttons evenly spaced along rem ribbing.

**

17 **V-Neck Argyle Vest (for intermediate knitters)**

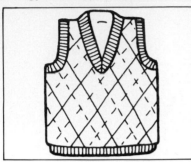

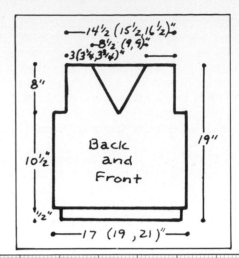

Finished Garment Measurements			
Women's	Small	Medium	Large
Bust	34"	38"	42"
Armhole	16"	16"	16"

Oversized cotton vest with solid color back, deep V-neck, notched armholes, and argyle motif. Shown in women's size 34" bust (small). Directions are for women's 8-10. Changes for 12-14 and 16-18 are in parentheses.

MATERIALS

Yarn: 4(5,6) 100 gr/3.5 oz (approx 109 yds) balls Tahki Creole Cotton, white (MC), 1 ball each same yarn yellow (A), peach (B), teal blue (C), and rose (D).

Needles: One pair each #7 and #9 (or size to obtain gauge), 1 29" #7 circular needle, 15 bobbins, 1 stitch holder, 1 crochet hook or tapestry needle.

GAUGE

4sts and 6rws = 1" (in St st on larger needles).
CHECK GAUGE TO ASSURE PROPER FIT.

STITCH PATTERN

Ribbing Stitch: Rw 1: *K1, P1*; rep between *'s to end of rw.
Rw 2: Knit the K sts, purl the P sts. Rep rw 2 for patt.
Stockinette Stitch: *K1 rw (RS), P1 rw (WS)*; rep between *'s for patt.

NOTES

When changing colors, be sure to twist new yarn around dropped yarn in back of work.

Prepare bobbins: 2 each of MC, A, and B, 3 of C, 6 of D.

INSTRUCTIONS

Back: Cast 68(76,84) on smaller needles in MC. Work in ribbing for ½". Change to larger needles. Work even in St st until piece measures 10½".
Armhole Shaping: Bind off 5(7,9)sts at beg of next 2rws. There are now 58(62,66)sts rem on needle. Work even until armhole measures 8(8½,9)".
Shoulder Shaping: Bind off 12,(13,15)sts at beg of next 2rws. Place rem 34(36,36)sts on holder.

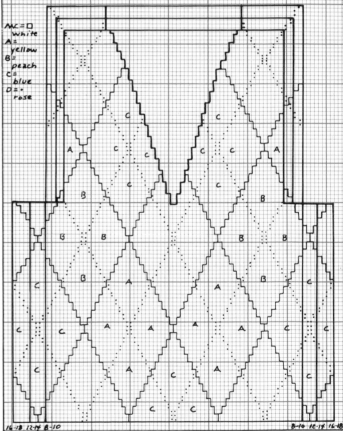

Front: Cast 68(76,84)sts on smaller needles in MC. Work in ribbing for ½". Change to larger needles. Work even in St st foll chart through rw 58. Piece measures 10½".
Armhole and V-Neck Shaping: Rw 59 (RS): Bind off first 5(7,9)sts, work in patt until there are 28(30,32)sts on needle, join another ball of yarn, and bind off center 2sts; complete rw. Rw 60: Bind off first 5(7,9)sts, work in patt across rem sts of first side; then across sts of second side. There are 28(30,32)sts on each side. Working both sides at once, cont to foll chart for color changes and dec 1 st at neck edge every 3rd rw until 12(13,15)sts rem. Work even until armholes measure 8(8½,9)". Bind off. Block pieces. Sew shoulders.

✳✳

18 | **Children's Baseball Cardigan (for intermediate knitters)**

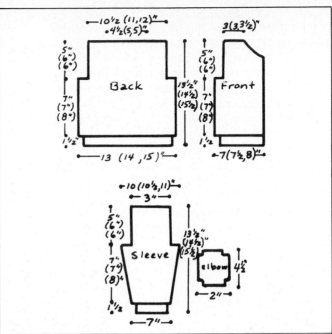

Finished Garment Measurements			
Children's Size	4	6	8
Chest	26"	28"	30"
Armhole depth	5"	6"	6"
Sleeve/Upper Arm	10"	10½"	11"

Button front, lined cardigan with fitted sleeves, elbow patches, and baseball motif. Shown in Children's size 4 (24" chest). Directions are for 4. Changes for 6-8 are in parentheses.

MATERIALS

Yarn: 5(6,6) 50 gr/1.8 oz (approx 90 yds) balls Melior ABC Cotton, turquoise (MC), 1 ball each same yarn white (A), yellow (B), and red (C).
Needles: One pair each #4 and #7 (or size to obtain gauge), 8 ½" buttons, 13 bobbins.

GAUGE

5sts and 7rws = 1" (in St st on larger needles).
CHECK GAUGE TO ASSURE PROPER FIT.

STITCH PATTERN

Ribbing Stitch: Rw 1: *K2, P2*. Rep between *'s to end of rw. Rw 2: Knit the K sts, purl the P sts. Rep rw 2 for patt.
Stockinette Stitch: *K1 rw (RS), P1 rw (WS)*. Rep between *'s for patt.

NOTES

When changing colors, be sure to twist new yarn around dropped yarn in back of work.

Prepare bobbins: 6 of MC, 1 of A, 2 of B, 4 of C.

INSTRUCTIONS

Back: Cast 64(68,74)sts on smaller needles in B. Work in ribbing for 3rws each with B, A, and B, inc 1 st at end of last rw. Change to larger needles and MC. Work even in St st on 65(69,75)sts until piece measures 7"(7",8").
Armhole Shaping: Bind off 4sts at beg of next 2rws. Dec 1 st at each end every other rw 3 times until 51(55,61)sts rem on needle. Rws 3, 4, 5, 6: Dec 1 st beg of each rw. Work even in patt foll chart 1 for baseball motif. Work even until armhole measures 5(6,6) from beg.

Shoulder Shaping: Bind off 5(5,6)sts at beg of next 6rws. Bind off rem 21(25,25)sts.
Right Front: Cast 36(36,40)sts on smaller needles in B. Work in ribbing same as for back, inc 0(2,0)sts at end of last rw. Change to larger needles and MC. Work even in St st on 36(38,40)sts until piece measures 7(7,8)", end on WS.
Armhole Shaping: Bind off 4sts at beg of next rw (armhole); then dec 1 st at same edge every other rw 3 times until there are 29(31,33)sts rem. Work even foll chart 2 for star motif. Work even until armhole measures 3½(4½,4½)" from beg, end on RS.
Neck Shaping: Bind off 6(7,6)sts at beg of next rw (neck) once, then 5(6,6)sts at same edge once. Dec 1 st at neck edge every other rw 3 times until 15(15,18)sts rem. Work even until armhole measures 5(6,6)" from beg, end on RS.
Shoulder Shaping: Bind off 5(5,6)sts at armhole edge 3 times until no sts rem.
Left Front: Work same as for right front, reversing shapings.
Sleeves: Cast 36(36,38)sts on smaller needles in B. Work in ribbing same as for back, inc 1 st at each end of last rw. There are 38(38,40)sts on needle. Change to larger needles and MC. Work in St st, inc 1 st at each end of every 8th(7th,7th) rw 6(7,7) times until there are 50(52,54)sts on needle. Work even until sleeve measures 10½(11½,12½)" from beg.
Cap Shaping: Bind off 4sts at beg of next 2rws. Dec 1 st at each end of every other rw 8(9,10) times until 26sts rem. Bind off 3sts at beg of next 4rws until 14sts rem. Bind off rem sts.
Left Front Ribbing: From RS with smaller needles and B, pick up and K48(58,58)sts along center front edge. Work in ribbing same as for back. Bind off. Sew 7 buttons evenly spaced along ribbing.
Right Front Ribbing: Pick up sts same as for left front rib. Work in ribbing same as for left front rib, working buttonholes on 4th rw to correspond to buttons (buttonholes: on RS bind

off 2sts at button; cast on 2sts over bound-off sts on next rw).
Bind off. Block pieces. Sew shoulder and side seams.

Neckband: From RS with smaller needles and B, pick up and
K52(56,56)sts along entire neck edge, including ends of front
ribs. Work in ribbing same as for back, working 1 buttonhole
on center stripe of ribbing at right front above other buttonholes. Sew button on opposite edge.

Elbow Patch: (make 2): Cast 10sts on larger needles in A.
Work in St st inc 1 st at each end of every other rw 3 times
until there are 16sts on needle. Work even for 6rws. Dec 1 st at
each end of every other rw 3 times until 10sts rem. Bind off.
Sew elbow patches on sleeves. Sew sleeve seams. Sew in
sleeves.

Cardigan Lining (optional): Cut fabric pieces using sweater
pieces for pattern, excluding ribbing and adding seam
allowances. Sew shoulder, side, and sleeve seams. Sew in
sleeves. Turn under seam allowances along all outer edges
and press. With an invisible stitch, sew lining in place, RS
facing out.

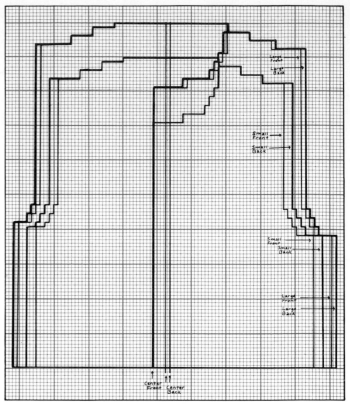

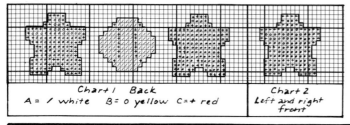

Chart 1   Back
A = / white   B = 0 yellow C = + red
Chart 2
Left and right
front

---

*

19 Men's V-Neck Cotton Vest (for beginning knitters)

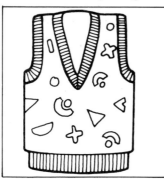

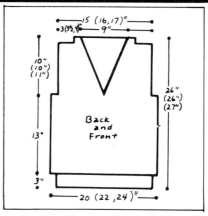

Finished Garment Measurements			
Men's	Small	Medium	Large
Chest	40"	44"	48"
Armhole	20"	20"	20"

Oversized cotton V-neck vest with fitted armholes and
brightly colored geometric shapes. Shown in men's size 38"
chest. Directions are for 34. Changes for 36–38 and 40–42 are
in parentheses.

MATERIALS

Yarn: 6(7,8) 100 gr/3.5 oz (approx 109 yds) balls 100% cotton
Tahki Creole, white (MC), and 1 ball each same yarn, red (A),
green (B), yellow (C), blue (D).

Needles: One pair each #8 and #10 (or size to obtain gauge), 1
29" #8 circular needle, 16 bobbins, 1 stitch holder.

GAUGE

4sts and 5rws = 1" (in St st on larger needles).
CHECK GAUGE TO ASSURE PROPER FIT.

STITCH PATTERN

Ribbing Stitch: Rw 1: *K1, P1*. Rep between *'s to end of rw.
Rw 2: Knit the K sts, purl the P sts. Rep rw 2 for patt.
Stockinette Stitch: *K1 rw (RS), P1 rw, (WS). Rep between *'s for patt.

NOTES

Prepare bobbins: 2 each of A, B, C, D, and 8 of MC.
When changing colors, be sure to twist new yarn around
dropped yarn on WS.

INSTRUCTIONS

Back: Cast 80(88,96)sts on smaller needles in MC. Work in ribbing for 3″. Change to larger needles. Work even in St st until piece measures 16″, end on WS.

Armhole Shaping: Bind off 4sts at beg of next 2rws, then 3sts at beg of next 2rws, and 2sts at beg of foll 2(4,2)rws. Dec 1 st at each end of next 1(1,3)rws. There are now 60(64,68)sts on needle. Work even until armhole measures 10(10,11)″.

Shoulder Shaping: Bind off 12(14,16)sts at beg of next 2rws. Bind off rem sts for back neck.

Front: Work same as for back foll chart for color design until piece measures 16″, end on WS.

Armhole and V-Neck Shaping: Work armhole shaping same as for back and **at same time** beg neck shaping on 2nd rw as foll: Work to center 2sts, join another ball of yarn, and bind off center 2sts; complete rw. Working both sides at once, cont armhole shaping and dec 1 st at neck edge every 3rd rw 5 times each side; then every other rw 12 times each side. There are now 12(14,16)sts on each side. Work even until armhole measures 10(10,11)″. Bind off.

Finishing: Weave in or tie all loose ends on WS of pieces. Block all pieces. Sew shoulders.

Neckband: From RS with circular needle and MC, pick up and K42(42,46)sts along each side of neck edge and 30sts along back of neck. There are 114(114,122)sts on the needle. Work in rnds of K1, P1 ribbing for 2″, dec 1 st on each side of 2sts at point of the V every rnd. (See page 150 for more details on this method.)

Armhole Bands: From RS with smaller needles and MC, pick up and K92(92,100)sts along entire armhole edge. Work in rws of K1, P1 ribbing for 2″. Bind off. Sew side seams, including armbands.

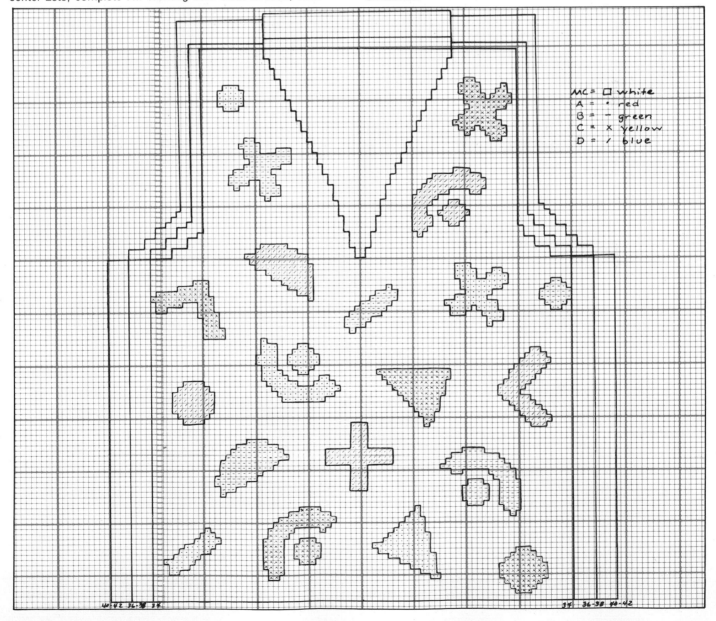

MC = □ white
A = · red
B = – green
C = x yellow
D = / blue

✱✱

20   **Men's V-Neck Argyle Vest (for intermediate knitters)**

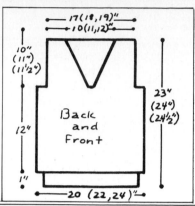

Oversized cotton vest with solid color back, deep V-neck, notched armholes, and argyle motif. Shown in men's size 36 (small). Directions are for size 34–36. Changes for 38–40 and 42–44 are in parentheses.

Finished Garment Measurements			
Men's	Small	Medium	Large
Chest	40"	44"	48"
Armhole	10"	11"	11½"

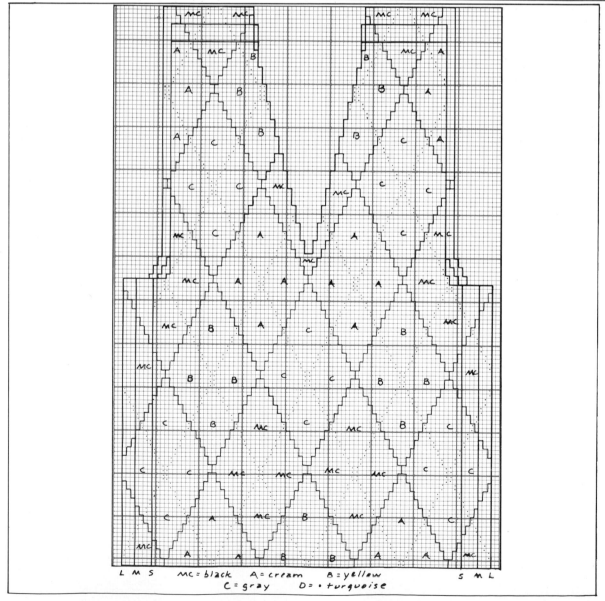

L M S   MC = black   A = cream   B = yellow   S M L
C = gray   D = turquoise

MATERIALS

Yarn: 4 100 gr/3.5 oz. (approx 109 yds) balls cotton Tahki Creole, black (MC), 1 ball each same yarn off-white (A), maize (B), gray (C), turquoise (D).
Needles: One pair each #7 and #9 (or any size to obtain gauge), 1 29" #7 circular needle, 15 bobbins, 1 stitch holder, 1 crochet hook or tapestry needle.

GAUGE

11sts = 3"; 5rws = 1" (in St st on larger needles).
CHECK GAUGE TO ASSURE PROPER FIT.

STITCH PATTERN

Ribbing Stitch: Rw 1: *K1, P1*. Rep between *'s to end of rw. Rw 2: Knit the K sts, purl the P sts. Rep rw 2 for patt.
Stockinette Stitch: *K1 rw (RS), P1 rw (WS)*. Rep between *'s for patt.

NOTES

When changing colors, be sure to twist new yarn around dropped yarn in back of work.

Prepare bobbins: 2 each of MC, A, B, 3 of C, 6 of D.

INSTRUCTIONS

Back: Cast 72(80,86)sts on smaller needles in MC. Work in ribbing for 1". Change to larger needles. Work even in St st until piece measures 13".
Armhole Shaping: Bind off 3(5,6)sts at beg of next 2 rws. Dec 1 st at each end of every other rw 1(3,3) times. There are now 64(64,68)sts rem on needle. Work even until armhole measures 10(11,11¾)".
Shoulder Shaping: Bind off 20(20,21)sts at beg of next 2 rws. Place rem 24(24,26)sts on holder for neck.
Front: Work ribbing same as for back. Change to larger needles. Work even in St st foll chart until piece measures 13", end on WS.
Armhole Shaping: Work same as for back.
V-Neck Shaping: Next rw (WS): Work in patt across first 31(31,33)sts, join another ball of color in progress and bind off center 2sts; complete rw. There are 31(31,33)sts on each side. Working both sides at once, dec 1 st at neck edge on 3rd rw and every 4th rw thereafter 11(11,12) times until 20(20,21)sts rem. Bind off.
Finishing: Block pieces. Sew shoulders.
Neckband: From RS with circular needle and MC, beg at base of V and pick up and K90(98,102)sts along entire neck edge, including sts on holder. Work in rws of ribbing for 1". Bind off. Overlap left end of ribbing on right and sew in place.
Armbands: From RS with smaller needles and MC, pick up and K62(68,72)sts along entire armhole. Work in ribbing for 1". Bind off. Sew side seams, including ribbing.

✳✳

21 | **Children's Mohair Cardigan with Hearts**
(for intermediate knitters)

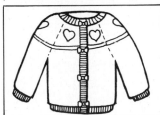

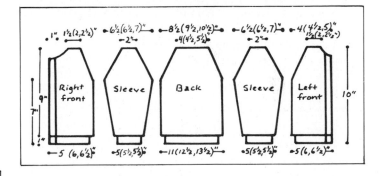

Finished Garment Measurements			
Children's Size	2	4	6
Chest	22"	25"	27"
Sleeve/Upper Arm	9"	9½"	10"

Button front cardigan in white mohair with red mohair heart motif at yoke. Raglan sleeves, ribbed bottom, collar, and cuffs with red stripe, satin ribbon bows, and 4 bow buttons at cardigan opening. Shown in children's size 2 (22" chest). Directions are for size 2. Changes for sizes 4 and 6 are in parentheses.

MATERIALS

Yarn: 5(6,6) 50 gr/1.8 oz (approx 165 yds) balls Tiber Super Kid Mohair, white (MC), 2 25 gr (approx 86 yds) balls Woollybear Mohair from Patricia Roberts, crimson (A).

Needles: One pair #8 (or size to obtain gauge), 1 29" #8 circular needle, 4 stitch markers, 11 bobbins, 1 yd red satin ribbon ¼" wide, 3 stitch holders, 4 bow buttons, 1 crochet hook or tapestry needle.

GAUGE

4sts and 6rws = 1" (in St st on larger needles).
CHECK GAUGE TO ASSURE PROPER FIT.

STITCH PATTERN

Ribbing Stitch: Rw 1: *K1, P1*. Rep between *'s to end of rw. Rw 2: Knit the K sts, purl the P sts. Rep rw 2 for patt.
Stockinette Stitch: *K1 rw (RS), P1 rw (WS)*. Rep between *'s for patt.

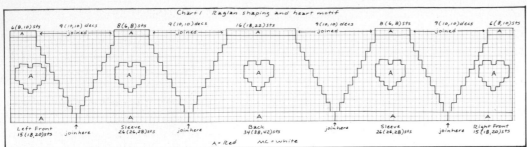

Chart 1 Raglan shaping and heart motif

A = Red   MC = white

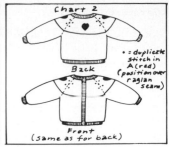

Chart 2

Back

• = duplicate stitch in A (red) (position over raglan seam)

Front (same as for back)

NOTES

When changing colors, be sure to twist new yarn around dropped yarn in back of work.

Prepare bobbins: 6 of MC, 5 of A.

INSTRUCTIONS

Back: Cast 44(50,54)sts on straight needles in MC. Work in K1, P1 ribbing for 1″. Work even in St st for 4rws. Change to A and work 2rws more. Change to MC and work even until piece measures 7(7,8)″.
Raglan Shaping: Dec 1 st at each end of every 3rd rw 5(6,6) times, end on WS. There are now 34(38,42)sts on needle. Place sts on stitch holder.
Left Front: Cast 20(24,26)sts on straight needles in MC. Work same as for back until piece measures 7(7,8)″, end on WS.
Raglan Shaping: Dec 1 st at beg of next rw and at same edge every 3rd rw 5(6,6) times, end on WS. There are now 15(18,20)sts on needle. Place sts on stitch holder.
Right Front: Work same as left front, reversing shaping.
Sleeves: Cast 20(22,22)sts on straight needles in MC. Work in K1, P1 ribbing for 1″. Work even in St st for 4rws. Change to A and work 2rws more. Change to MC. Work in patt, inc 1 st at

each end of every 3rd rw 8(8,9) times. There are now 36(38,40)sts on needle. Work even until piece measures 7(9,10)″.
Raglan Shaping: Dec 1 st at each end of every 3rd rw 5(6,6) times, end on WS. There are now 26(26,28)sts on needle. Place rem sts on stitch holder.
Yoke: Place pieces on circular needle to accommodate sts, as follows. Placing a marker between each section: right front, sleeve, back, sleeve, left front. Next 2rws: With A, work even in patt across 116(126,138)sts. Change to MC. Cont in rw of St st and foll chart 1 for heart motifs; dec 1 st on each side of every marker every K rw 9(10,10) times until 44(46,58)sts rem. Change to A and work even for 2rws more. Change to MC.
Neck: Work in K1, P1 ribbing for 1″. Bind off loosely.
Center Front Ribbing: From RS with MC, pick up and K72(76,82)sts along entire left front edge. Work in K1, P1 ribbing for 1″. Bind off loosely. Sew 4 buttons evenly spaced along rib. Rep ribbing along right front edge, working buttonholes on 3rd rw to correspond to buttons. (Buttonhole: Bind off 2sts; on next rw cast on 2sts over bound-off sts) Sew sleeve and side seams. Thread tapestry needle with red satin ribbon. Weave ribbon through red stripe at neck edge and at cuffs. Tie bow at cardigan opening and at center of each sleeve. Using red mohair, work sts at raglans in duplicate st foll chart 2.

✻✻✻

22 **Red Silk Evening Sweater (for advanced knitters)**

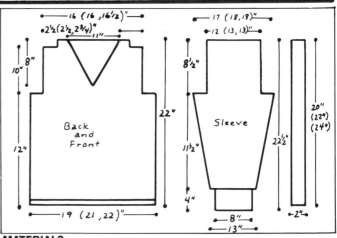

Finished Garment Measurements			
Women's	Small	Medium	Large
Bust	38″	42″	44″
Sleeve/Upper Arm	17″	18″	18″

Silk pullover with deep-collared V-neck, tucked and fitted sleeves, scalloped edge formed by pattern stitch, and self-belt at back. Shown in women's size 36″ bust (medium). Directions are for 34. Changes for 36 and 38 are in parentheses.

MATERIALS

Yarn: 9(10,11), 50 gr (approx 125 yds), balls 100% silk Crystal Palace Mandarin, red.
Needles: One pair each #6 and #8 (or size to obtain gauge), 1 #6 circular needle, stitch markers, about 90 ¼″ crystal beads, 4 ½″ crystal buttons, shoulder pads (optional).

GAUGE

5sts and 6rws = 1″ (in St st on larger needles).
CHECK GAUGE TO ASSURE PROPER FIT.

STITCH PATTERN

Ribbing Stitch: Rw 1: *K1, P1*. Rep between *'s to end of rw.
Rw 2: Knit the K sts, purl the P sts. Rep rw 2 for patt.

Dragon Skin Pattern Stitch:
Rw 1 (WS) and alt rws: P.
Rw 2: *K1, lift running thread between st just worked and next st and K into back of this thread—make one (M1); skpo, K4, K2tog, K3, M1, K2, M1, K3, skpo, K4, K2tog, M1, K1*; rep between *'s.
Rw 4: *K1, M1, K1, skpo, K2, K2tog, K4, M1, K2, M1, K4, skpo, K2, K2tog, K1, M1, K1*; rep between *'s.
Rw 6: *K1, M1, K2, skpo, K2tog, K5, M1, K2, M1, K5, skpo, K2tog, K2, M1, K1*; rep between *'s.
Rw 8: *K1, M1, K3, skpo, K4, K2tog, M1, K2, M1, skpo, K4, K2tog, K3, M1, K1*; rep between *'s.
Rw 10: *K1, M1, K4, skpo, K2, K2tog, K1, M1, K2, M1, K1, skpo, K2, K2tog, K4, M1, K1*; rep between *'s.
Rw 12: *K1, M1, K5, skpo, K2tog, K2, (M1, K2) twice, skpo, K2tog, K5, M1, K1*; rep between *'s.
Rep rws 1–12 for patt.

INSTRUCTIONS

Back: Cast 94(106,112)sts on larger needles. K2rws. Next rw (WS): P8(1,4), place marker, work in patt st across next 78(104,104)sts, place marker, P8(1,4). Work even with center sts in patt st and side sts in St st until piece measures 12″, end on WS.
Armhole Shaping: (On RS rws, bind off sts and K to first (M1, K2, M1) ridge, then cont with set patt st and work to end of rw foll patt. On WS rws, bind off sts normally.) Bind off 3(5,6)sts at beg of next 2rws, then 2(3,3)sts at beg of next 4rws and 0(2,2)sts at beg of next 2rws. There are now 80(80,84)sts rem on needle. Work even until armholes measure 10″, end on WS.
Shoulder Shaping: Bind off 6(6,7)sts at beg of next 4rws. Bind off rem sts.

Front: Work same as back until piece measures 14″, end on WS.
V-Neck Shaping: Next rw (RS): Work in patt across first 39(39,41)sts, place these sts on a holder, then bind off 2 center sts; complete rw in patt. There are 39(39,41)sts on needle. Dec 1 st at neck edge every rw 3(3,5) times, then every other rw 22 times. Now 14sts rem on needle. Work even until armhole measures 10″ from beg, end at armhole edge.
Shoulder Shaping: Bind off 6(6,7)sts at beg of next rw and at same edge once more until no sts rem. Place sts from holder on needle and work other side of neck in the same manner.
Sleeves: Cast 40sts on smaller needles. Work in ribbing for 4″, inc 28sts evenly spaced across last rw. There are 78sts on needle. Change to larger needles. Working the 78sts in patt st, inc 1 st at each end of every 7th(5th,5th) rw 4(6,6) times, with the inc sts in St st. There are now 86(90,90)sts on needle. Work even until piece measures 11½″.
Cap Shaping: Bind off 3(5,5)sts at beg of next 2rws, then 2(3,3)sts at beg of next 4rws and 1(2,2)sts at beg of next 2rws. Work even on 60(64,64)sts until cap measures 8½″. Bind off.
Finishing: Block all pieces. Sew side and shoulder seams. Sew sleeve seams. Sew tucks in sleeve caps as indicated on page 46. Sew sleeves into body of sweater.
Collar: Rw 1 (RS): From WS of neck opening with circular needle, beg at bottom of V, and pick up and K54sts along left neck edge, 53sts across back neck, and 54sts along right neck edge. There are 161sts on needle. (Remember that the RS of the collar emerges from the WS of the sweater.) With RS of collar facing you, *K1, P1, K1*, rep to end of rw. Work these 3sts as a border on each end. All inc will occur to the inside of this border. Work in ribbing for 32rws, inc 1 st in 4th st from each end of every RS rw (to inc: M1). Bind off.
Belt: Cast 7sts on smaller needles. Work 1 rw in ribbing. Next rw: Work in ribbing, inc 1 st at each end. Cont in ribbing until piece measures 20(22,24)″. Dec 1 st at each end of next rw. Then work even for 1 rw more. Bind off.
Randomly sew ¼″ crystal beads onto sweater. Sew belt at waist, easing in fullness and attaching 2 ½″ buttons to each end of belt in front.

✳

| 23 | **Polar Bear Sweater (for beginning knitters)** |

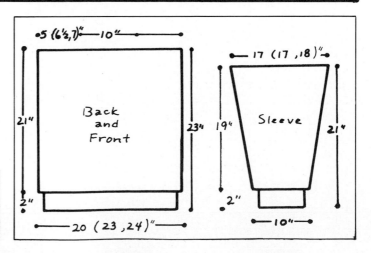

Finished Garment Measurements			
Women's	Small	Medium	Large
Bust	40″	46″	48″
Sleeve/UpperArm	17″	17″	18″

Mohair and angora pullover with polar bear motif. Worked in stockinette stitch with ribbed borders, side button collar which can be worn buttoned up or open. Collar is lined on inside with black-and-white flecked novelty wool worked in stockinette stitch. Polar bear, which is worked in angora, has a black round button nose and rhinestone button eye. Buttonloops are chain stitch crochet for neck closure. Polar bear is approximately 10". Shown in women's size 45" bust (medium). (This is an oversized garment.) Directions are for 8–10. Changes for 12–14 and 16–18 are in parentheses.

MATERIALS

Yarn: 4(5,6) 1½ oz (90 yds) balls Elite La Gran Mohair (with wool nylon mixture), black (MC), 5 10 gr/⅓ oz (approx 97 yds) balls ACA Supreme Angora (rabbits hair), white (A), 2 50 gr/1¾ oz (yardage varies, sold by weight) balls Tahki Cabaret Mohair (with polyester mixture), white with black flecks (B).
Needles: One pair #9 (or size to obtain gauge), 1 16" #9 circular needle, 1 black round (glass/onyx) button for polar bear nose, 1 rhinestone (oval or round) button for polar bear eye, 2½" black buttons for neck closure, 6 bobbins, 1 crochet hook and tapestry needle.

GAUGE

4sts = 1"; 9rws = 2" (in St st on larger needles).
CHECK GAUGE TO ASSURE PROPER FIT.

NOTES

Prepare bobbins: 4 of MC, 2 of A. When changing colors, be sure to twist new yarn around dropped yarn in back of work. When working on circular needle (in stockinette stitch), do not work in rnds; work 1 K rw, turn work, 1 P rw (WS).

STITCH PATTERN

Ribbing Stitch: *K2, P2* Rep between *'s to end of rw. Rw 2: Knit the K sts, purl the P sts. Rep rw 2 for patt.
Stockinette Stitch: *K1 rw (RS), P1 rw (WS)*. Rep between *'s for patt.

INSTRUCTIONS

Back: Cast on 72(80,86)sts in MC. Work in ribbing for 2", inc 9(11,11)sts evenly spaced across last rw. There are now 81(91,97)sts on needle. Work in St st until back measures 23". Bind off.
Front: Work same as for back, foll chart for polar bear motif.
Sleeves: Cast on 40sts in MC. Work in ribbing for 2", inc 4sts evenly spaced across last rw. There are now 44sts on needle. Work in St st, inc 1 st at each end of every 5th rw 12(12,14) times. There are now 68(68,72)sts on needle. Work even until sleeve measures 21". Bind off.
Finishing: Block pieces. Sew shoulders, leaving a 10" neck opening. Mark side edges of front and back 8½"(8½",9") from shoulders for armholes (see diagram). Sew sleeves to sides of garment between armhole markers. Sew side and sleeve seams.
Collar: From RS with circular needle and MC, pick up and K40sts along front neck edge and 40sts along back neck edge. There are 80sts on needle. Do not join. Work even in rws of St st for 4". Change to B. Work in St st for 4" more. Bind off. Fold color B section of collar to inside and stitch in place along neck edge. Tuck rw edge of collar in and sew open ends closed. Block collar. Sew rhinestone button at eye and black button at nose. Sew 2 rem buttons to end of front collar ½" from top bottom.
Buttonloops: Using crochet hook, make a simple chain st (see page 152) large enough to accommodate button and secure to opposite edge of collar.

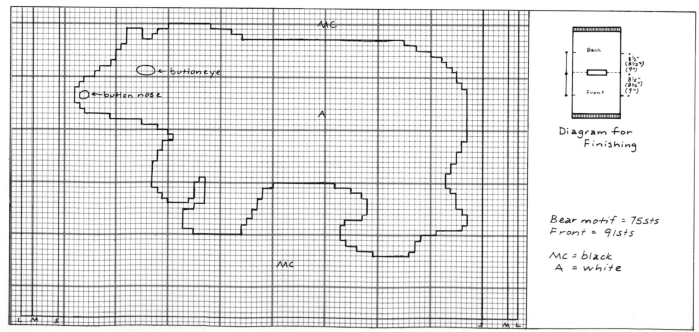

Diagram for Finishing

Bear motif = 75sts
Front = 91sts

MC = black
A = white

**

24 Red Reindeer Sweater (for intermediate knitters)

Finished Garment Measurements			
Women's	Small	Medium	Large
Bust	41"	45"	47"
Sleeve/Upper Arm	17"	18"	18"

Wool turtleneck ski sweater, with classic, fitted armholes, mohair reindeer and snowflakes, and a triangular applied collar. This design can be adapted for beginners by omitting the collar. Sweater is shown in women's size 36" bust (medium). Directions are for 8–10. Changes for 12–14 and 16–18 are in parentheses.

MATERIALS

Yarn: 9(10,11) 3.5 oz/100 gr (approx 180-200 yds) balls 100% wool knitting worsted, red (MC), 2 25 gr balls each 100% mohair, black (A) and white (B).
Needles: One pair each #6 and #8 (or size to obtain gauge), 1 16" #6 circular needle, 8 bobbins, 4 stitch holders.

GAUGE

4sts and 5rws = 1" (in St st on larger needles).
CHECK GAUGE TO ASSURE PROPER FIT.

STITCH PATTERN

Ribbing Stitch: Rw 1: *K2, P2*. Rep. between *'s to end of rw.
Rw 2: Knit the K sts, purl the P sts. Rep rw 2 for patt.
Stockinette Stitch: *K1 rw (RS), P1 rw, (WS). Rep between *'s for patt.

NOTES

When changing colors, be sure to twist new yarn around dropped yarn in back of work to avoid holes.

Prepare bobbins: 5 of MC, 3 of A.

INSTRUCTIONS

Back: Cast on 82(90,94)sts on smaller needles in MC. Work in ribbing for 3". Change to larger needles. Work in St st, foll chart 1 for color changes to rw 84, end on WS. Piece measures 17".
Armhole Shaping: Bind off 3(4,5)sts at beg of next 2rws, then 2(3,4)sts at beg of next 2rws, and 2sts at beg of next 2rws. There are now 68(72,72)sts rem on needle. Work even until armholes measure 8(8,8½)" from beg, end on WS.

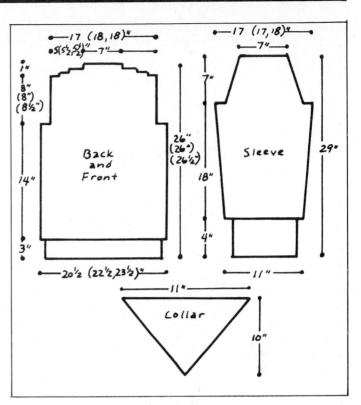

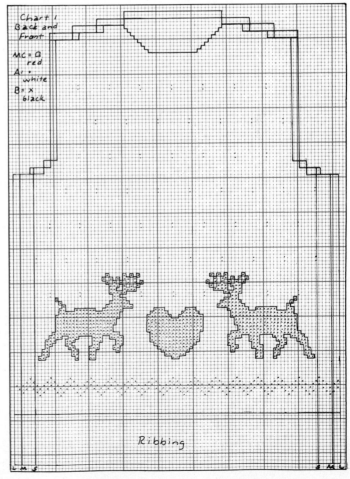

Shoulder Shaping: Bind off 7sts at beg of next 4rws, then 6(8,8)sts at beg of next 2rws. There are now 28sts rem on needle. Bind off.

Front: Work same as for back foll chart 1 for color changes, until armhole measures 7(7,7½)″ from beg, end on WS.

Neck Shaping: Next rw: Work across first 27(29,29)sts, join another ball of yarn, and bind off center 14sts; complete rw. Working both sides at once, dec 1 st at neck edge every rw 7 times each side, and **at same time** work even at armhole edges for 4rws, then bind off 7sts at armhole edge twice each side, then bind off 6(8,8) rem sts each side.

Sleeves: Cast on 40sts with smaller needles in MC. Work in ribbing for 4″, inc 2sts at each end of last rw. Change to larger needles. Work in St st, foll chart 2 for color changes for left sleeve, and chart 2a for color changes for right sleeve, inc 1 st at each end of every 5th rw 10(12,12) times, then every 10th rw twice. There are now 68(72,72)sts on needle. Work even until piece measures 22″.

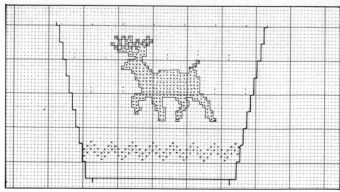

Chart 2a Right sleeve

Cap Shaping: Bind off 3(4,4)sts at beg of next 2rws, then 3(0,0)sts at beg of next 2rws, and 2sts at beg of next 4(2,2)rws. There are now 54sts on needle. Dec 1 st at each end every 3rd rw 6 times; then every other rw 6 times. There are now 30sts rem on needle, and the sleeve cap measures 7″. Bind off.

Collar: (make 2): (Border sts indicated in symbolcraft below the solid line on chart 3 are worked in ribbing and rem sts are worked in St st.) Cast on 2sts on larger needles in MC. Work in K2, P2 ribbing as shown on chart 3, inc 1 st at each end every rw twice, *work 1 rw even, then inc 1 st each end every rw 4 times*. Rep between *'s foll chart 3 for color changes until there are 84sts. Bind off 24sts at beg of next 2rws. Place the center 36sts on a holder.

Finishing: Block all pieces. Sew shoulders. Sew collar at shoulder, leaving center 35sts of each side for neck opening. Matching shoulders, place neck edges of collar around neck edges of sweater.

Neckband: From RS with circular needle and MC, pick up and K36sts along front and 36sts along back neck edges, working through both thicknesses and including sts on holders. There are 72sts on needle. Work the matching st from collar and st from sweater tog as 1 st when you begin ribbing. Work in rnds of ribbing for 3″. Bind off loosely.

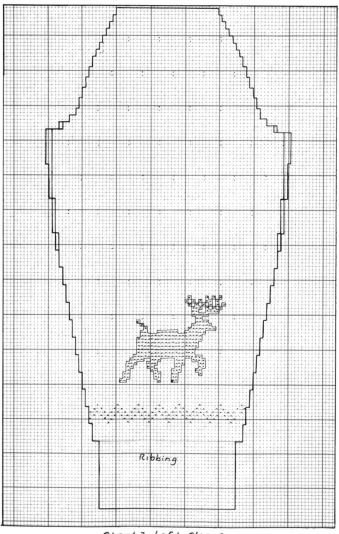

Chart 2 Left Sleeve

MC = ☐ red   A = • white   B = x black

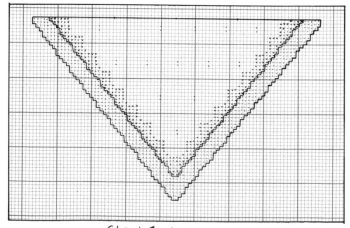

Chart 3 Collar

MC = ☐ red   A = • white   B = x black

Symbolcraft Chart → ⊞ = Knit   ⊟ = Purl

✳✳

25 | **Peach Taos Sweater (for intermediate knitters)**

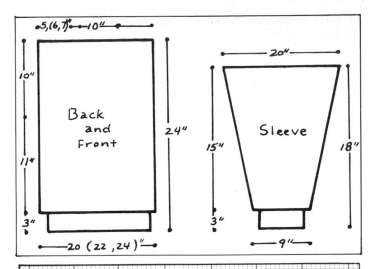

Finished Garment Measurements			
Women's	Small	Medium	Large
Bust	40"	44"	48"
Sleeve/UpperArm	20"	20"	20"

Drop shoulder sweater with split asymmetrical collar and tapered sleeves. For a simpler pattern, follow the written instructions, not the chart for the border treatments. This handspun, vegetable-dyed yarn is a Taos specialty; you can re-create the look by finding a yarn with the same gauge. Shown in women's size 36" bust (medium). Directions are for 8–10. Changes for 12–14 and 16–18 are in parentheses.

MATERIALS

Yarn: 23(24) 1¾ oz (yardage varies, sold by weight) balls LaLana Wools, peach (MC), 1 ball each same yarn aqua (A) and white (B).
Needles: One pair each #8 and #10½ (or size to obtain gauge), 6 bobbins.

GAUGE

3sts and 4rws = 1" (in St st on larger needles).
CHECK GAUGE TO ASSURE PROPER FIT.

STITCH PATTERN

Ribbing Stitch: Rw 1: *K1, P1*. Rep between *'s to end of rw.
Rw 2: Knit the K sts, purl the P sts. Rep rw 2 for patt.
Stockinette Stitch: *K1 rw (RS), P1 rw, (WS). Rep between *'s for patt.

NOTE

Bobbins aren't necessary for random strands of color. Use a length of yarn instead. Do use bobbins for larger triangular shapes. When changing colors, be sure to twist new yarn around dropped yarn in back of work.

INSTRUCTIONS

Back: Cast 60(66,72)sts on smaller needles in MC. Work in ribbing for 3". Change to larger needles. Work in St st foll chart 1 until piece measures 24". Bind off.
Front: Work same as for back foll chart 1 to rw 92.
Neck Shaping: Next rw: Work across 23(26,29)sts, join another

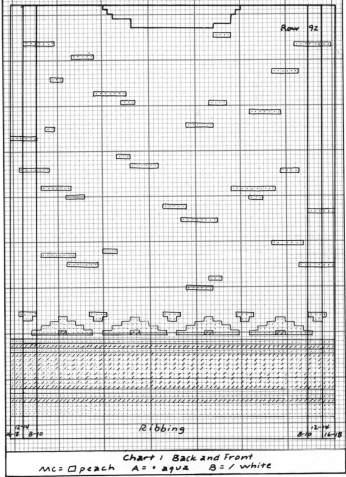

Chart 1 Back and Front
MC = □ peach   A = • aqua   B = ∕ white

ball of yarn, and bind off center 18sts; complete rw. Working both sides at once, bind off 4sts at neck edge once each side, then dec 1 st at neck edge every rw twice each side. There are now 15(18,21)sts on each side. Bind off.
Sleeves: Cast 24(26,26)sts on smaller needles in MC. Work in ribbing for 3", inc 8(6,6)sts evenly spaced across last rw. There are now 32sts on the needle. Change to larger needles. Work in St st foll chart 2 and inc 1 st at each end every 3rd rw

14 times. There are now 60sts on the needle. Work even until piece measures 18″. Bind off.

Finishing: Weave in or tie all loose ends on WS. Block all pieces. Sew right shoulder. Mark neck edges of left shoulder.

Collar: From RS with smaller needles and MC, pick up and K 62sts along entire neck edge, beg and end at left shoulder markers. Next rw: Work in K1, P1 rib across first 2sts, work in

St st fol chart 1 to last 2sts, P1, K1. Cont in patt fol chart #3 with first and last 2sts in ribbing until piece measures 9″. Change to smaller needles and work in ribbing across all sts for 1″. Bind off.

Sew left shoulder. Mark side edges of front and back 10″ from shoulders. Sew sleeves between markers. Sew side and sleeve seams.

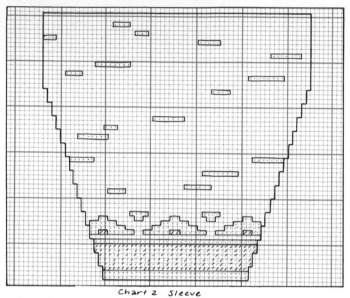

Chart 2 Sleeve

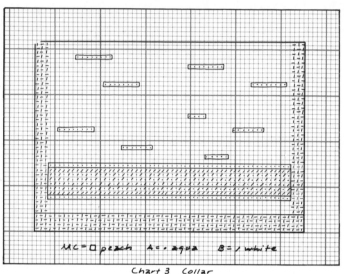

MC=□ peach   A=∙ aqua   B=/ white

Chart 3 Collar

*

26 **Taos Vest (for beginning knitters)**

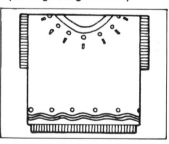

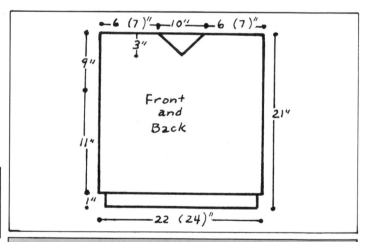

Finished Garment Measurements		
Women's	Small/Medium	Medium/Large
Bust	44″	48″
Armhole	19″	19″

An oversized drop shoulder shape, with a modified, shallow V-neck. Look for a yarn of the same gauge to achieve this look. Shown in women's size 32″–36″ bust. Directions are for small-medium. Changes for medium-large are in parentheses.

MATERIALS

Yarn: 12(13) 1¾ oz (yardage varies, sold by weight) 100% wool La Lana, off-white (MC), 1 ball each same yarn peach (A) and light blue (B).

Needles: One pair each #8 and #10½ (or size to obtain gauge).

TIP

• *Hand-dyed yarns are one-of-a-kind finds. One of the great things about handmade yarn is its uniqueness: no two skeins are the same. The real challenge is to knit a garment that has cohesiveness from yarns that have changing colors. The answer is to create your own variegated yarn. Try this: Make each skein into a ball and begin to mix the yarns by taking several yards from one ball and tying it to the next. Switching the yarn systematically lets you "homogenize" your lot. Try not to cut the lengths too short or you will end up with a lot of knots throughout the back of your knitting sweater).*

GAUGE

3sts and 4rws = 1" (in St st on larger needles).
CHECK GAUGE TO ASSURE PROPER FIT.

STITCH PATTERNS

Ribbing Stitch: Rw 1: *K1, P1*. Rep between *'s to end of rw.
Rw 2: Knit the K sts, purl the P sts. Rep rw 2 for patt.
Stockinette Stitch: *K1 rw (RS), P1 rw, (WS). Rep between *'s for patt.

NOTE

The "random" strands of color are achieved by using a length of yarn, not a bobbin. When changing colors, be sure to twist new yarn around dropped yarn in back of work to avoid holes.

INSTRUCTIONS

Back: Cast 66(72)sts on smaller needles in MC. Work in ribbing for 1". Change to larger needles and work in St st foll chart until piece measures 21". Bind off.
Front: Work same as for back foll chart until piece measures 17", end on WS.
V-Neck Shaping: Next rw: Work in patt st across 32(35)sts, join another ball of yarn, bind off 2sts, complete rw. Working both sides of front at the same time and foll chart, dec 1 st at neck edge every rw 14 times each side. There are 18(21)sts rem on each side of neck edge. Bind off rem sts.
Finishing: Block all pieces. Sew one shoulder.
Neckband: From RS with smaller needle and MC, pick up 18sts along left front edge, 30sts along back, and 18sts along right neck edge. There are 66sts on needle. Work in ribbing for 1". Bind off all sts.
Sew other shoulder. Mark side edges of front and back 9" from shoulders.

Armbands: From RS with smaller needles and MC, pick up 88sts between armhole markers. Work in ribbing for 1". Bind off. Sew sides, including armbands.

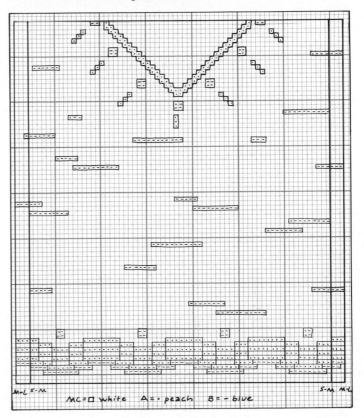

MC=□ white   A=· peach   B=- blue

---

27   **Women's "Nantucket Yarn" Pullover Sweater**
(for beginning knitters)

✳

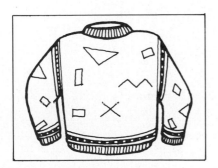

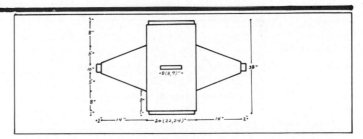

Oversized pullover with random geometric shapes and checked border. Ribbed bottom, cuffs, and wide crew neck. Front and back are knit in one piece. Sleeves are knit out from sides of garment. Shown in women's size 44" bust (medium). Directions are for 8–10. Changes for 12–14 and 16–18 are in parentheses.

MATERIALS

Yarn: 6(7,8) 3.5 oz (yardage varies, sold by weight) balls 100% handspun wool Nantucket Looms yarn, cream, (MC), 2 balls each same yarn yellow (A) and blue (B), 1 ball same yarn dark red (C).

Needles: One pair each #9 and #11 (or size to obtain gauge), 1 16" #9 circular needle, 1 crochet hook or tapestry needle, 7 bobbins.

Finished Garment Measurements			
Women's	Small	Medium	Large
Bust	40"	44"	48"
Sleeve/Upper Arm	22"	22"	22"

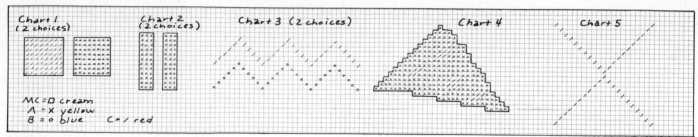

GAUGE

7sts = 2"; 5rws = 1" (in St st on larger needles).
CHECK GAUGE TO ASSURE PROPER FIT.

STITCH PATTERN

Checked Border: Rw 1: (RS) *K2 with B, K2 with MC*. Rep between *'s across, end with B. Rw 2: *P2 with B, K2 with MC*. Rep between *'s across, end with B.
Ribbing Stitch: Rw 1: *K2, P2*. Rep between *'s to end of rw. Rw 2: Knit the K sts, purl the P sts. Rep rw 2 for patt.
Stockinette Stitch: *K1 rw (RS), P1 rw (WS)*. Rep between *'s for patt.

NOTES

When changing colors, be sure to twist new yarn around dropped yarn in back of work.

Prepare bobbins: 1 of A, 3 each of B and C.

When knitting checked border work with 1 ball of each color and carry yarn on WS.

INSTRUCTIONS

Back: Cast 70(78,86)sts on smaller needles in MC. Work in ribbing for 1". Change to A and larger needles. Work in St st for 2rws. Then work checked border for 2rws. Change to A. Work in St st for 2rws. Change to MC. Cont in St st, using charts 1–5 to place geometric shapes randomly over entire back until piece measures 18", end on WS.

Neck Shaping: Next rw: Work in patt across first 21(25,27)sts, join another ball of yarn, and bind off center 28(28,32)sts; complete rw. There are 21(25,27)sts on each side. Working both sides at once, cont in St st for 10rws, end on WS. Next rw: K across first side, cast on 28(28,32)sts, K across second side. There are now 70(78,86)sts on needle.

Front: Cont on St st, using charts 1–5 to place geometric shapes randomly over entire front until piece measures 16", end on WS. Change to A. Work in St st for 2rws; then in checked border for 2rws. Change to A and work in St st for 2 more rws. Change to MC and smaller needles. Work in ribbing for 1". Bind off. Block piece. Mark side edges of front and back 8" up from ribs.

Sleeves: From RS with larger needles and A, pick up and K78sts evenly spaced between markers. Work in St st for 1 rw; then in checked border for 2rws. Change to A and work in St st for 2 more rws. Change to MC and smaller needles and cont in St st using charts 1–5 to place geometric shapes randomly over entire sleeve, and **at same time** dec 1 st at each end of every 5th rw 10 times; then at each end of every 3rd rw 3 times. Work even on 52sts until piece measures 13" from beg, end on WS. Change to A. Work 2rws in St st; then work checked border for 2rws. Change to A and work in St st for 2rws more. Change to MC and smaller needles. Work in ribbing for 2". Bind off.

Finishing: Block pieces.
Collar: From RS with circular needle and MC, pick up and K64sts. Work in rnds of ribbing for 2". Bind off. Sew side and sleeve seams.

✳

| 28 | "Nantucket Yarn" Straight Skirt (for beginning knitters) |

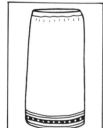 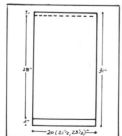

Straight skirt with checked border. Mid-calf length with gathered (elasticized) waist and side seams. Shown in women's size 36" hips (small). Changes for 39" and for 43" hips are in parentheses.

MATERIALS

Yarn: 8 1¾ oz (yardage varies, sold by weight) balls 100% handspun wool "Nantucket Looms," 1 ball each cream (MC), yellow (A), and blue (B).
Needles: One pair each #9 and #11 (or size to obtain gauge), 1 tapestry needle or crochet hook, 1 yd ¾" elastic.

GAUGE

7sts = 2"; 5rws = 1" (in St st on larger needles).
CHECK GAUGE TO ASSURE PROPER FIT.

Finished Garment Measurements			
Women's	Small	Medium	Large
Waist	25"	28"	32"
Hips	36"	39"	43"
Length to mid-calf	32"	32"	32"

STITCH PATTERN

Checked Border: Rw 1: (RS)*K2 with B, K2 with MC*, rep between *'s, end with MC. Rw 2: *P2 with MC, K2 with B*. Rep between *'s, end with B.
Ribbing Stitch: Rw 1: *K2, P2*, rep between *'s to end of rw. Rw 2: Knit the K sts, purl the P sts. Rep rw 2 for patt.
Stockinette Stitch: *K1 rw (RS), P1 rw (WS)*, rep between *'s for patt.

NOTE

When knitting checked border, work with 1 ball of each color and carry yarn on WS.

INSTRUCTIONS

Back: Cast 64(68,76)sts on larger needles in MC. Work even in St st for 28", end on WS. Change to A. Work in St st for 2rws, then in checked border for 2rws. Change to A and work in St st for 2rws more. Change to MC. Work even for 2". Then change to smaller needles and work in ribbing for 1". Bind off.
Front: Work as for back.
Finishing: Block pieces. Sew side seams.
Waistband: Fold 1" at top of garment to inside and sew in place, leaving a 3" opening. Cut elastic to fit waist plus 2". Thread elastic through top casing. Sew ends together. Then sew rem casing closed.

✱✱✱

29 **Indigo-Dyed Cotton Western Dress (for advanced knitters)**

Finished Garment Measurements			
Women's	Small	Medium	Large
Bust	32"	34"	38"
Waist	30"	32"	35"
Hips	34"	36"	40"

Mid-calf-length cotton dress of indigo-dyed yarn with contrasting trim and triangular motif. Loose-fitting top with V-neck polo button-down collar; false skirt is knit down from ribbed waist and has horse motif patch pockets and false front button closure. Skirt remains open from knee down. Top can be knit alone. Shown in women's size 34" bust (medium). Directions are for size 4–6. Changes for 8–10 and 12–14 are in parentheses.

MATERIALS

Yarn: 16(18,20) 100 gr/3.5 oz (approx 215 yds) balls cotton Crystal Palace Jeans Yarn, light blue (MC), and 3 balls each same yarn, medium blue (A) and dark blue (B). (For top only, purchase half of MC and 2 balls each of A and B.)
Needles: One pair #8 (or size to obtain gauge), 1 29" #8 circular needle, 1 crochet hook and tapestry needle, 8 bobbins, 1 yd ¾" elastic, 1 stitch holder, 11 ¾" buttons, 2 ¼" buttons.

GAUGE

5sts and 6rws = 1" (in St st on larger needles).
CHECK GAUGE TO ASSURE PROPER FIT.

STITCH PATTERN

Ribbing Stitch: Rw 1: *K2, P2*. Rep between *'s to end of rw. Rw 2: Knit the K sts, purl the P sts. Rep rw 2 for patt.
Stockinette Stitch: *K1 rw (RS), P1 rw (WS)*. Rep between *'s for patt.

NOTES

When changing colors, be sure to twist new yarn around dropped yarn in back of work.

Prepare bobbins: 3 each of MC and B, 2 of A.

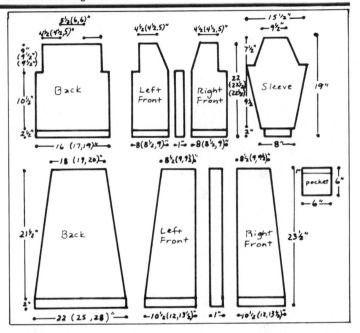

INSTRUCTIONS

Back: Cast on 80(86,94)sts in B. Work in ribbing for 2½". Change to MC. Beg with a P rw, work in St st foll chart 1 for color changes and using bobbins to work motifs until piece measures 13", end on WS.
Armhole Shaping: Bind off 3(3,4)sts at beg of next 2rws; then 1(2,3)sts at beg of next 2rws until 72(76,80)sts rem on needle. Rep between *'s once, foll chart for increases and armhole shaping. Cont in patt and foll chart until armholes measure 8½(9,9)" from beg, end on WS. Work until piece measures 19½".
Neck Shaping: Next rw: Work across first 25(26,28)sts, join another ball of yarn, and bind off center 22(24,24)sts; complete rw. Working both sides at once, bind off 3sts at neck edge once each side until 22(23,25)sts rem on each side. Bind off.
Top Right Front: Cast on 40(43,47)sts in B. Work in ribbing for 2½". Change to MC. Beg with a P rw, work in St st foll chart 2 for color changes and using bobbins to work motifs until piece measures 13", end on RS.
Armhole Shaping: Bind off 3(3,4)sts at beg of next rw (armhole) once; then 1(2,3)sts at same edge once until 36(38,40)sts rem. Work even until piece measures 13", end on RS.

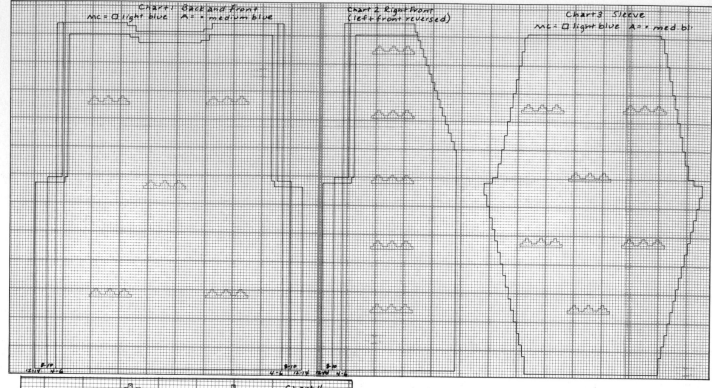

Neck Shaping: Next rw: Work in patt, dec 1 st at end (neck). Cont in patt foll chart and dec 1 st at neck edge every 3rd rw 13(14,14) times more, until 22(23,25)sts rem. Bind off.

Top Left Front: Work same as right front, reversing shapings.

Sleeves: Cast on 40sts in B. Work in ribbing for 2″, inc 7sts evenly spaced across last rw. There are 47sts on needle. Change to MC. Work in St st foll chart 3 for color changes, using bobbins to work motifs, and inc 1 st at each end of 7th rw and then every 4th rw thereafter 15 times in all until there are 77sts on needle.

Cap Shaping: Bind off 3sts at beg of next 2rws; and 2sts at beg of next 2rws. Then dec 1 st at each end of every 5th rw 10 times until 47sts rem. Bind off.

Finishing: Block pieces. Sew shoulders.

Collar: From WS with circular needle and B, beg at base of left front neck shaping and pick up and K41(45,45)sts along left neck, 28(30,30)sts across 45sts, 31sts from holder, and 45sts from right front back neck and 41(45,45)sts along right neck. There are 110(120,120)sts on needle. Work in ribbing for 1½″. Bind off loosely.

Right Mock Buttonband: From RS with straight needles and MC pick up and K90sts along center front beg above bottom rib. Work in ribbing for 1″. Bind off loosely. Sew center front edge of left front to WS of first rw of right front mock buttonband. Sew ends of bottom ribbing closed at center front.

Sew 6 buttons evenly spaced along mock buttonband. Sew side and sleeve seams. Sew in sleeves, easing in fullness at shoulders. At collar points, sew ¼″ buttons.

Skirt Back: Cast on 89(95,101)sts in MC. Work in St st, inc 1 st at each end of every 6th row 10(15,19) times. Work even on 109(125,139)sts until piece measures 21½″. Change to B and work in ribbing for 2″. Bind off loosely.

Skirt Left Front: Cast on 42(45,47)sts in MC. Work in St st inc 1 st at end of 7th rw (K rw) and same edge every 6th rw thereafter 9(14,18) times more. Work even on 52(60,66)sts until piece measures 21½″. Change to B and work in ribbing for 2″. Bind off loosely.

Skirt Right Front: Work same as for left front, reversing shapings.

Pockets: Cast on 30sts in MC. Work in St st foll chart 4 for horse motif. Change to B and work in ribbing for 1″. Block pockets. Sew to right and left fronts (horses facing), from inside edges.

Skirt Right Mock Buttonband: From RS with MC, pick up and K120sts along entire center front edge. Work in ribbing for 1″. Bind off loosely.

Skirt Left Mock Buttonband: Work same as for skirt right mock buttonband. Overlap buttonband closures (left on inside and right on outside). Sew together from top of skirt to 9½″ from hem. Sew 5 buttons evenly spaced along 14″ of sewn band.

Finishing: Sew top of skirt to bottom of sweater, matching side and center fronts and easing fullness. Cut elastic to waist measurement plus 2″. Sew ends of elastic together. With B and tapestry needle, sew elastic in place on inside of ribbing, using a zigzag stitch across elastic width and catching ends of stitches on WS of ribbing to form a thread casing to hold elastic.

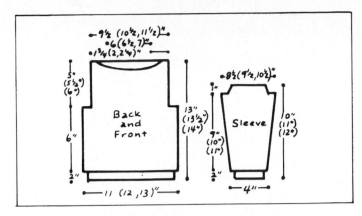

30 | Children's Pink Pullover with Cow Motif (for beginning knitters)

Finished Garment Measurements			
Children's Size	2-3	4-5	6-7
Chest	22"	24"	26"
Sleeve/Upper Arm	8½"	9½"	10½"

Crew neck pullover with notched armhole, shoulder and neck button closure, ribbed bottom, collar, and cuffs, and black and white cow motif with applied bell. Directions are for children's size 2. Changes for size 4 and size 6 are in parentheses.

MATERIALS

Yarn: 4(5,6) 50 gr/1.8 oz (approx 90 yds) balls Conshoken Softball Cotton, pink (MC), 1 ball each same yarn white (A), black (B), and dark pink (C).

Needles: One pair #8 (or size to obtain gauge), crochet hook or tapestry needle, 12 bobbins, 3 stitch holders, 3 black heart buttons, jingle bell.

GAUGE

4sts = 1"; 13rws = 2" (in St st).
CHECK GAUGE TO ASSURE PROPER FIT.

STITCH PATTERN

Ribbing Stitch Rw 1: *K1, P1*, rep between *'s to end of rw.
Rw 2: Knit the K sts, purl the P sts. Rep rw 2 for patt.
Stockinette Stitch: *K1 rw (RS), P1 rw (WS)*.

NOTE

When changing colors, be sure to twist new yarn around dropped yarn in back of work.

INSTRUCTIONS

Back: Cast on 38(42,46)sts in MC. Work in ribbing for 8rws, inc 6sts evenly spaced across last rw. There are now 44(48,52)sts on needle. Work even in St st until piece measures 6", end on WS.
Armhole Shaping: Bind off 3sts at beg of next 2rws. There are 38(42,46)sts on needle. Work even in St st until armhole measures 5(5½,6)".
Shoulder Shaping: Bind off 5sts at beg of next 2rws, 2(3,4)sts at beg of next 2rws; then 6sts at beg of next 2rws. There are 12(14,16)sts rem on needle. Bind off.
Front: Work as for back until piece measures 4", end on WS. Cont in St st and foll chart for cow motif, and **at same time**, when piece measures 6", work armhole shapings same as for back. Work even until armhole measures 4½(5,5½)", end on WS.

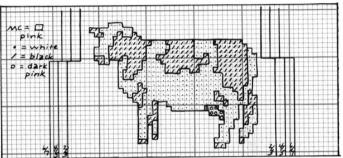

Neck Shaping: Next rw: K15(16,17)sts, place center 8(10,12)sts on holder, join another ball of yarn; K15(16,17)sts. Working both sides at once, dec 1 st at neck edge twice each side until 13(14,15)sts rem on each side.
Shoulder Shaping: (Work both sides together): Bind off 5sts at armhole edge once each side; then 2sts at armhole edge once each side until 6sts rem on each side. Bind off the 6sts of left shoulder; then place the 6sts of right shoulder on stitch holder.
Sleeves: Cast on 16(18,20)sts in MC. Work in ribbing for 8rws, inc 4sts evenly spaced across last rw. There are now 20(22,24)sts on needle. Work in St st, inc 1 st at each end of every 5th rw 7(8,9) times. There are now 34(38,42)sts on needle. Work even until piece measures 9(10,11)".
Cap Shaping: Bind off 3sts at beg of next 2rws until 28(32,36)sts rem. Then work even in St st for 4 more rws. Bind off.
Neckband: Sew left shoulder. From RS with MC, beg at right shoulder and pick up and K36(40,44)sts along entire neck edge, including sts from front neck holder. Work in ribbing for 3rws. Next rw: Work in ribbing to last 4sts, end at front neck, bind off next 2sts for buttonhole; complete rw. Cont in ribbing for 3 more rws and cast on 2sts over bound-off sts.
Right Shoulder Buttonband: From right side with MC, pick up and K14(15,16)sts across right front shoulder, including 6sts from holder; do not pick up sts across end of neckband. Work in ribbing for 4rws. Rw 5: *K1, P1, bind off 2sts*, for buttonhole. Rep between *'s across to last st, end with P1(K1,P1). Cont in ribbing for 2 more rws and cast on 2sts over bound-off sts. Bind off. Overlap right shoulder band over back shoulder and tack tog at armhole. Sew side and sleeve seams. Sew in sleeves. Sew buttons at neckband and shoulder and jingle bell on cow's neck.

✳✳✳

31 **Fiesta Sweater (for advanced knitters)**

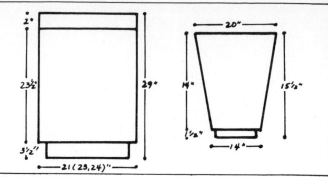

Finished Garment Measurements			
Women's	Small	Medium	Large
Bust	42"	46"	48"
Sleeve/Upper Arm	20"	20"	20"

Oversized, drop shoulder boatneck sweater. To knit easier version, use one color and follow written instructions only. Shown in women's size 36" bust (medium). Directions are for 8–10. Changes for 12–14 and 16–18 are in parentheses.

MATERIALS

Yarn: 15(17,18) 100 gr/3.5 oz (approx 109 yds) balls 100% cotton Tahki Creole, white (MC), 1 ball each same yarn, olive (A), lavender (B), pink (C).
Needles: One pair each #8 and #10 (or size to obtain gauge), 19 bobbins.

GAUGE

4sts and 5rws = 1" (in St st on larger needles).
CHECK GAUGE TO ASSURE PROPER FIT.

STITCH PATTERN

Ribbing Stitch: Rw 1: *K2, P2*. Rep. between *'s to end of rw.
Rw 2: Knit the K sts, purl the P sts. Rep rw 2 for patt.
Stockinette Stitch: *K1 rw (RS), P1 rw, (WS). Rep between *'s for patt.

NOTES

When changing colors, be sure to twist new yarn around dropped yarn in back of work to avoid holes.

Prepare bobbins: 10 of MC and 3 each of A, B, and C.

INSTRUCTIONS

Back: Cast 84(92,96)sts on smaller needles in MC. Work in ribbing for 3½". Change to larger needles. Work even in St st until piece measures 27". Change to smaller needles and work in ribbing for 2". Bind off.
Front: Work same as for back foll chart 1 for color changes in St st.
Sleeves: Cast 56sts on smaller needles in MC. Work in ribbing for 1½", inc 1 st at each end of last rw. There are 58sts. Change to larger needles and work in St st foll chart 2 for color changes, inc 1 st at each end of every 5th rw 11 times. There are now 80sts on needle. Work even until sleeve measures 15½". Bind off.
Finishing: Weave in or tie all loose ends on WS of each piece. Block all pieces. Sew shoulders. Mark side edges of front and back 10" from shoulders. Sew sleeves between markers. Sew side and sleeve seams.

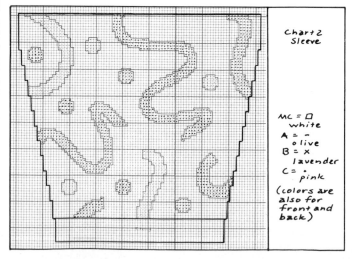

✱✱

32 | **Fiesta Vest (for intermediate knitters)**

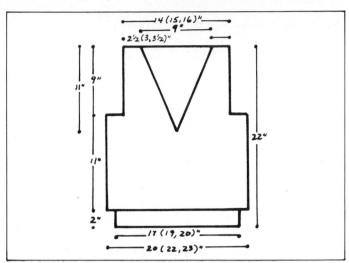

Finished Garments Measurements			
Women's	Small	Medium	Large
Bust	40"	44"	46"
Armhole	18"	18"	18"

Deep V-neck cotton vest with fitted armhole. For a simpler sweater, follow only the written instructions and use a solid color. Shown in women's size 36" bust (medium), this is an oversized sweater. Directions are for 8–10. Changes for 12–14 and 16–18 in parentheses.

MATERIALS

Yarn: 5(6,7) 100 gr/3.5 oz (approx 109 yds) balls 100% cotton Tahki Creole, white (MC), 1 ball each same yarn pink (A), lavender (B), olive (C).
Needles: One pair each #8 and #10 (or size to obtain gauge), 1 29" #8 circular needle, 15 bobbins, 1 stitch holder.

GAUGE

4sts and 5rws = 1" (in St st on larger needles).
CHECK GAUGE TO ASSURE PROPER FIT.

STITCH PATTERN

Ribbing Stitch: Rw 1: *K1, P1*. Rep between *'s to end of rw.
Rw 2: Knit the K sts, purl the P sts. Rep rw 2 for patt.
Stockinette Stitch: *K1 rw (RS), P1 rw, (WS). Rep between *'s for patt.

NOTES

Prepare bobbins: 3 of A, 2 each of B and C, and 8 of MC.

When changing colors, be sure to twist new yarn around dropped yarn on back of work to avoid holes.

INSTRUCTIONS

Back: Cast 68(76,80)sts in MC on smaller needles. Work in ribbing for 2", inc 12sts evenly spaced across last rw. There are now 80(88,92)sts. Change to larger needles. Work even in St st until piece measures 13", end on WS.
Armhole Shaping: Bind off 4sts at beg of next 2(4,4)rws, then 3sts at beg of next 2rws and 2sts at beg of next 4(2,2)rws. Dec 1 st at each end of next rw. There are now 56(60,64)sts rem on needle. Work even until armhole measures 9". Bind off.
Front: Work same as for back and foll chart until piece measures 11", end on RS.
V-Neck and Armhole Shaping: Next rw: Work in patt across 39(43,45)sts, join another ball of yarn, and bind off next 2sts

for base of V; complete rw. Working both sides at once, dec at neck edge as shown on chart, and **at same time**, when piece measures 13", beg armhole shaping as for back. When piece measures 22" and 10(12,14)sts rem on needle for shoulder, bind off.
Finishing: Weave in all loose ends on WS. Block all pieces. Sew shoulders.
Neckband: From RS with circular needle and MC, beg at base of V and pick up and K64sts along left edge of neck, 34sts across back of neck, and 64sts along right edge of neck. Do not join sts. Work in rws of ribbing for 1¼". Bind off. Crosslap ends of ribbing and sew in place.
Armbands: From RS with smaller needles and MC, pick up and K88sts along entire armhole edge. Work in ribbing for 1¼". Bind off. Sew side seams, including armbands.

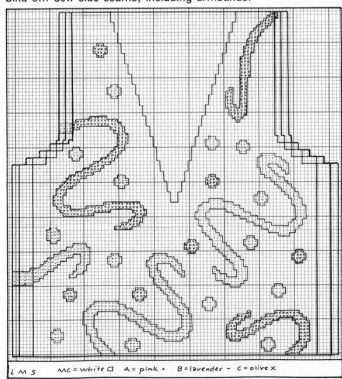

L M S   MC = white □   A = pink •   B = lavender –   C = olive X

CHAPTER FOUR
KNITTING PSYCHOLOGY

Help! My sleeves are too long, my collar's too big, my ribbing's too baggy . . . What can I do to *save* my sweater?

Have you ever felt your original enthusiasm for a project begin to wane as you encounter a problem? You may have spent your hard-earned cash on yarn and been hoping to wear your new creation to an upcoming party. What should you do? The sweater won't fix itself, so let's explore what you can do to make this sweater a success.

We have several different techniques for you to try, from basic problem-solving techniques to several "quick knits" that are guaranteed to pull you out of the doldrums. The most important thing is to get re-energized. Sometimes this means starting a new project that can be knit quickly. *Behold: The Instant Gratification Sweater!* Here are four different quick and easy I.G.S.'s to whet your appetite:

- The knit-up-all-your-odds-and-ends-into-a-summer-shell sweater (the "Rag" sweater)
- The Miami Beach or condo sweater
- The tear-up-some-old-fabric sweater
- The patchwork sweater (the gauge swatch sweater)

These sweaters are designed for fast knitting, they don't cost a lot of money, and you don't have to think too much. The main goal is to start knitting again. The next step is creative pattern making of your own designs.

WHAT TO DO WHEN THINGS GO WRONG

In any project, there is always a chance that something will go wrong. One way to avoid this is by playing it safe. That's why we've recommended that beginners choose simple shapes, patterns, and stitches and remember always to check gauge. As you begin to learn more about knitting and designing, half the fun comes from exploring new areas and learning new skills. In order to learn, you have to be willing to take a few risks, and that can mean making mistakes. The important thing is to realize there *is* a way to correct mistakes. It may mean ripping out a few rows, but the next time you knit it you'll probably get it right.

Let's start with some questions to ask yourself about your problem sweater:

Materials:
• How does the weight of yarn work with the design?
• How do the colors work with the type of yarn and the design?
• How does the stitch pattern work with the weight of yarn, or the type of yarn?
• Is the tension too tight? Too loose? Is the knitted fabric too stiff or not holding its shape well?

Color:
• Are the colors too subtle? Too bold?
• Are the colored shapes too busy? Too bland?

Stitch:
• Is the stitch pattern working with the design of the garment?
• Is the stitch pattern too busy?
• Are there errors in the stitch pattern?
• Is the stitch pattern too difficult?
• Is the stitch pattern too simple?

Shape:
• Is the shape too complicated? Too simple?
• Is the body of the garment knitting up too small? Too large?
• Does the type of neck (collar, sleeve, cuff, waist) not seem to be working on the garment?
• Is there any way I can make this thing work?

THINK IT THROUGH

The best way to solve a problem is to define it. Try this: sit down with paper and pen and make a list of what is not working with your project. Use our list of questions to get started. Go into as much detail as possible about the problem. The more clearly defined the problem is, the closer you are to finding the solution. Now put the list away for 24 hours.

After a day, read the list over again, adding any thoughts or possible ideas for solutions. Again, put the list away for 24 hours.

The next day, take your list, a new sheet of paper, and jot down ideas and thumbnail sketches for possible solutions. You may be amazed at the ideas that have popped into your mind. If you still are not satisfied, give the whole thing a rest for a few days and see what happens.

Allow your unconscious to do the work for you: as you go about your daily activities, your unconscious is percolating the information. When you're least expecting it, it may throw out an answer or two. Maybe you're watching a movie and the heroine is wearing a garment with the exact detail that will solve your problem. Because you temporarily let go of worrying about it, you were more open to creative suggestion.

KEEP A KNITTING DIARY

Another way to keep yourself stimulated and receptive to new design ideas is to keep a knitting diary in your Workbook. You might start a special section devoted to clippings from fashion or knitting magazines regarding special techniques, design ideas, or pictures of garments that strike your fancy. Cut them out, take them down, and jot down any special ideas you have about them. Not only is this a great way to discover what you like, but it's a great way to get "unstuck." Next time you can't figure out how to solve a problem, consult your Workbook for inspiration.

BRAINSTORM

Do you have a friend who likes to knit? If you've hit a snag, ask someone else for suggestions. One of your coworkers might have a great solution, or what about your aunt? After all, she's been knitting all of her life! You'll discover that it can be fun to "brainstorm."

Or go to your local yarn store and find out if there is a knitting group that you could join. If there isn't, you might consider starting one that meets once every few weeks.

HOW TO FIX MISTAKES

Did you know you can shorten or lengthen a garment after it's completely finished? What if the ribbing turns out to be too loose and the sweater doesn't hold its shape? Add some elastic thread to pull it tighter. Or unravel the old ribbing and reknit new, tighter ribbing. If the garment is too baggy or too large, take in the side seams. If it is too small, add panels along the sides.

These are just a few of the techniques we are presenting. The main thing to remember is that there *is* a solution to every problem. You may be surprised at the interesting sweater design you create from a mistake. It may be your best sweater yet!

HOW TO PICK UP DROPPED STITCHES

This is one of the most frequent problems encountered by beginners and is quite simple to repair in stockinette or garter stitch. When working with a more complex pattern stitch, it is usually easier to rip back to the mistake and start over because complex pattern stitches often have a series of slipped and passed over stitches or increases and decreases within a group of stitches. It is difficult to re-create a complicated pattern if the dropped stitch is several rows down.

If the error is one row down, drop the stitch off the needle directly above it, then pick it up with a crochet hook as shown. Or, if you feel comfortable, you can use your needle to pick up the stitch.

When it is a few rows down, knit to the stitch directly above the dropped stitch and let the fabric "run" down to the place of the mistake. Pick up the dropped stitch with a crochet hook as shown, and continue to loop each row through as you progress up the fabric. Refer to page 149 for the correct way to insert the crochet hook for the knit or purl side of the garment.

One row down

On the knit side

On the purl side or in garter stitch

MENDING A CIGARETTE BURN OR MOTH HOLE

If you have any of the original yarn left over, it's easy to pick up the top of the loop that's open and reconnect the missing stitches with a crochet hook (see page 148). If you don't have the original yarn left, consider embroidering a small design on top of the hole. Any motif will work, or try several letters to make your own monogram. We have provided an alphabet in the Workbook chapter as reference (see page 163, and page 155, Embroidery). Or if you're a seamstress, try darning the hole with a needle and thread.

Make a single crochet chain (see page 149) to the open loop on the other edge of the hole, and tie the ends together.

Enlargement of a Moth Hole

Pull a loop with the new yarn through one open loop.

WHAT IF YOU RUN OUT OF YARN?

If the store where you purchased the yarn is out of the dye lot, or you purchased the yarn on vacation and can't go back to get more, you will have to improvise. The solution you choose depends on how far you've progressed on the sweater. It is always best to knit the front and back first. That way if you run out of yarn on the sleeves, you have several alternatives: either eliminate the sleeves altogether and make a vest, or integrate other colors into the sleeves to make the yarn stretch farther. If you knit the sleeves first and run out of yarn on either the front or back, you will be forced to rip the sleeves out in order to get enough yarn to finish the body.

If you decide to integrate several other colors into the sleeve design, you can then go back and embroider, or duplicate stitch (see page 155), a similar motif in the new color on the front and back, or use them as a border treatment.

If you've knit the front and are halfway through the back and run out of yarn, you might want to consider a multi-colored sweater. Knit one sleeve out of red, the other out of yellow, the front out of green, and the back out of purple. Or knit the ribbing the same color on all the pieces to achieve unity in the design. Rethink why you ran short of yarn. Next time, ask the advice of the salesperson, or use the formula we've provided (see page 12).

SHORTENING AND LENGTHENING TECHNIQUES

You thought you measured your garment properly, but after sewing it together and trying it on, you find it's too short. Rather than relegate it to the bottom drawer and never wear it again, you can lengthen it. There are several different ways of doing this; the method you choose will depend on the design of the garment. The same technique for separating the two sections will be used for all the methods of shortening or lengthening.

HOW TO SEPARATE A KNITTED GARMENT INTO TWO SECTIONS

Rip the seam open to the point at which you want to separate. Cut one strand of yarn at the seam edge and pull gently. This should create a gathered effect all the way to the end of the row. Cut the other end of the row and pull the strand of yarn out completely; in essence, you pull out that row. An edge of open loops is created which can be picked up with a needle and knit upward or downward. Or if you feel nervous about using this technique, try cutting straight across the row with a pair of scissors. Two rows of yarn will be lost this way, and any excess scraps of yarn will have to be carefully removed before you begin knitting upward or downward.

 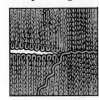 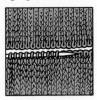

LENGTHENING A SWEATER WITHIN THE BODY

This is more difficult to incorporate without the alteration looking like a patch. The best place to add length in the body of the sweater is along the lower edge, as a border pattern. Study some of the Scandinavian jacquard motifs for interesting border ideas. The colors can be very different from the body of the sweater as long as they are complimentary.

Follow the diagrams below for adding a border treatment. Remember it's not necessary to rip out the bottom section. After separating the two pieces, insert the knitting needle into the loops at the top of the bottom piece and knit the border upward. When you have knitted as much as you need for added length, do not bind off. Use the "grafting" technique shown on page 148.

LENGTHENING A SWEATER FROM THE RIBBING DOWN

It's very easy to remove the ribbing, unravel it, wind it into a ball, or mix it with another color in a stripe motif, to create a longer ribbing. Of course, if you have any of the original yarn left, it's always best to use that first. Knit the ribbing downward to the length you desire and bind off loosely.

LENGTHENING A SKIRT

It's best to use the original yarn for lengthening. If this yarn is not available, choose a color that is different but complimentary. One of the problems with lengthening is to make the adjustment look like it was meant to be that way, not an afterthought. If the skirt is part of a knitted outfit and there is a way to pick up a color from the top, do so. Or knit a band of the matching color across the bottom using an interesting pattern stitch or border treatment.

SHORTENING A SKIRT

Rip out the seam to the cut-off point and follow the instructions for separating the garment into sections. Unravel the yarn from the lower section you just separated, and roll it into a ball. After picking up the loops along the bottom edge of the skirt, either knit a hem or a new kind of edging, with the unraveled yarn (see page 79 for hems).

SHORTENING A SWEATER

Follow the instructions for separating a garment into two pieces, but knit ribbing downward from the body of the garment to the desired length. Remember to bind off loosely because bind-off stitches have a tendency to be tighter than cast-on stitches.

If you plan ahead, this skill can be very helpful in creating versatile fashions. We all know how often a misplaced hemline can ruin a garment that is otherwise beautiful. Buying extra yarn will ensure that you won't be caught short in the event hemlines drop. Rather than just leave the yarn in a trunk, knit up a large swatch and wash it at the same time the garment is washed. In the event that you need the additional yarn for adjustments or repairs, the yarn will have the same coloration as the original garment.

  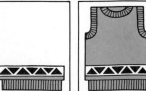

Original sweater. | Use the technique described above for separating two pieces. | Pick up stitches and knit a border treatment upward from the lower portion. | Weave the two sections together.

LENGTHENING A SLEEVE

The same technique described for lengthening a sweater works well for lengthening a sleeve. The lower portion of a sleeve is a good place for a border treatment. If you are lengthening your sweater, you may want to consider adding the same border treatment to the sleeves for continuity.

If you are *just* lengthening the sleeves and you do have the original yarn left, separate into two pieces as described on page 139. Pick up the loops from the top piece and knit down to the desired length.

The easiest method of lengthening a sleeve is to extend the ribbing on the cuff. Separate the ribbing on the sleeve by either cutting it with scissors or using the technique described on page 139. Or you can just cut off the cast-on row, pick up the loops, and knit to the desired length.

SHORTENING A SLEEVE

Separate the sleeve at the length you desire. Unravel the yarn from the lower section and roll into a ball. Pick up the loops along the bottom edge of the sleeve and knit the ribbing downward to the desired length. Bind off loosely.

SHORTENING OR LENGTHENING A COLLAR

The best method for this is to remove the collar from the garment and reknit the collar to the length you prefer.

MAKING A GARMENT SMALLER

If your gauge or measurements are inaccurate, you can end up with a garment that is too large. This doesn't have to be a problem if you rethink the design so the proportions will fit your figure. Consider tapering the sides so the waist is snugger, or tapering the hips so the shoulders have a broader appearance. Be careful to taper the seam gradually to the underarm area, which is more difficult to adjust after the garment has been sewn together.

Take a tapestry needle and yarn of the same color if possible, and resew the seam (backstitch is preferable), to the desired width (see page 147). Cut the excess seam off to within ¼″ of the new seam. Take a needle and thread and close off the trimmed edge so the fabric won't fray. This last step is very important because if a loose end breaks through the seam, an entire row could unravel across the sweater.

If the yarn is very bulky, it's better to rip the seam out, cut the knitted fabric to the correct size, bind each edge with a needle and thread, and sew a flat seam.

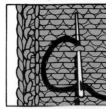

Sewing up new seam

normal seam new seam

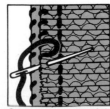

New seam

Overcast the edges of the new seam with needle and thread to secure edges.

ADDING WIDTH TO A GARMENT

It's more difficult to integrate this type of alteration into a design and have it look natural. The aim of any good alteration is to look like it was originally designed that way, not like an afterthought. To add width to the body of a sweater or sleeves, knit new panels that will go between the side seams, under the arm, and between the bottom seams of the sleeves.

A good way to integrate this new panel, if you do not have any of the original yarn left, is to choose a colorful yarn to create a stripe on either side. Obviously this works with some designs and not others. The main idea is to make these new panels look like they were created as a point of interest for the design and not as a way to salvage a mistake. Use your imagination and see what you come up with.

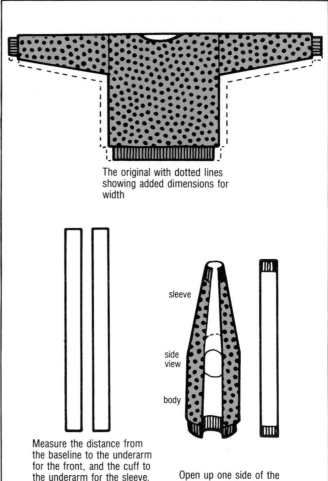

The original with dotted lines showing added dimensions for width

sleeve

side view

body

Measure the distance from the baseline to the underarm for the front, and the cuff to the underarm for the sleeve. Add the two measurements. This is the length of the panel. The width of the panel depends on how many inches you want to add to each side. Multiply the width you want for one side by the stitch gauge to determine how many stitches wide to make the panel.

Open up one side of the sweater and the sleeve seam for the same side. Sew the new panel into each side of the sweater and sleeve. Once you have completed one side, open up the other side and repeat.

BAGGY RIBBING

There are several simple and effective ways of dealing with baggy ribbing, which can be done at any time in a sweater's life. Elastic thread comes in many colors, so choose one that matches your yarn color. With a tapestry needle, weave the elastic thread through the back of the ribbed stitches on each row. You'll be amazed at the difference.

This also works well for the waistband of a skirt and can be knitted in by twisting with the yarn as you knit.

Another way to create a tighter ribbing is to remove the old ribbing as described previously and reknit downward using fewer stitches. If you originally had 36 stitches for the ribbing, your gauge is 6sts = 1″, and you want to reduce the ribbing by one inch, reknit downward with 30 stitches. Remember, if you take one inch off both the front and back, you'll remove a total of two inches from the ribbing.

Sewing Elastic Into Ribbing

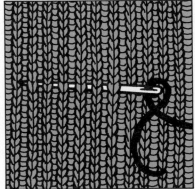

Insert needle through back of ribbing

WHAT ABOUT SAGGING ELSEWHERE?

You may need to add extra stability to other areas of the garment, such as the front openings on a cardigan, a stand-up collar, or a shoulder seam on a jacket or heavy cardigan. Purchase twill seam tape or grosgrain ribbon in ³⁄₈″ or ¹⁄₂″ widths at the notions counter of a fabric store. Be sure to get a matching color. Tack it down to the garment with a needle and thread, using a loose running stitch. If you are reinforcing a seam, be sure to center the tape directly over the seam. Once you have the proper length and positioning, cut to size and sew securely onto the garment. This acts as a good backing for buttons and buttonholes on cardigan front openings.

WORN RIBBING, EDGING, ELBOWS, AND CUFFS

It's easy to replace old ribbing. Choose a yarn that is the same weight. Consider replacing all of the ribbing (cuffs, neck edge, and bottom edge) with a contrasting color to give the sweater a continuity. This is a great way to perk up an old sweater and make it look like new. It's also a good opportunity to change the neck style: add a turtleneck to a crew neck.

TIPS FOR OLDER GARMENTS

What about that fabulous sweater you made ten years ago that you can't bear to part with, even though you haven't worn it in eight years? Consider recycling it!

Rip out all the seams and prepare to unravel: Take a wire hanger and reshape as shown above. Wind the yarn around the hanger as you unravel it, making sure not to pull too tightly. You may have to do this on several hangers to accommodate a large sweater. In order to get the kinks out you'll have to apply steam. Heat a large kettle of water or a teapot and bring to a boil. When there is a lot of steam rising, hold the yarn over the water until you see all of the kinks relax. The important thing to notice is that the steam penetrates all the way to the center of the skein.

Allow the yarn to dry in a room with a moderate temperature and then rewind into balls.

You will know the approximate size of the garment you can expect to make with the yarn from the size of the garment you unravel. If you unravel a tight-fitting sweater, don't expect to make an oversized bulky unless you have several other types of yarn to mix together to give the added volume.

Reusing Old Yarn

> **TIP**
> • *The unraveling technique also works well for commercially made sweaters. The main thing to look for is the general condition of the yarn. If it's heavily matted, it will be difficult to rip out and has probably lost most of its elasticity.*

Badly worn sleeves can be patched at the elbow with either leather patches or knitted patches of a contrasting color. If the sleeves are really beyond repair, cut them off and make short sleeves, or take them off altogether and make a vest. Unravel some of the sleeve you have just removed, pick up the stitches around the armhole with a circular needle, and knit new ribbing onto the armhole using the yarn that you salvaged. Of course, you can also knit new sleeves using a contrasting color.

INSTANT GRATIFICATION SWEATERS

And now, what we've all been waiting for, the Instant Gratification Sweaters! Start a fun weekend project that will pull you out of the doldrums and presto: a new sweater to wear to work on Monday. The most exciting thing about an IGS is that you probably won't even have to go to the knitting store to buy yarn. Rummage through your closet and gather all the leftover odds and ends from your various knitting projects. Choose the colors and weights of yarn that will work well together, a good pair of needles (preferably large), and start knitting. The simpler the shape the better. Remember, you don't want to think too much for this one. A drop shoulder with a boat neck is a simple rectangle with no armhole or neck shaping (no increasing or decreasing), which is perfect for an IGS. All you need to do is take your hip or bust measure (whichever is larger) to see how many stitches to cast on. From there, just knit away until you reach a length you like and bind off.

For instance, your hips measure 36″ and your bust measures 34″. Take the larger measurement and add 2″ for ease on each side. That gives you a total of 40″ (20″ each for front and back). If your gauge is 3sts = 1″, then 20 x 3 = 60 sts. All you need to know to knit this sweater is that you need to cast on 60 stitches.

Knit to whatever length you desire. The whole point is that you shouldn't have to think too much for this one—just enjoy wearing it!

Pay attention to your choices of yarns for combining. Naturally, don't combine wool and cotton if you are making a summer sweater. If you want a winter vest, a little cotton thrown in for good measure won't hurt.

The color choices are up to you. What do you like? If you don't mind a "crazy quilt" effect, you can combine anything and everything. If you want to go for a more "tasteful" coloration, you might limit yourself to a certain number of colors. Ultimately, it will depend on how much yarn you have of each color.

Circular needles work very well for an IGS because if you run out of a color, you have already used it equally on the front and back. Just knit to the armhole and break for the upper body shaping. (Spaghetti straps eliminate the need for anything above the underarm. Simply twist several strands together and sew onto the front and back.)

And now for the "patterns," really a loose framework for the sweaters rather than a set pattern. Just a few things to think about when you're preparing your quick masterpiece.

PATCHWORK (OR GAUGE SWATCH) SWEATER

If you have been following our advice to knit a gauge swatch for each project you work on and you decide to keep them for easy reference, you have an instant sweater waiting at your fingertips. All you have to do is get out a tapestry needle and some yarn and sew them all together. You can turn the swatches in different directions to create interesting textural effects, or keep the stitches in the same direction for a more cohesive look. Sew up the seams on the right side of the garment to create a patchwork quilt effect. With this type of sweater, anything goes.

If you are the kind who rips

Two Variations on the Patchwork Sweater

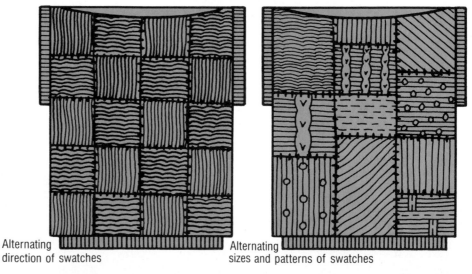

Alternating direction of swatches

Alternating sizes and patterns of swatches

out your gauge swatch in order to incorporate the yarn back into the sweater, think about knitting up some new swatches for this sweater. It's a great way to try out some new stitch patterns and increase your repertoire at the same time. Just be sure to photocopy each swatch with the pertinent information (stitch pattern or symbolcraft chart of the stitch pattern, type of yarn, gauge, and needle size) and enter into your Workbook for future reference.

If you decide to make a new set of swatches for this sweater, you can still use up a lot of old odds and ends, and you may have more control over the combination of elements. For instance, you might decide to use several different stitch patterns, one for each color of yarn, and alternate them when sewing up.

The basic drop shoulder boat-neck works very well with this type of IGS because each swatch is basically a square. Plan out the widest measurement and multiply by the average stitch gauge to determine the basic proportion of each swatch. If you decide to make the width 20″ (for each front and back) and you are knitting 4″ x 4″ gauge swatches, you would need five swatches across to create that width. If the length was also going to be 20″, the 4″ x 4″ swatch would work out perfectly in each direction. If, however, you wanted to make the length 25″ and the width 20″, you might consider making each swatch more vertical than square.

Since each swatch has its own finished edges, you don't have to add ribbing to the sweater, although the choice of one-color ribbing for the bottom and neck edges (and sleeve cuff if you're doing sleeves) will always help to tie a design together. Also, nonribbed edges have a tendency to roll instead of lying flat. Be sure that you want this effect if you make that choice.

RAG SWEATER #1

This version of the rag sweater is made from remnants of old fabrics or used clothing that you're tired of wearing as is but whose fabric you still love. The fabric is a perfect candidate for shredding.

We gave you instructions on page 11 on how to cut fabric on the bias. Bias strips have more elasticity and create a garment that has ease of movement. Keep the strips somewhere between ¼″ and ½″ wide, depending on the fabric. If it's a heavier fabric, keep the strips narrower, unless you want to knit a very bulky sweater. Lightweight fabrics can be cut in wider strips to give them more volume. Firmly woven cottons or cotton blends work well for shredding, as do silks, rayons, and lightweight wools. If the fabric has a right and wrong side, remember that you will get a multicolored effect as the wrong side shows up.

After you have cut the strips you can either sew the ends together or tie them for a different effect. Roll the strips into balls as you would any skein of yarn. If you're worried about shrinkage, wash the fabric first in hot water.

One of the great things about the fabric rag sweater is that it can be sewn up on the sewing machine. Use any kind of tape, ribbon, or contrasting fabric as sewn-on edgings. Of course, it can also be sewn up as you would any other sweater.

One yard of 45″ fabric will yield about 50 yards of strips. You need about 500–600 yards for most medium-sized, long-sleeve sweaters, or about 10–12 yards of 45″ fabric. If you're in the mood for a quick fix and just want to make a summer shell, halve that amount. And remember that mixing and matching different fabrics is part of the "anything goes" approach of this version of an IGS.

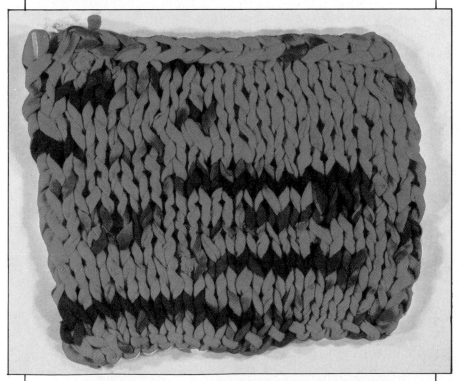

Rag Sweater #1 Swatch Made with Tie-Dyed T-Shirt Fabric

RAG SWEATER #2

A rag sweater is a wonderful way to experiment with color and texture. This remnant sweater combines two to three yarns as one to create the look of a rag rug. The rag effect is created by tying on a new color every two to three rows. Change one color at a time for a variegated look or all colors at once for a striped effect. Go through your yarn box (see page 164, Fiber File) and select all of the yarn types and colors that work well together. Don't worry about how much of each color there is because you will change colors often. Just make sure you are always using the same number of strands throughout the sweater.

Begin your rag sweater by swatching with medium-sized needles until you achieve the right gauge and tension for the yarn weights you are using. Determine how much yarn you have to work with by using our method of calculating yarn by yardage (see page 12) when rolling up your "combination ball." You will usually need large needles when using two or more strands of yarn.

Rag Sweater #2 Made with Three Strands of Cotton String Yarn

TIP
• *Use different yarn types in combination, but pay close attention to yarn types that may not work well together. For example, cotton, linen, silk, rayon, and metallic (synthetics) combine nicely. Try thick and thin yarns twisted or knit together as one strand. Wools work well with silk, some linens, and synthetics. Don't combine cotton and wool, as they have different degrees of shrinkage when washed. Also, when you're combining any group of yarns, a good idea is to wash a test swatch to see whether or not the colors bleed.*

JOINING YARN
When you get to the end of one ball of yarn you will have to join the next ball. It's always best to join the yarn at the outer edge of the knitted piece by tying a loose knot which can later be undone and woven into the seam. Join the yarn at the beginning or end of a row, if possible, because a knot in the center of the row will leave a hole.

If you get to the middle of the row and run out of yarn, rip back to the beginning of the row and tie in the new yarn at that point. The immediate inconvenience of taking the yarn back to the beginning of the row will be greatly outweighed by a better-looking garment.

MIAMI BEACH OR CONDO SWEATER

This type of sweater was inspired by the women who live in Miami Beach and knit oversized lacy sweaters on large needles. This style is more suitable to leftover mohair or lightweight novelty yarn than a heavier wool or cotton because the large stitch pattern would look stringy in a normal "worsted" type of yarn.

To knit your own Miami Beach sweater you will need two pairs of knitting needles of drastically different sizes. For the large size, choose #17, #19, #35, or #50 (12½, 16, 19, or 25½mm). The small size can vary from a #7 to a #10, using the #7 for the #17 or #19 and the #10 for the larger-sized needles. Knit with one needle of the smaller size and one needle of the larger size, creating a row of large loopy stitches and a row of smaller, normal-sized stitches. The small row will help to anchor the large row so that the stitches hold their shape.

The best stitches to choose for your sweater are stockinette, garter, or a slip stitch pattern where you knit one stitch and slip one stitch alternately across the first row, for the front of the sweater. Purl the rows on the back of the sweater.

Choose a simple shape such as a drop shoulder with a boat neck to avoid having to increase or decrease. The sleeves can even be "knit out from" the shoulder area of the garment by picking up as many stitches as you want and knitting straight down to the desired sleeve length. (Be sure to sew your shoulder seams together first, then pick up the sleeve stitches.)

Another advantage to the Miami Beach sweater is that you won't need as much yarn as you would for an average sweater of this size. So it's a well-suited alternative for your IGS clean-up-the-odds-and-ends-box approach!

Condo Sweater Swatch Using K1, s1 1 Stitch and Paper Yarn

CHAPTER FIVE
FINISHING TECHNIQUES

Now that you understand how to design and knit your own garments, you are ready to learn how to put all the pieces together. You've come this far, so take the extra time to make sure the seams lie flat and the border looks just the way you want. The right finishing techniques make the difference between the amateurish- and professional-looking garment.

In this chapter we'll take you through blocking and sewing techniques, how to pick up stitches, and create different border treatments. If you've never made a buttonhole before, we'll show you how, as well as how to make pockets and put in zippers. Duplicate stitching and embroidery are good ways to add motifs after the garment is finished. You will learn how to create these stitches and also how to sew or knit in beads for an expensive-looking evening sweater. Last but not least, you will find a maintenance chart to help you take the best care of your very special knits.

Remember, these techniques are provided as a starting point. You may want to try one approach to see how it looks on your garment. If you are not satisfied, don't be afraid to rip it out and try again. Each garment will have its own special finishing needs, so find the ones that work best.

BLOCKING

This is a technique of "setting" your knitting to give it a finished look. The most professional way to block is on a hard yet porous surface such as homosote board. Buy a piece at least 19" x 24" at your local lumberyard and use it as a base for blocking.

You can also block by layering blankets or towels on a table or the floor to make a soft, padded surface.

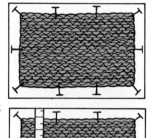

Step 1 —Pin each piece right side down, making sure not to stretch the fabric. (If the garment is a bit small, you may want to stretch it.) Be careful to keep rows and stitches in straight lines.

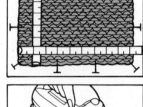

Step 2 —Recheck measurements for accuracy.

Step 3 —Refer to the directions on the yarn label to see where to set the heat on your iron.

Step 4 —Place a slightly damp cloth over the work, excluding the ribbed areas, and lay the iron gently on top of the cloth. Be gentle, as heavy pressing can damage many textured and novelty yarns. Ribbing loses its elasticity if pressed so be sure to avoid touching the iron to ribbed areas.

Step 5 —Repeat this procedure over the entire garment area.

Step 6 —Allow the fabric to cool and remove the pins.

TIP
• It's best to use nonrusting T-pins for blocking.

SEWING UP

Once the pieces are blocked, they're ready to be sewn together. Use the same yarn to sew up the seams that was used to knit the garment. If the yarn is very bulky or textured, consider substituting a similar-colored four-ply yarn. Or you can split the yarn. Tapestry needles are recommended because they have blunt ends and won't split the yarn.

SEAMS

The two most popular stitches for seams are backstitch and flat seams. We will also discuss invisible seams, invisible weaving, lapped seams, grafting (or Kitchener's stitch), slipstitch, and crocheting a seam.

BACKSTITCH

This is the most common for sleeve and side seams and for set-in sleeves.

Step 1 —Place the two pieces with right sides together on a flat surface.

Step 2 —Pin each end and the middle to keep the fabric from shifting.

Step 3 —To begin, secure yarn with two or three running stitches on top of each other (instead of tying a knot).

Step 4 —Put needle into right end of running stitch and bring out one stitch ahead. Pull yarn through to front.

Step 5 —Reinsert needle at the right, back at the point of the last stitch.

Step 6 —Continue until seam is complete.

FLAT SEAM

Good for joining ribbed areas and bulky fabrics.

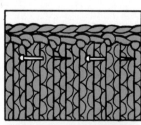

Step 1 —Put right sides together, making sure to line up rows that match. Pin the pieces together at each end and in the middle to prevent shifting.

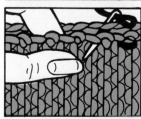

Step 2 —Secure yarn at beginning of seam by several running stitches on top of each other, then put your left forefinger between the two pieces.

Step 3 —Insert the needle first on the underside piece then through the same stitch on the top piece and pull the yarn through.

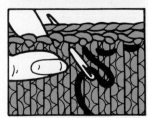

Step 4 —Work back through the next stitch on the top piece to the corresponding stitch on the underside piece.

Step 5 —Continue this weaving process until the seam is complete.

GRAFTING (OR KITCHENER'S STITCH)

A great way to create an almost invisible seam by weaving stitches together directly from the needles, rather than binding off the stitches at the end of the piece. It's important to have the same number of stitches on each needle. This method works especially well for shoulder seams and for joining two pieces together for alterations.

Step 1 —If the stitches are on holders, place them on two needles and lay the pieces flat on a table, right side up, in position to be sewn together.

Step 2 —Either secure the yarn at the edge of the seam or pick up the strand of yarn that was used to knit the last row and use to sew the seam.

Step 3 —Insert the needle through the first stitch on the other needle, slip stitch off needle.

Step 4 —Insert needle through next stitch on front needle as shown and leave on needle. Repeat through next stitch on back needle, but let the stitch off the needle.

Step 5 —Continue in this way until all the stitches have been woven together.

Stockinette stitch

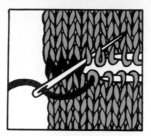

Garter stitch
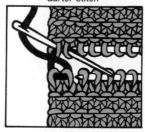

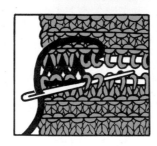

INVISIBLE SEAM

Creates a soft edge.

Step 1 —Place both pieces right side up on the table and secure the yarn at the beginning of seam.

Step 2 —Pick up the first stitch from one side and pull through.

Step 3 —Pass the needle back to the first stitch on the other piece, pick up, and pull the yarn through.

Step 4 —Continue alternating sides in this way, making sure to pull stitches tightly.

How To Sew an Invisible Seam
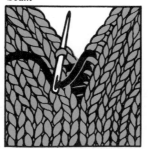

INVISIBLE WEAVING

Good for shoulder seams that have a bound-off edge.

Step 1 —Place the two pieces on a table right side up and in position.

Step 2 —Secure yarn at seam edge and work from one piece to the other, placing the needle under each two strands of the stitch. This recreates the look of the knit stitch and covers up the bound-off edges.

How To Do Invisible Weaving
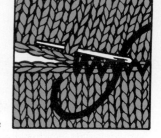

LAPPED SEAMS

Step 1 —Place the two pieces right sides together with the underneath piece extending ¼" beyond the upper piece.

Step 2 —Backstitch close to the edge.

Step 3 —Turn the pieces to the right side and backstitch through both layers of fabric ½" from the original seam, using small stitches.

HOW TO SEW SIDE SEAMS IN RIBBING

Step 1 —Work with pieces right sides together.

Step 2 —Secure yarn at beginning of the seam.

Step 3 —Insert needle through the centers of the first two corresponding rib stitches from the bottom side, pull through.

Step 4 —Move to the center of the next two stitches and reinsert needle down through the centers of the stitches. When the seam is finished, each half of each rib stitch creates the look of one rib stitch.

TIP
• *If working on bulky garments, reinforce seams with twill tape on the inside to add strength to the seam.*

SHOULDER SEAMS

Can be done in invisible weaving stitch or grafting stitch, described previously, or with a backstitch by placing right sides together, pinning each end, and backstitching across shoulder to end of seam.

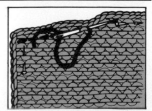
Sewing up a Shoulder Seam

JOINING WITH SINGLE CROCHET

Step 1 —Place the two pieces together right sides up on a table. Secure the yarn at the beginning of the row.

Step 2 —Work a row of single crochet by inserting the hook within the inner loop of each bound-off stitch. This is created by yarning over and through all the loops.

HOW TO SINGLE CROCHET

Step 1 —Make a loop as you would to begin casting on.

Step 2 —Hold crochet hook as you would a pencil. Insert crochet hook through the loop.

Step 3 —Hold yarn in your other hand and pull yarn through the loop.

Step 4 —Repeat until you have the number of loops needed. This makes a single chain and gives you the most basic crochet stitch.

How to make a loop for crochet

How to begin single crochet chain stitch

SLIPSTITCH

This stitch is useful for sewing one article onto another rather than for closing a seam. It is perfect for applying pockets to the front of a sweater, applying ribbon to the inside of a cardigan front border, sewing up a hem, or sewing on an appliqué. It's also good for closing a seam edge that has been resewn together for an alteration.

Step 1 —Secure yarn (or thread) at seam edge or on wrong side of piece.

Step 2 —Insert needle through fabric and whatever is being sewn on and pull through.

Step 3 —Reinsert needle through wrong side and back into whatever is being applied and pull through.

Step 4 —Repeat until seam is complete.

How To Slipstitch

HOW TO PICK UP STITCHES

You've blocked your pieces and sewn them together. Now it's time to pick up the stitches to create the ribbed border treatments. Follow these simple instructions to create a beautiful pick-up row.

The easiest method is to have the stitches placed on a holder rather than binding off. This works well on straight horizontal rows—simply pick up with a needle and begin knitting.

For curved edges, such as necklines or armhole openings for vests, place pins at equally spaced 1″–2″ intervals and pick up the same number of stitches within each interval. A good rule of thumb is to pick up one stitch for every stitch and three stitches for every four rows. This works best with stockinette stitch. When picking up stitches along a bound-off edge, pick up one stitch for every bound-off stitch.

There are two ways to create the first pick-up row: (1) insert the needle into each loop on the garment edge until you've picked up the desired number of stitches; or (2) knit the first row as you pick up the stitches.

TIPS
• *Remember, for borders it's best to use needles that are two sizes smaller than those used for the body of the garment. This will ensure a flat, firm, yet elastic edge.*
• *If you're using a contrasting color for the border, use the original color of the garment for the pick-up row.*

SECOND METHOD

Step 1 —With a circular needle and a ball of yarn (usually the same color, unless you're making the ribbing in a contrasting color) and the right side of the garment facing you, insert the needle under the loop from front to back. With the new yarn, wrap the yarn around the needle as if to knit a stitch and pull through the loop to the right side. You have just created the first stitch on the new pick-up row.

Step 2 —Repeat this process along the edge to create the entire pick-up row.

When you have picked up all the stitches, begin the first row of rib, seed, or garter stitch for the border. Other stitches can be used, but these are the most common. Bind off loosely, keeping the tension consistent. If the bound-off stitches are too tight, it may be difficult to get the sweater over your head!

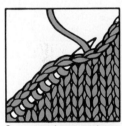

On a curved row, such as an armhole or neck edge

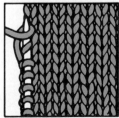

On a vertical row, such as a cardigan front

NECKLINE BORDERS

SQUARE NECK WITH MITERED CORNERS

Step 1 —Sew shoulder seams together.

Step 2 —Pick up stitches across the front, work in chosen stitch, decreasing one stitch each end of right side rows for 1–1½".

Step 3 —Pick up stitches with a circular needle, working up one side of the neck, around the back neckline, and down the other neck edge. Decrease one stitch each end every right side row.

Step 4 —Sew sections together at corners.

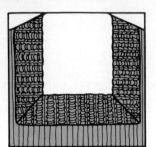

Square Neck with Mitered Corners

SQUARE NECK WORKED SQUARE

Step 1 —Sew shoulder seams together.

Step 2 —Pick up all center stitches and work to desired length in either rib or garter stitch.

Step 3 —With circular needles, pick up stitches as in Step 2 above.

Step 4 —Work in chosen stitch to same depth as border on front stitches. Bind off loosely.

Step 5 —Sew edges of border together.

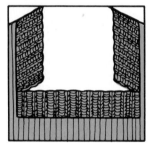

Square Neck Worked Square

TURTLENECK

Step 1 —Work with needles two sizes smaller for the first third of the ribbing.

Step 2 —Switch to needles one size smaller for second third.

Step 3 —Switch to same size needles for the last third.

Step 4 —Bind off loosely. This will allow the fabric to expand as it folds over.

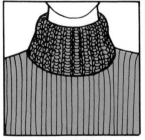

Turtleneck

V-NECK WITH RIBBED BAND AND TWO CENTER STITCHES

Step 1 —Sew shoulder seams.

Step 2 —Pick up stitches around the neck edge with a circular needle two sizes smaller than that used to knit the sweater. Begin on one side of the V and end on the other side. The two center stitches at the point of the V become the central stitches, with the decreases working as diagonals converging at this point. (This could also be knit on straight needles working just the front.)

Step 3 —Work around the entire neck edge in a rib or garter stitch to the desired depth. (For the slant to the left, sl1, k1, psso. For the slant to the right, K2tog.

V-neck with two center stitches

Close-up of V-neck with two center stitches

V-neck with overlapping edges

V-NECK WITH OVERLAPPING EDGES

Step 1 —Sew shoulder seams.

Step 2 —Pick up stitches around neckline as in Step 2 above.

Step 3 —Rather than decreasing at the neck edge, work each side straight up to the desired depth and bind off.

Step 4 —Sew one side overlapping the other, with a slipstitch.

BOATNECK

There is no neck shaping on a boatneck. There are several ways to create finishing for the top edge.

Ribbed top: 2"–3" before shoulder edge, change to smaller needles and work in rib stitch to shoulder.

Turned-under edge: knit to shoulder, make a turning edge, as for a hem, by making one row of reverse stockinette stitch, and change to smaller needles. Work in same stitch as for sweater for ½"–1". Bind off loosely. Slipstitch facing to sweater on the wrong side.

Straight bind-off is the simplest way to create the neck shaping. Just bind off all stitches at the shoulder seam.

CREW NECK

Step 1 —Sew shoulder seams together.

Step 2 —Pick up all neck stitches with a circular needle two sizes smaller than those used to knit garment.

Step 3 —Knit either a single or double neckband. For single, work 1½"–2" in rib stitch and bind off. For double, work twice the amount of ribbing and bind off loosely. Roll the fabric inward and slipstitch to the sweater.

SLEEVES, COLLARS, BORDERS, AND HEMS

CLASSIC SET-IN SLEEVES

Step 1 —Sew shoulder and side seams of sweater.

Step 2 —Sew sleeve seam.

Step 3 —Position two pieces together with right sides facing each other; work on wrong side.

Step 4 —Pin together at shoulder, underarm seam, and in the middle of each, to keep the pieces from shifting.

Step 5 —Backstitch the seam, as near to the edge as possible, using small stitches and gently easing any fullness that may occur around the sleeve cap.

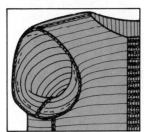

Sewing up a Classic, Set-In Sleeve

TIP
• *If sleeve cap has too much fabric and is difficult to sew in smoothly, remove from pins and run a thread across the top of the cap. Pull gently to create gathers and repin. Now when you sew the sleeve in, you will have soft, consistent gathers around the cap.*

RAGLAN SLEEVES

Step 1 —Lay all pieces flat on table, right sides together.

Step 2 —Pin the raglan seams at each end and in the middle.

Step 3 —Sew raglan seams first, then sew side and sleeve seams all in one piece.

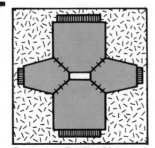

Sewing up Raglan Sleeves

SEWN-ON COLLARS

Step 1 —With right side of collar facing wrong side of piece, pin center of collar to center of neckline and each end of collar to neckline edges. Be careful not to stretch the neckline.

Step 2 —Sew seam as close to the edge as possible in a backstitch.

BORDERS FOR CARDIGAN OPENINGS

A border of ribbing is an extension of knitted fabric that is decorative and also helps the garment to retain its shape. Either (1) knit these borders along with the garment, (2) pick up stitches along garment edges and knit the border separately, or (3) knit as an entirely separate piece and sew on. The first type (knit-in) was discussed in Chapter Two on page 40. We will now discuss the other two.

SEPARATE SEWN-ON BORDER

For a straight border either cast on the number of stitches for the length of the garment and knit a piece to the desired depth or cast on the number of stitches for the desired width of the border band and knit to the length of the garment. With either treatment, then lay the garment and the border edge side by side, right sides up, and sew on using a flat seam.

BORDER KNIT FROM PICKED-UP STITCHES

For a single straight seam, pick up the same number of stitches that are on the garment edge. Work in a rib, garter, or seed stitch to desired length (usually not more than 2″).
For a curved border (as in a curved neckline), use a long circular needle to pick up stitches along both fronts and the back neck edge. Follow same instructions for other borders.

If you want to knit **a doubled border**:

Step 1 —Knit to desired length.

Step 2 —Knit a row in reverse stockinette stitch (for the turning edge) and change to smaller needles.

Step 3 —Continue in stockinette stitch for the same depth as the front border.

Step 4 —Bind off loosely.

Step 5 —Fold border in half, press lightly, and slipstitch in place.

HEMS

Step 1 —Press hem in place by covering with damp cloth and gently using iron at recommended setting.

Step 2 —Pin in position.

Step 3 —Slipstitch in place.

Step 4 —Repress lightly with damp cloth.

FRONT BANDS

A flat seam is the best method for sewing on. Be sure to stretch the band slightly to prevent sagging after it's been sewn on.

Cardigan Borders

Single straight border

Single curved border

Double border

BUTTONHOLES

Buttonholes are always formed in relation to the design of the garment and the size of the buttons. Some questions to ask yourself when charting your design are:

• Where do I want the buttons to be?
• What will the orientation of the buttonholes be? Horizontal or vertical?
• How large do I want the buttons to be? Therefore, how large should the buttonholes be?

This last question will affect the size of the ribbed band that holds the buttonholes.

Once you have made the buttonholes, you can either leave them as they are or add reinforcement for strength and finish. Use the same yarn or thread, and the buttonhole stitch. Remember when placing the buttonholes that the neck, the bust, and the bottom of the garment are the most important closure points. The other buttons should fall evenly spaced between these three positions.

VERTICAL BUTTONHOLES

Step 1 —Work garment to the buttonhole edge. Tie on new ball of yarn and continue knitting to end of row.

Step 2 —Work back on next row to the buttonhole edge and pick up original ball of yarn and continue working to end of row.

Step 3 —Repeat this process until the buttonhole reaches the desired length. For example, if a buttonhole is to be 1″ long and your gauge is 5 rows = 1″, make the buttonhole 5 rows long.

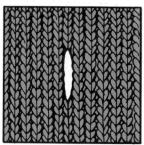
Vertical buttonhole

Step 4 —At the desired length, knit straight across the row, with one ball of yarn.

Step 5 —(optional) After the garment has been sewn up, work the finishing around the buttonhole edge.

EYELET BUTTONHOLE (THE EASIEST)

Step 1 —Work to the position of the buttonhole, on right side of the fabric.

Step 2 —Yo (yarn over), and K2tog (knit 2 together).

Step 3 —Finish by overcasting around the hole (between the stitches) to strengthen.

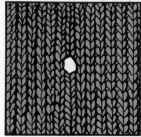
Eyelet buttonhole

HORIZONTAL BUTTONHOLES

Plan your buttonholes in advance.

Step 1 —Work garment to the placement of the first buttonhole. On the right side, bind off three or more stitches to accommodate the size of the button. Figure out the length by multiplying the inches by the stitch gauge.

Step 2 —Next row, at the point of bind-off, cast on the same number of stitches that were bound off, and rejoin to the stitches of the previous row.

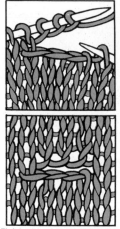
Finished horizontal buttonhole

LOOP BUTTONHOLES

These are good to use for double-breasted sweaters.

Step 1 —Mark the buttonhole position with two straight pins.

Step 2 —Secure the yarn at one end and crochet a line of single crochet (see page 149) to the end point, secure, snip end with scissor close to the buttonhole. (Or thread a needle with two strands of yarn, making a loop long enough for the button to pass through.) Secure tightly on each end, and work the buttonhole stitch over it.

FINISHING A BUTTONHOLE

Most buttonholes should be finished to add strength and for a neater appearance. Work a buttonhole stitch with sewing thread of a matching color. Make sure the stitches you sew around the buttonhole are neither too close nor too far apart.

OVERCAST STITCH

With either the yarn used for the garment or matching thread, stitch with diagonal strokes over the edges at a consistent depth and distance apart.

BUTTONHOLE STITCH

Using matching thread, secure and work along both edges of buttonhole as shown. Seal off each end with three straight stitches. This gives a firm finish and works best with tape or ribbon facing.

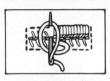
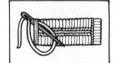

RIBBON FACING

Some sweaters may be reinforced along the front openings. This will help strengthen the fabric for the buttons and buttonholes and will prevent the ribbing from stretching.

Step 1 —Choose grosgrain ribbon or twill tape in a color to match the yarn. Allow at least ¼" hem at the top and bottom of both bands.

Step 2 —Lightly tack the ribbon onto the inside edge of the ribbing with pins, making sure the lengths are identical.

Step 3 —Slipstitch the ribbon onto the ribbing with matching cotton thread.

Step 4 —Cut buttonholes along the grain of the ribbon, sew over the ribbon and buttonhole with the buttonhole stitch.

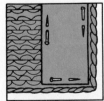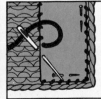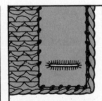

How to slipstitch ribbon onto sweater inside for facing.

TIP
• Soak twill tape in warm water and squeeze out excess moisture. Press with hot iron to preshrink. Without this precaution, the tape could shrink on the first washing.

POCKETS

Pockets are another element in the design of the garment, and they serve both functional and decorative purposes. Consider how the size of the pockets relates to the size of the garment; they shouldn't be too large or too small. If the pocket is going to be on the inside of the garment, be sure that it doesn't extend below the bottom edge.

Here are three pocket designs: patch pockets, horizontal inserted, and vertical inserted.

PATCH POCKETS

Use any shape you like on this type of pocket. Old gauge swatches can make fun pockets, but add some ribbing at the top so the edge doesn't curl.

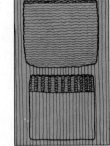

Step 1 —Place the wrong side of the pocket onto the right side of the garment, making sure the lower edge lines up with one row of the main fabric to keep it straight.

Step 2 —Carefully slipstitch the pocket down on three sides.

HORIZONTAL INSERTED POCKETS

Determine where the pockets are to be positioned. Plot this area on your chart. Begin by knitting the pocket lining.

Step 1 —With the same size needles and yarn as the garment, cast on the number of stitches you have determined you will need for the size of the pocket.

Step 2 —Knit in stockinette stitch to the desired length and hold.

Step 3 —On the main garment, knit to the position of the pocket and place the stitches for the pocket opening on a holder.

Step 4 —On the next row, work to the same place and transfer the pocket lining to the needle in place of the stitches that have been placed on the holder.

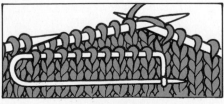

Transferring the pocket lining to the body of the sweater

Step ⑤ —Knit the body of the garment to completion.

Step ⑥ —Pick up the stitches from the holder and knit downward to the same length as the lining.

Step ⑦ —Pick up loops where the stitches were on the holder and with smaller needles work ¼″–1″ of ribbing or garter stitch for finishing off the pocket and stitch down with slipstitch.

Step ⑧ —Sew the three sides of the pocket together on the wrong side.

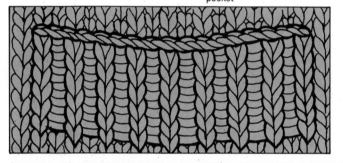

Completed horizontal inserted pocket

VERTICAL INSERTED POCKETS

Make this as deep as you want, as long as the pocket lining doesn't hang lower than the hem of the garment. A good way to determine proper positioning is to sew the shoulder seams and try on the sweater.

Place your hands where they would naturally fall into a side pocket. Mark with pins, and sew side seams to that point (from the hemline up and from the armhole down).

Step ① —Pick up the remaining stitches on the front side of the sweater with a smaller needle size and work in rib or garter stitch for 1″–1½″ for the flap.

Step ② —Pick up the stitches on each side of the opening and work two separate pieces of fabric to the desired depth, for the lining. Bind off.

Step ③ —Sew the three sides together.

Step ④ —Slipstitch the ribbed facing on the outside to the sweater body.

Vertical Inserted Pocket

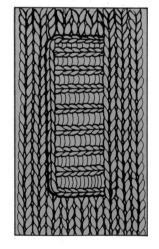

ZIPPERS

Nylon zippers are the best to use for knitwear.

Step ① —Place the zipper to the inside of the knitted edges, making sure the top of the zipper lines up with the top of the piece.

Step ② —Carefully pin in place, taking care not to stretch the fabric.

Step ③ —With sewing needle, matching thread, and right side facing you, sew zipper in place using backstitch. Be sure to keep the seam as close to the knitting as possible.

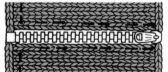 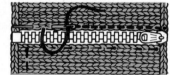

TIP

• *If the zipper will be closed at one end, as in a skirt, you should sew up the seam first to the point where the zipper will be inserted and then position the zipper.*

YARN ENDS

At the completion of the garment, there will be many little yarn ends that have to be woven into the garment to create a finished inside and also to prevent unraveling. Use a crochet hook and weave the ends into the back of the stitches of the same color. Trim ends close to the piece.

BEADS

Beads and sequins can be a festive and decorative way to spice up any plain yarn or design. Either knit them in as you go or sew them on top of the finished garment as you would sew on a button. To knit them in, thread the beads onto your ball of yarn. Here is the easiest method:

Step ① —Cut a 12″ piece of sewing thread and have the ball of yarn on hand.

Step ② —Thread the needle and place the knitting yarn through the loop of thread.

Step ③ —Insert the beads onto the needle, slide onto the sewing thread and then onto the yarn. If the opening in the bead is large enough, keep the supply of beads on the yarn until you need one for your knitting. Then simply pull the bead up and onto the stitch, and to the front of the garment. This works best on a right-side row.

If you want to plan a design, chart the positions of the beads onto the graphed chart so you'll know the right time to place each bead.

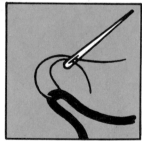

Place the knitting yarn through the loop of thread

Insert beads onto needle and sewing thread and onto yarn

DUPLICATE STITCHING OR EMBROIDERY

Duplicate stitching is an easy form of embroidery that gives the impression that the design has been knitted. Many people feel it's easier to duplicate a stitch pattern on a completed garment than to try to carry many different colored yarns as they're knitting. This is also a great way to perk up an old sweater that needs some new life, or to reinforce an area that may be worn, as it strengthens the fabric.

Step ☐1 —Thread a tapestry needle with yarn of the same ply as the sweater.

Step ☐2 —Secure the yarn at the base of the first stitch.

Step ☐3 —Insert the needle from right to left through the base of the stitch above.

Step ☐4 —Reinsert the needle into the base of the original stitch and through the base of the next stitch to the left.

Step ☐5 —Continue this retracing the paths of the original stitches.

Duplicate stitching

TIPS

• *Be aware of the gauge of the sweater. Are the stitches wider than they are tall? Or taller than they are wide? Either of these would change the look of your design from what you have charted. Use the knitter's graph paper provided in the Workbook chapter for exact proportion of the image you chart (see pages 166–168).*

• *If you like to embroider, use the same stitches that you would for embroidering on fabric. Be sure not to split the yarn and to keep it twisted as you go.*

APPLIQUÉ

This refers to applying a cut-out shape onto fabric. Many different fabrics and textures can be applied to knit garments, from leather to felt, cotton, silk, or any fabric you like. The best method to use for sewing is slipstitch, done with matching sewing thread. Appliqués work well over worn fabric or moth holes. Do take into consideration how the appliqué will clean with the sweater. Be sure the dyes won't bleed.

CARE OF YOUR KNITWEAR

The one piece of advice we give you in terms of care of your precious knitwear is **Read yarn labels!** Since care instructions vary greatly for different types of fibers, the only way to be sure of the proper cleaning techniques is to check the label. Consider including the care instructions on your pattern instructions in your Workbook for a permanent record. Also, jot down ironing instructions. Usually a warm iron is recommended for synthetics, warmer for wool, and hot for cotton. Of course, it's never recommended to put the iron directly onto the knitted fabric. Always place a damp towel between the garment and the iron.

Here are some guidelines for hand-washing:

• Turn the garment inside out.

• If the label advises, wash in a machine on the gentle cycle; otherwise wash by hand in cold water.

• Never wring out knitwear! Squeeze gently to remove moisture, place on a flat dry towel, and gently pull into shape and let dry naturally, out of direct sunlight.

TIPS

• *Have the original measurements handy when laying the garment flat for drying. Make sure to pull it back gently to its original dimensions.*

• *Save a few yards of the original yarn, roll it into a small ball, and attach securely to an inside seam. This yarn will then get washed along with the garment and will be similarly discolored if it's needed for a mending job.*

• *Pilling refers to the little balls of fiber that appear on the surface of the garment. They can usually be removed with tape. If they're really tenacious, go over the surface gently with a clothes brush, or razor blade.*

• *Remember that hand-knit garments shouldn't be hung on hangers because they will get pulled out of shape. Always fold flat and keep in plastic bags for storage. Punch a few holes in the bag for the yarn to breathe.*

Can be washed by machine or hand. Above line, number represents washing process for machines. Below line, number represents water temperature in ° centigrade.	Do *not* wash.	△ If triangle contains "CL," bleaching is permitted. If triangle is crossed out, do *not* use bleach.	Do *not* tumble dry.
	(A) Dry clean with any solvent.		Use hot iron up to 210°C.
Hand-washable only.	(P) Dry clean with perchlorethylene or petroleum-based solvents.	Do *not* dry clean.	Use warm iron up to 160°C.
	(F) Dry clean with fluorocarbon or petroleum-based solvents.	Okay to tumble dry.	Use cool iron up to 120°C. 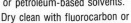 Do *not* iron.

CHAPTER SIX
WORKBOOK

This chapter will guide you in creating your own Workbook for keeping records of completed projects and for planning new ideas. We make suggestions about how you might want to organize your Workbook, but feel free to improvise.

We suggest you use a three-ring binder notebook with divider (tab) pages. Here are some ideas for the various sections, along with the pages in this chapter that relate to each. Feel free to photocopy all these pages so you don't run out.

YOUR KNITTING DIARY

Whenever you see a photograph you like, clip it out and put it in your diary. This could be sweaters and dresses or a painting that has an image you find interesting. You may be at a restaurant and take a fancy to their matchbook cover, or a cocktail napkin that has a unique design on it. The idea is to focus in on what you like in terms of fashion, color, shape, and design. When you're wondering what you might want to create for your next project, go back over your diary for visual inspiration.

We've provided some pages that will help with this process, the Stencil Page and the Alphabet Page. Once you've decided on a design, use the Prep Page to do all the calculations, and the Graph Paper pages to chart the design.

THE CUT-OUT PAGE

A quick tool to use to show the shape of your design without having to draw it. Choose the elements you like to create a sweater, and tape them on the Fill-in-the-Blank Pattern Page as a reminder of your design.

PATTERN INSTRUCTIONS FOR YOUR DESIGNS

We have provided a blank pattern page. Fill in the spaces to create your own instructions.

MEASUREMENTS DATA BANK

Here you can record the measurements of family and friends, so you have a record of their sizes for making special gifts.

THE FIBER FILE

Clip and record all the remnants of yarn you own. No more wondering what's in that big trunk in the attic! You'll soon have immediate access to your own inventory, so designing can be more economical as well.

ARAN SWATCH LIBRARY

Knit swatches of Aran stitch patterns that you like and photocopy them along with the written instructions for the stitch. Compile these photocopies to remind yourself of stitches that you have knit. When the time comes to create an Aran sweater, cut and paste the photocopies together to make a one-of-a-kind Aran design from your own library.

Although this is the final chapter in our book, it's the first chapter in yours. Now you are graduating into the rewarding world of being your own designer. Patience and perseverance are the keys to success, and remember, if you have the desire, you can do anything. Even though you may occasionally feel confused, remember to stay focused on your goal of that beautiful masterpiece, and you *can* make it happen.

THE PREP PAGE

BOX#1 THUMBNAIL SKETCH

BOX#2 AND BOX#4 SCHEMATIC WITH MEASUREMENTS

BOX#3

MEASUREMENTS		
a	Baseline: ½ of hip or waist measurement	
b	length of ribbing	
c	length of ribbing to underarm	
d	length of armhole to shoulder	
e	total length	
f	shoulder width	
g	neck width	
h	width of sleeve at cuff	
i	length of cuff ribbing	
j	length of top of cuff ribbing to underarm	
k	sleeve cap length	
l	width of upper arm at armhole	
m	total length of sleeve	

BOX#5   STITCH PATTERN

SYMBOLCRAFT CHART

WRITTEN INSTRUCTIONS

BOX#6   YARN

BOX#7   NEEDLE SIZES

BOX#8   4″ × 4″ GAUGE SWATCH + RIBBING

BOX#9

GAUGE
___ sts =1″   ___ rws =1″

BOX#10   MATH

MEASUREMENTS × GAUGE = STITCHES + ROWS	
STITCHES PER ROW (HORIZONTAL MEASUREMENTS)	**ROWS PER INCH (VERTICAL MEASUREMENTS)**
a	b
	c
f	d
g	e
	i
h	j
	k
l	m

BOX#11

		STITCHES/INCH ROWS/INCH
a	Baseline: ½ of hip or waist measurement	
b	length of ribbing	
c	length of ribbing to underarm	
d	length of armhole to shoulder	
e	total length	
f	shoulder width	
g	neck width	
h	width of sleeve at cuff	
i	length of cuff ribbing	
j	length of top of cuff ribbing to underarm	
k	sleeve cap length	
l	width of upper arm at armhole	
m	total length of sleeve	

BOX#12 AND BOX#13 YOU WILL FILL IN ON YOUR OWN BLANK SHEET OF PAPER

CUT-OUT PAGE

Cut and Combine to create the style you like.

Drop shoulder sleeve

Fitted sleeve

Raglan sleeve

These styles may be used on the fill-in-the-blank pattern page.

RECORD THE MEASUREMENTS IN THE BOXES

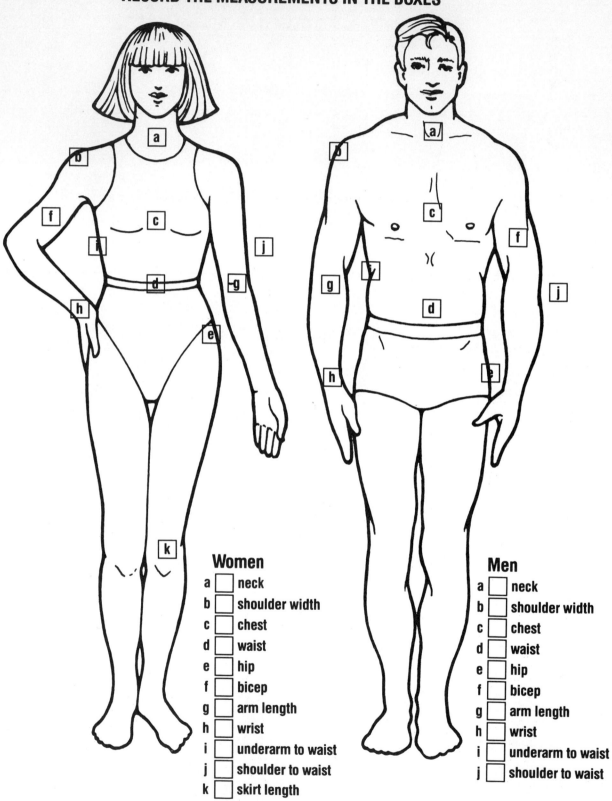

Women

a ☐ neck
b ☐ shoulder width
c ☐ chest
d ☐ waist
e ☐ hip
f ☐ bicep
g ☐ arm length
h ☐ wrist
i ☐ underarm to waist
j ☐ shoulder to waist
k ☐ skirt length

Men

a ☐ neck
b ☐ shoulder width
c ☐ chest
d ☐ waist
e ☐ hip
f ☐ bicep
g ☐ arm length
h ☐ wrist
i ☐ underarm to waist
j ☐ shoulder to waist

FILL-IN-THE-BLANK PATTERN PAGE

Date: _____   Sweater for: _____

Type of yarn: _____

Gauge: _____   Needle size: _____

Size: _____   **Measurements:** shoulder width ☐ ″ chest ☐ ″ waist ☐ ″ hips ☐ ″ wrist ☐ ″

upper arm ☐ ″ length of arm ☐ ″ length of back ☐ ″

Stitch pattern: _____

_____

_____

Back: _____

_____

_____

Front: _____

_____

_____

Sleeves: _____

_____

_____

Finishing: _____

_____

_____

Notes: _____

_____

Begin by charting your garment shape onto graph paper, then choose one or more of these stencils for motifs. Trace the stencil, position it where you want it on your garment's chart, and tape in place. Draw the image onto the chart first, then go over it creating the stepped lines for the grid. Remove the stencil and check to see if the overall shape reads well. If it doesn't, you may have to adjust the squares.

If the image doesn't fit onto your chart because it's either too large or too small, scale it either up or down (see page 55) for scaling instructions).

Remember, the smaller the gauge the more detail you'll achieve in a visual motif. If you want to use a complex image, choose a yarn that gives you a gauge of 4sts=1″ or more.

ABCDEFG
HIJKLM
NOPQRS
TUVWXYZ
abcdefg
hijklmnop
qrstuvwyxz
1234567890

Use the Fiber File to keep track of all those odds and ends of yarn that are stashed in bags, boxes, trunks, closets, attics, basements. No one likes to part with even a ball of that gorgeous bouclé or the angora which was a perfect trim for the evening sweater you made two years ago. But the problem always has been, "Where did I put it?" or "I wonder how much of that I have left?"

Here is the solution. Snip a piece of every ball of yarn you own. Tape each piece of yarn in its own box and make a notation next to it of how many skeins or scraps you have left. It might be a good idea to put any coordinating fibers together on the same page so you can begin to brainstorm about that fabulous sweater you're going to design.

To create the Aran section of your Workbook, knit swatches of stitch patterns that you like, lightly press each one with a steam iron, and staple it onto a piece of paper. Record all the information that applies, such as the gauge, needle size, written instructions for the stitch, and a symbolcraft graph if you prefer. This is a catalogue of the stitches and cables that you know how to knit, and an instant reference for gauge and texture.

To design an Aran sweater, photocopy each swatch, and choose stitches for a central panel, two side panels, and divider stitches. Remember, cables and bobbles can be integrated into any of these main sections.

Tape the swatches together in the proper order to illustrate your sample design.

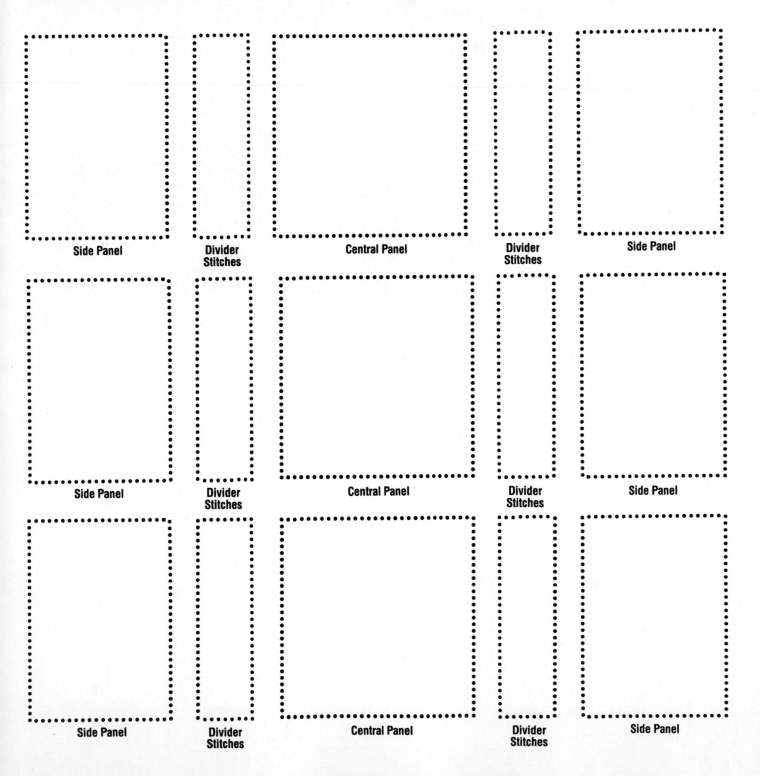

Side Panel Divider Stitches Central Panel Divider Stitches Side Panel

Side Panel Divider Stitches Central Panel Divider Stitches Side Panel

Side Panel Divider Stitches Central Panel Divider Stitches Side Panel

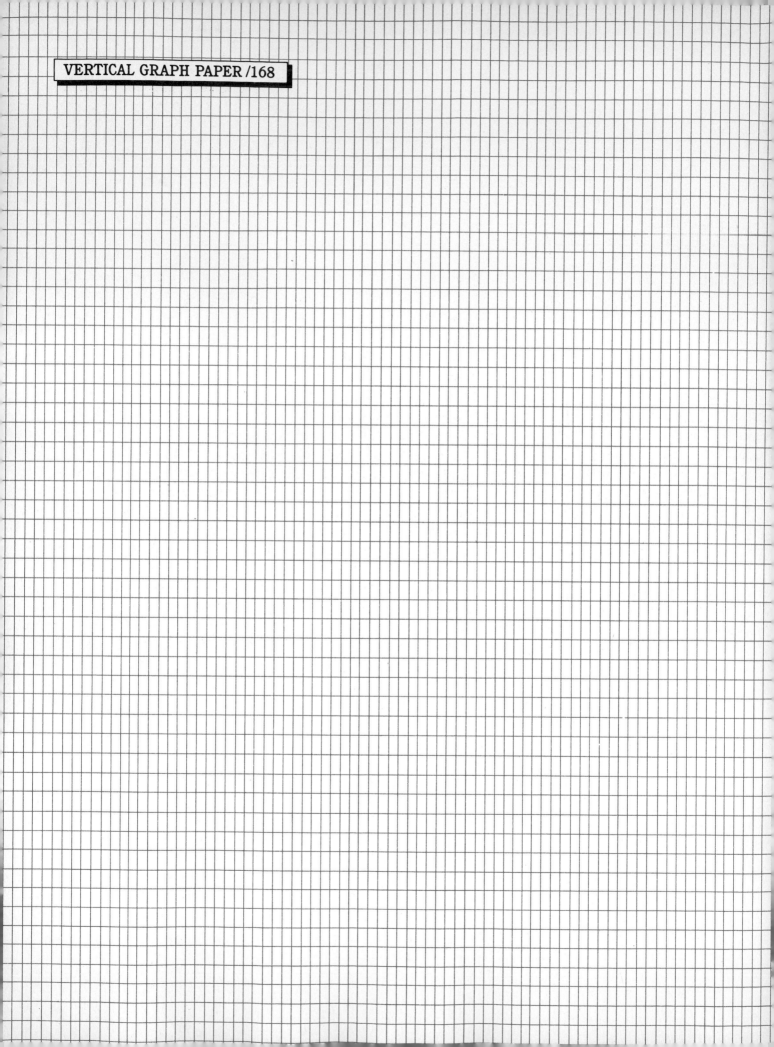
VERTICAL GRAPH PAPER /168

YARN MANUFACTURERS AND DISTRIBUTORS

- **AARLAN, INC.**
128 Smith Place
Cambridge, MA 02138
(617) 491-6744/To order: (800) 343-5080
    Imported knitting yarns from Europe. Many different kinds of angora and angora blends, cottons, mohairs, silks, alpaca, novelties, wools, blends, and acrylics.

- **Amcan Feather Co., Inc.**
45 East Street
South Salem, NY 10590
(203) 834-2450
    Worldwide wholesale dealers in raw and dyed fancy feathers. Feather yarns made from turkey feathers with rayon cord, for hand and machine knitting, weaving, and sewing.

- **The Armen Corporation**
1400 Brevard Road
Asheville, NC 28806
(704) 667-9902
    Importers and distributors of Chat Botte brand hand-knitting yarns. Cost of shade book: $20, refunded on yarn order.

- **Stanley Berroco**
Elmdale Road
PO Box 367
Oxbridge, MA 01569
(800) 343-4948 or (617) 278-2527
    Specialty yarns for knitting, crocheting, and weaving. A collection of fashion yarns and ribbons, bouclés, brushed wools, twists, and spacedye variations in cotton and rayon.

- **Berger du Nord-Brookman and Sons, Inc.**
12075 NW 39th Street
Coral Springs, FL 33065
(800) 327-2770
    Fashion hand-knitting yarns from France, novelties, wool and wool blends, kid mohair, 100% angora, metallic, and cottons.

- **Brunswick Yarns**
Off Sangamo Road
PO Box 276
Pickens, SC 29671
(803) 878-6375
    Wool, cotton, blends, and synthetics in all weights. Brunsana Persian yarn.

- **Crystal Palace Yarns**
3006 San Pablo Avenue
Berkeley, CA 94702
(415) 548-9988/(800) 227-0323
    100% silks—Silk Tweed, Country Silk, Mandarin, Bouclé, Allegro. Silk blends—Creme, Silk Rustique, Colorado. Cottons, linen blends, fashion yarns. Emphasizing natural fibers.

- **Dariff Design Associates, Inc.**
238 Prospect Avenue
Cedarhurst, NY 11516
    Own yarns of cotton, silk, wool, and rayon. Sample cards available upon request.

- **The DMC Corporation**
107 Trumbull Street
Elizabeth, NJ 07206
(201) 351-4550
    Cotton knitting and crocheting yarns, art needlework threads, six-strand embroidery floss, matte and pearl cottons, three-ply Persian wool, tapestry wool, metallic threads.

- **Classic Elite Yarns, Inc.**
12 Perkins Street
Lowell, MA 01854
(617) 453-2837
    Quality-fibered hand-knitting yarns, featuring mohair, wool, cotton, rayon, silk, cashmere, and others. The primary line is brushed and looped mohair available in over 80 colors.

- **Fiesta Yarns**
PO Box 2548
Corrales, NM 87048
(505) 897-4485
    Hand-dyed rayon, two-strand cotton, silk, and mohair yarns.

- **Frederick J. Fawcett, Inc.**
Dept. F
320 Derby Street
Salem, MA 01970
(617) 741-1306
    Wool, worsted, and cotton yarns. Leclerc looms and equipment.

- **Gemini Innovations Ltd.**
720 East Jericho Turnpike
Huntington Station, NY 11746
(516) 549-5650
    Ribbons for knitting and crocheting including ¼" and ½" charmeuse and dazzle ribbon, novelty imported and domestic yarns, beads, appliqué, fur, and novelty trim.

- **Grandor Industries, Ltd.**
4031 Knobhill Drive
Sherman Oaks, CA 91403
    Mail order only fiber company specializing in quality weaving and knitting yarns.

- **Green Mountain Spinnery**
PO Box 54
Putney, VT 05346
(802) 387-4528
    100% virgin wool from New England. Natural, undyed and unbleached yarns, and colored yarns. Each lot is unique.

- **Halcyon Yarns**
12 School Street
Bath, ME 04530
(800) 341-0282
    Three dozen sample cards of 100 different kinds of yarns, all natural fibers. Wools, cottons, silks, and linens. Bulk orders wholesale.

- **Kiwi Imports, Inc.**
54 Industrial Way
Wilmington, MA 01887
(617) 656-8566
    Hand-knitting yarns from New Zealand. Perendale Worsted Softwist, Quicknit (Bulky) 100% wool, Hanna and Glencairn yarns.

- **Knitting Fever, Inc.**
  180 Babylon Turnpike
  Roosevelt, NY 11575
  (516) 546-3600/(800) 645-3457
    Exclusive distributor of Noro, Dorothee Bis, and Lanas Katia yarns. Creator of Watch & Learn Videos and Knitting Instructor Computer Program.

- **Lana Moro, Inc.**
  260 Fifth Avenue
  New York, NY 10001
  (212) 683-5290
    Hand-knitting yarn manufacturer supplying yarn to chains such as Zayre, Bradlees, McCrory, F.W. Woolworth, and Ames. Yarns range from 100% acrylic to mohair blends and knitting ribbons. They do not sell directly to consumers but upon request will supply a list of retail outlets in the consumer's immediate area.

- **Les Fils Crystal Yarns, Inc.**
  01260 Rue Richmond
  Suite 105
  Montreal, Quebec H3K 2H2, Canada
  (514) 937-6111
    Classic and trend-setting worsted and novelty yarns formulated from natural fiber and blend combinations. Contact Jeffrey Frank for retail outlets, or send for catalog.

- **Lion Brand Yarn Company**
  1270 Broadway
  New York, NY 10001
  (212) PE6-7937
    Complete line of hand-knitting yarns ranging from 100% French angora, 100% wool, wool acrylic blends, cotton blends, and 100% acrylics.

- **Manos del Uruguay**
  Distributed by Simpson Southwick
  421 Hudson Street
  New York, NY 10014
  (212) 620-0053
    Unique hand-dyed and hand-spun wool yarn, Romney fleece, and horn buttons.

- **Mark Distributors Inc.**
  5239 Commerce Avenue
  PO Box 179
  Moorpark, CA 93020-0179
  (805) 529-0755
    Welcomme and Pernelle knitting yarns. Zweigart material, Persian yarn, Boye and Clover needles.

- **Melrose Yarn Co., Inc.**
  1305 Utica Avenue
  Brooklyn, NY 11203
  (718) 629-0200
    Imported and designer hand-knitting yarns, 100% wools, mohairs, angora, chenilles, cottons, rayons, metallics, bouclé, loop mohair, dress mohair, and color-coordinated fashion yarns. Offers skirts and pants loomed by hand in matching yarn, upon request.

- **Merino Wool Co., Inc.**
  230 Fifth Avenue
  Suite 2000
  New York, NY 10001
  (212) 686-0050
    Importers of quality knitting yarns, specializing in novelty twists and fine natural fibers. Exclusive distributor of European brands such as George Picaud, Emu, Tiber, plus the Merino brand.

- **Mohair Council of America**
  1412 Broadway
  New York, NY 10018
  (212) 382-2444
    Resource library for mohair yarns. Call for appointment or write for retail outlets.

- **Neveda—Martek Craft Industry**
  199 Trade Zone Drive
  Ronkonkoma, NY 11779
  (516) 467-1195
    Complete line of fashion and hand-knitting yarns, including silk blends, mohair, 100% cotton, Shetland, sock yarns, Newolon, acrylic blends, all weights of 100% wool, linen blends, cotton blends, nylon blends, silver and gold.

- **C.M. Offray & Son, Inc.**
  Route 24,
  PO Box 601
  Chester, NJ 07930-0601
  (201) 879-4700
    Quality woven-edge designer ribbons: satins, grosgrains, velvets, plaids and checks, novelties, feather-edge and double-face satin, taffeta fancies, knitting ribbon, and webbing.

- **Phildar USA**
  6438 Dawson Boulevard
  Norcross, GA 30093
  (404) 448-7511
    Classic and novelty hand-knitting yarns from France. Over 40 qualities and 700 fashion colors. Phildar needle line is also available.

- **Plymouth Yarn Company**
  500 Lafayette Street
  Bristol, PA 19007
  (215) 788-0459
    Domestic and imported hand-knitting yarns: craft yarns, weaving yarns, yarns on cones for home machine knitting. "Indicity" alpaca dyed and natural shades, angora and angora blends, 100% wools, cottons, Persian yarn in skeins and cones.

- **Rainbow Mills, Inc.**
  5539 Fair Oaks Street
  Pittsburgh, PA 15217
  (412) 422-7012
    Unusual and creative materials for hand-knitting and crochet: hand-dyed handspun "Candy" yarns of mohair and wool, hand-dyed "Butterfly Silks," Feather yarn, and ribbons.

- **Santa Fe Yarns (formerly Crawford-McKelvey-Dryden, Inc.)**
  1570 Pacheco C-1
  Santa Fe, NM 87501
  (505) 982-4798
    Worsted wool, silk, cotton, and blends in a variety of textures and colors, both solid and variegated. Many yarns are hand-dyed. Two European imports: 100% lamb's wool and 70% cashmere/30% silk.

- **Schaffhauser/Qualitat, Ltd.**
  3489 N.W. Yeon, Building 3
  Portland, OR 97210
    Imported luxury yarns from Switzerland. Many different kinds of superwash (machine washable) wool, silk, mohair, cotton, sock yarns, blends and acrylics.

- **Scheepjeswool USA Inc.**
  155 Lafayette Avenue
  White Plains, NY 10603
  Wholesale only. Scheepjeswool and Thorobred/Scheepjeswool fine knitting yarns: fashion, novelty, superwash, wool, mohair, cotton, and all blends. Hundreds of patterns, buttons.

- **The Sheepish Grin**
  40 Fairfield Road
  Kingston, NJ 18528
  (609) 924-YARN
  Manufacturers of Serendipity Skeins. Hand-dyed, one-of-a-kind, and limited edition silk knitting ribbon, silk bouclés, silk chenille, lustrous silk cords, silk-wool, silk-linen, brushed mohairs, mohair bouclé, alpaca, cashmere, angora, wools, cottons, and marabou feathers.

- **Shepherd Wools, Inc.**
  711 Johnson Avenue
  PO Box 2027
  Blaine, WA 98230
  (206) 332-8144
  Samband Lava and Samband Saga 100% Icelandic wool yarns. Chinook Indian sweater yarn. Hawaii, Hawaii Chunky, Grousemoore, Baroque, Grampian Chunky, Vanity Fair and Rendezvous from Hayfield Textiles Ltd., England.

- **Silk City Fibers**
  155 Oxford Street
  Paterson, NJ 07522
  (201) 942-1100
  Dyed silk, viscose, wool, linen, cotton, and metallic yarn—color-coordinated in solid and variegated groupings, novelty and smooth styles, cones and skeins, domestic and imported. Over 485 items in 47 styles in stock available for immediate delivery. The exclusive North American distributor of the Mokuba collection of ribbons and tapes—18 styles, 1243 colors.

- **Spring House Yarns**
  649 Wexford Bayne Road
  Wexford, PA 15090
  (412) 935-5266
  Wholesale only
  Hand-dyed fibers, natural plant materials, and exotic woods are used to obtain richness of color and sheen. The "Cloudspun" series designed for large needle projects such as #13 and #15. Custom spinning is available for those who have yarns and fibers in mind.

- **Spinrite Yarns & Dyers, Limited**
  320 Livingstone Avenue South
  Listowel, Ontario N4W 3H3
  Canada
  Contact: Mr. Robert Hay, Vice President
  (519) 291-3780
  Manufacturer of a complete range of acrylic, wool and blended yarns, classic and fashion, hand-knitting and domestic machine knitting yarns, under the brand name "Bouquet."

- **Tahki Yarns**
  92 Kennedy Street
  South Hackensack, NJ 07601
  (201) 489-9505
  Imported luxurious and classic natural fiber yarns for hand-knitting, weaving, and machine knitting. The Tahki Collection features pure wool Donegal homespun and Soho bulky tweeds, tweedy alpaca and angora, Chelsea and other top quality silk/wool blends, French ombres, mohair/silk blends, 100% cotton, cotton/linen blends, in hundreds of fashion colors.

- **Treenway Crafts, Ltd.**
  3841 Duke Road
  RR 1, Victoria, British Columbia, V8X 3W9
  Canada
  (604) 478-3538/383-1413
  Luxurious silk in many weights and 30 colors. Also supply other wools, cottons, mohair, and cottonlin. Spinning fibers, spinning and weaving books, carding equipment, spinning wheels, loom accessories. Mail order only. Dealer inquiries welcome.

- **W. West Designs**
  2305 Main Street
  Santa Monica, CA 90405
  (213) 392-4809
  Exciting collection of unique hand-knitting yarns. A quality selection of silk, cotton, alpaca and wool fibers. The latest stock and colors from France, Italy and the United States.

- **Wilde Yarns**
  John Wilde & Brother, Inc.
  3705 Main Street
  Philadelphia, PA 19127
  (215) 482-8800
  Many weights and colors of wool for hand-knitting. Since 1880.

- **Wonder Craft**
  1 Constitution Street
  Briston, RI 02809
  (401) 253-2030
  Rug wools, synthetics, novelty yarns, and cottons.

- **Yarnville, Inc./Sasha Yarns**
  230 Ferris Avenue
  White Plains, NY 10603
  (914) 997-5653
  Distributors of Argentine hand-knitting yarns, 100% wool and blends.

NEEDLE COMPANIES

- **Susan Bates, Inc.**
  Route 9A
  Chester, CT 06412
  (203) 526-5381
  Knitting needles, crochet hooks, accessories, frames, hand sewing needles, embroidery hoops.

- **Boye Needle Company**
  4343 North Ravenswood
  Chicago, IL 60613
  (312) 472-0354
  Crochet, afghan hooks, crochet hook needles, double- and single-point knitting pins, circulars, tatting, looms, hand sewing needles, plastic, cotton canvas.

- **Clover Needlecraft, Inc.**
  1007 East Dominguez Street
  Suite N
  Carson, CA 90746
  (800) 621-0849 ext. 203/ (213) 516-7846
  Manufacturers and importers of the Clover "TAKUMI" bamboo knitting needles and accessories. Available in single point, double point, circular, and flex (jumper type).

RETAIL AND MAIL ORDER

- **Amaryllis**
PO Box 63
Department KW
Brookline, MA 02146
(617) 566-5686
  Natural fiber yarns, patterns, books, magazines, and accessories for the machine and hand knitter. Catalog with color strips of yarn and actual 2″ × 2″ knitted swatches, with gauge, yardage, needle sizes, and washing instructions for each yarn costs $25 ($15 refundable with first order of $35 or more).

- **Andean Yarns, Inc.**
54 Industrial Way
Wilmington, MA 01887
(617) 657-7680
  Finest quality 100% alpaca in four different weights on balls and cones. 55 colors on cones and 130 colors on balls. Also, pima cotton in 17 shades. Write for color cards.

- **The Artisan's Accomplice**
201 East Lancaster Avenue
Wayne, PA 19087
(215) 688-6658
  Precious fibers (silk, alpaca, mohair, and angora) as well as old favorites. All weaving equipment. Instruction in weaving, knitting, and basketry. No catalog.

- **Art Yarn by Ruht**
909 N.W. 5th Avenue
Fort Lauderdale, FL 33311
(305) 522-4203
  Novelty yarns, sweater kits, furs, feathers, ceramic buckles, and more. All yarns are custom blended and come with or without kits.

- **Susan Bates, Inc.**
212 Middlesex Avenue
Chester, CT 06412
(203) 526-5381
  Knitting needles and accessories: manufacturer of Susan Bates (R) products. Catalog $3. Susan Bates (R) aluminum, plastic and "Quicksilver" with "Silkon" finish—complete U.S./metric size range of single points, double points, circulars (now available in 11½″ lengths), and gift sets in zippered case. Accessories include stitch-count markers, cablestitch holders, point protectors, stitch holders, yarn bobs, knit stands, yarn needles. Hand-knitting yarns: Patons and Jaeger basic and fancy novelty yarns.

- **Bell Yarn Company**
10 Bell Street
Brooklyn, NY 11222
  Distributors of Wonoco, Fox Brand, and Coronation hand-knitting yarns. Wholesale and retail. For wholesale, color card sent free upon request; for retail, send $2.50 for color card set.

- **Brown Sheep Company**
Route 1
Mitchell, NE 69357
(308) 635-2198
  Manufacturers of wool yarn for hand-knitters, weavers, and crocheters. 100% wool yarn and 85% wool/15% mohair blend. Sample card is $2.50.

- **China Silk Company, Inc.**
PO Box 283
Butler, NJ 07405
(201) 838-6603
  All-silk yarns imported from China. All processing, dyeing and packaging is done in the United States. Write for retail store information. If no stores are available in your area, they will sell directly to retail customers.

- **Cosmos Rabbit Factory**
Dept. K
Box 1002
Silverdale, WA 98383
  Finest quality 100% angora and angora blends, made for textural quality in natural and dyed colors.

- **Cotton Clouds**
Desert Hills 16
Route 2
Safford, AZ 85546
(602) 428-7000
  100% cotton yarns and related products. Send $3 for complete catalog and samples.

- **Dyed in the Wool**
Suite 1800
252 West 37th Street
New York, NY 10018
(212) 563-6669
  All yarns are handpainted, variegated in one-of-a-kind sweater quantities, from 100% Australian merino wool. Also available in solid colors. 100% pima cotton, cotton shoelaces, cotton bouclé, 100% silk, wool/silk blend, and mohair. Retail sample/price list is $3.

- **Eaton Yarns**
c/o Craft Skellar
Marymount College
Tarrytown, NY 10591
(914) 631-1550/946-9180
  Yarn from Finland, exclusive agent in Eastern United States for Helmi Vuorelma and Matteil-Yhtyma wool, cotton, and linen. Sample cards are $1 each. Wholesale price list available.

- **Elsie's Exquisiques**
513 Broadway
Niles, MI 49120
(616) 684-7034
  Laces, trims, ribbons, notions, doll accessories, miniatures, handmade roses from ribbon, rosettes, ruffles, satin bows, flower appliqués.
  Wholesale catalog, no charge. Retail catalog, $2. refundable with first purchase.

- **The Fiber Studio**
Foster Hill Road
PO Box 637
Henniker, NH 03242
(603) 428-7830
   Retail shop and mail order business specializing in knitting and weaving yarns, spinning fibers, looms, spinning wheels and equipment, books, handmade buttons. Samples $3.

- **Florida Fiber Co-op**
PO Box 7693
Jacksonville, FL 32238-0693
(904) 264-4810
   Mail order only. Natural colors, novelty and luxury yarns, including alpaca, cashmere, wools, cottons, linens, and blends. Feature a custom "yarn packaging" service that allows one to buy yarns in smaller amounts than usually offered. Phone orders welcome.

- **Great Scot**
5606 Mohican Road
Bethesda, MD 20816
(301) 229-3632
   Scottish knitting wools, spun in the Shetland Isles. Items for argyle and plaid knitting including the patented ARGYLER. Special kits designed for any project. Yarn samples cost $2.00 Each skein costs $2.50, including postage.

- **Martha Hall**
46 Main Street
Yarmouth, ME 04096
(207) 846-9746
   Alpaca, hand-dyed silks, mohair, ribbons, cashmere, camelhair, cotton, linen, and Maine wools. Handmade buttons, knitting books from around the world, and gift items for knitters. Catalog is $1. The complete set of over 250 yarn samples is $10 postpaid.

- **Jamie Harmon**
391 Plain Road
Jericho, VT 05465
   Kits for hats, mittens, leg warmers, sweaters, and scarfs. Kits packaged with handspun, naturally dyed wool yarn and pattern. Yarn sample card and brochure is $3.50.

- **Helga's Needlecraft/Yarns by Mail**
PO Box 30282
Cleveland, OH 44130
   Yarns from the fashion centers of Europe. Send $3 for sample catalog, redeemable with first order.

- **La Lana Wools**
PO Box 2461
Taos, NM 87571
(505) 758-9631
   Handspun and plant-dyed yarns. Sample cards are $12 for a selection of all the yarns carried or can be purchased separately as follows: native plants—$2 (indicates plant dyes); exotics—$2.50; carded blends—$2; silk—$6; natural-colored fleeces and textured yarns—$2.50. Also available, a machine-spun yarn from the local mill, dyed with natural colors. Yarns are sold retail with bulk purchases of $150.00 or more, and wholesale is available to qualified stores, retail outlets, groups, and schools. (Wholesale purchases require a tax certificate.)

- **Maine Maid**
13 Bow Street
Freeport, ME 04032
(207) 865-9202
   Fine quality wool yarns in four-ounce skeins for $2.95. Knitting kits available. All yarns, supplies, and kits are mail order. Yarn chart is $1.00 and catalog is 50¢.

- **The Mariposa Tree, Inc.**
PO Box 336
Stapleton
Staten Island, NY 10304
   Mail order only. Cashmere, mohair, wool, and silk. Imported wool fibers from New Zealand, natural dyes and mordants for dyeing available, as well as Cushing synthetic dyes in a range of colors. Hand-turned walnut knitting needles and crochet hooks in sizes 6–10½. Send $1 for catalog or $5 for yarn color card samples plus catalog.

- **Morris Cottage Inc.**
2121 Walker Road
Palmyra, NY 14522
(315) 597-6333
   100% pure British wool including tweedspun and chunky weight. Brochure is $2.50 and refundable with first purchase.

- **Norwegian Yarns/Ellen Church**
Box 393
Bartlett, NH 03812
   Mail order only. "Rauma" Norwegian wool in 50 colors, two- and three-ply. $1.50 for sample card.

- **Pacer Yarns Inc.**
PO Box 2003
Northbrook, IL 60065
(800) 248-7250
   Lesotho Handspun Mohair is produced by self-employed villagers from the mountain regions of Lesotho, South Africa. Contact Stuart Starky for stores in your area that sell this product.

- **Rio Grande Wool Mill**
PO Box B
Tres Piedras, NM 87577
(505) 758-1818
   Sample card is $3 and all yarns are 100% wool spun in the tradition and colors of the Southwest: carding services for handspinners and woolmark quality.

- **River Farm—Banks of the Shenandoah**
Route 1
Box 401
Timberville, VA 22853
   Clean American fleece in brown, black, gray or white for spinning. Handspun wools. Some yarns are dyed with vegetal from flowers and bark. Ten spinning workshops per year. Farm visits by appointment. Free brochure and workshop schedule.

- **Santa Fe Weaving and Knitting Center**
821 Canyon Road
Santa Fe, NM 87501
(505) 983-5003
   Handspun and hand-dyed silks, wools, and cottons. Knitting and weaving equipment. Inquiries welcome. No sample cards available as yarn and colors vary. Many bargains and millends available.

- **Scott's Woolen Mill, Inc.**
Hecla Street and Elmdale Road
Uxbridge, MA 01569
Contact: Sandra Saviano
(617) 278-6571
Wholesale only. Novelty hand-knitting yarns, coned yarns for machine knitting, weaving. Over 20 qualities of imported and domestic yarns. Natural fibers and blends in cotton, rayon, and wool, and synthetic blends. Full color pattern leaflets available. Special design group collection of custom plied yarns. Complete sample sets available for both groups, $5 each.

- **The Sensuous Fiber/Arlene Mintzer**
Parkville Station
PO Box 44
Brooklyn, NY 11204
Unusual and exotic knitting and crocheting supplies, which include needles, books, and unusual yarns. Color card is $7.50 and mail order information is $2.

- **The Silk Tree (A division of Select Silks Inc.)**
Box 78
Whonnock, British Columbia V0M 150
Canada
Over 45 silk and silk-blend yarns in a wide range of weights and textures. Retail and wholesale, mail order only. Sample cards are $3 each.

- **Linda Snow—Fibers**
3209 Doctors Lake Drive
Orange Park, FL 32073
(904) 264-4235
A retail shop that does mail order business in the United States and worldwide. Weaving and knitting yarns, equipment, books, and a complete line of basketry materials. Samples: yarn—$2.50; spinning fibers—$1.50; basketry—$1.50; millend mailing list— $3 for one-year subscription.

- **Studio Spun**
2124 Kitteredge #108
Berkeley, CA 94704
(415) 658-5157
Handspun cotton mixed with linens and silks and naturally dyed colors. Samples and price list available for $1.50. 10% discount offered for orders over $100.00. No wholesale.

- **Sugar River Yarns**
PO Box 663
New Glarus, WI 53574
(608) 527-5157
Yarns made from their own sheep and from Norwegian wool. Unique sheepskin/sweater jacket kits, a complete line of high-quality looms, and weaving equipment. Free wool care pamphlet. Send $2 for catalog and $1 for samples.

- **Yarns by Mills**
Box 28
Wallback, West VA 25285
(304) 587-2561 (phone orders accepted)
Large selection of handspun yarns, specializing in silks, silk blends, hand-dyed mohairs, wool, and angora. Sample card is $2.50.

- **Yarn Yard**
1779 St. Johns Avenue
Highland Park, IL 60035
(312) 432-4455
All types of yarn from around the world; many not available in the United States. Mail order knitting club. Membership includes imported and domestic yarns at sale prices ranging from 10% to 50% off retail prices. Patterns are supplied and a newsletter of fashions, sketches, and hints. Six mailings per year. Membership fee is $12 per year and $21 every 2 years.

BUTTONS

- **The Hands Work**
PO Box 386
Pecos, NM 87552
(505) 757-6730
Unique, handmade buttons of porcelains, stoneware, nontoxic glazes, and underglazes. Send a yarn or fabric swatch and a description of your project so they can create the perfect compliment. Catalog is $2 and shows a large sampling of designs. Sell wholesale and retail.

- **Randy Miller**
North Road
East Alstead, NH 03602
(603) 835-2924
Handmade pewter buttons are unique for their miniature pictorial scenes in relief. Send $1 for catalog of designs.

- **Tender Buttons**
143 East 62nd Street
New York, NY 10021
(212) PL8-7004
Buttons from around the world, including rare antique buttons, ten-cent shirt buttons, Japanese Satsuma porcelains, French enamels, fur coat buttons from Italy and France, horn from England, painted glass from England, American Indian silver buttons and buckles, and European couturier buttons. Wholesale and retail, but wholesale accounts must be set up in person.

- **Wildwood Works**
Lasqueti Island, British Columbia V0R 2J0
Canada
(604) 333-8881
Natural wooden buttons, both conventional type with holes and shanked buttons with solid brass shank.

LABELS

- **The Designery**
PO Box 2887
Kalamazoo, MI 49003-2887
CRAFTags Care Labels provide your name and care instructions. Options include color choices, quantity discounts, yarn, special orders, and more. For brochure send $1.

- **Sterling Custom Labels**
Sterling Name Tape Company
9 Willow Street
Winsted, CT 06098
(203) 379-5142
Create your own label, use your own artwork. Many colors backgrounds, and inks. 100 labels minimum order for white, black, cream, ecru, or gray backgrounds. For special colors, the minimum order is 1,000. Prices range from $15.50 to approximately $60.

ABBREVIATIONS

alt: alternate

approx: approximately

beg: begin(ning)

bo: bobble(s)

c: cable

CC: contrasting color

C6B: slip 3 stitches onto cable needle and hold to back of work, knit 3 stitches, knit the 3 stitches from cable needle

C6F: slip 3 stitches onto cable needle and hold to front of work, knit 3 stitches, knit the 3 stitches from cable needle (the number in the center of this abbreviation refers to the number of stitches worked in the cable)

ch: chain

cm: centimeter

cn: cable needle

cont: continued

cross 2 R: pass righthand needle in front of first stitch, slip 2nd stitch to righthand needle purlwise, knit 2nd stitch, and drop both stitches off needle together

cross 2 L: knit 2nd stitch on lefthand needle, slip 1 stitch to righthand needle purlwise, and drop both stitches off needle together

cross 2 RK: cross 2 stitches to the right, knitting

cross 2 LK: cross 2 stitches to the left, knitting

cross 2 RP: cross 2 stitches to the right, purling

cross 2 LP: cross 2 stitches to the left, purling

cross 5 R: slip 2 stitches on cable needle and hold to back, knit 3, then purl 2 stitches from cable needle

cross 5 L: slip 3 stitches on cable needle and hold to front, purl 2 stitches, then knit 3 stitches from cable needle

dc: double crochet

dec: decrease(ing)

dpn: double-pointed needles

foll: follow(s), (ing)

g: gram(s)

grp: group(s)

g st: garter stitch

hdc: half double crochet

": inch(es)

inc: increase(ing)

K: knit

K up: pick up and knit

K-wise: knitwise

Kfb: knit into front and back of next stitch

K1B: insert needle into the next stitch to be knitted and knit

L: left

LH: lefthand

lp(s): loop(s)

m: meter(s)

mm: millimeter(s)

M1: make one stitch by taking yarn over or around needle

MC: main color

no(s): number(s)

oz: ounce(s)

P: purl

patt(s): pattern(s)

psso: pass slip stitch over

p2sso: pass 2 slipped stitches over

pfb: purl into front and back of next stitch

P up: pick up and purl

P-wise: purlwise

R: right

RH: righthand

RS: right side(s)

rem: remain(s)(ing)

rep: repeat

rev St st: reverse stockinette stitch

rib: ribbing

rnd(s): round(s)

sc: single crochet

sk: skip

SKP or skpo: slip 1, knit 1, pass slipped stitch(es) over

sl: slip

sl st: slip stitch

sp(s): space(s)

st(s): stitch(es)

St st: stockinette stitch

tbl: through back of loop(s)

tog: together

tr: triple

w1bk or ybk: wool back or yarn back

w1fwd or y.fwd: wool forward or yarn forward

WS: wrong side

wyib: with yarn in back

wyif: with yarn in front

y.fwd: yarn forward

yd: yard

yo: yarn over (needle or hook)

yon: yarn over (or round) needle

yrn: yarn round needle

*(asterisk): directions immediately following * are to be repeated as many times as indicated

[ ] (brackets): repeat directions inside as many times as indicated.

GLOSSARY

Baseline: the lowest edge of a garment, used in charting.

Bar: simplest increase made by knitting stitch and placing the needle into the back of the same stitch.

Bind off: a method of closing the knitted stitch by lifting one loop over the next, and so on.

Bind off in ribbing: closing off stitches on a row of ribbing by continuing the rib pattern as each loop is lifted over the next.

Blocking: ironing technique that "sets" the knitted fabric to give it a finished look.

Bobbin: a small yarn holder used in multicolored knitting to help keep yarn from tangling.

Bobble: a round, raised "bump" formed by knitting several times into the same stitch.

Bouclé: type of yarn created when strands of different sizes are combined at different speeds in the manufacturing process.

Cap: the curved top part of a sleeve.

Cast on: making loops on a knitting needle to form the base for the first row of knitting. Tie a knot in the first loop to begin.

Charting: a way of visually drawing pattern instructions using one square to represent one stitch and one row.

Colorwork: a knitting pattern or design using more than one color.

Decrease: reducing the number of stitches in a row, usually by knitting two stitches together.

Ease: the extra inches one builds into a garment's design to allow for movement and comfortable fit.

Eyelet: a hole created in the knitted fabric by making a yarn over, then knitting two stitches together.

Garter stitch: *straight needles*: knit every row; *circular needles*: knit one row, purl one row, repeat.

Gauge: a length and width measurement of the number of *stitches* per inch and the number of *rows* per inch.

Gathering: added width in a garment's sleeve cap, waist, or shoulder to make pleats or gathers. Done by increasing and decreasing the number of stitches.

Grafting: joining two pieces of a garment by weaving the edges together with a tapestry needle.

Hem: the bottom edge of a garment, also edge of a collar. To mark a hemline, knit the first row after the hemline in a different stitch. Then knit the remaining rows (to make however deep a hem you want) in the regular stitch.

Increase: adding to the number of stitches in a row of knitting.

Joining: tying the end of one ball of yarn to the beginning of another. Also, joining two pieces of knitting. See *Grafting*.

Knitting together: knit two loops together; decreases one stitch.

Knitwise: insert needle into stitch as if you would knit it.

Multiple: the number of stitches required to complete a stitch pattern. Always shown between two asterisks.

Notched armhole: type of armhole where all the stitches are bound off in one row. Creates a geometric, square armhole.

Pattern: instructions needed to knit a garment; *pattern stitch:* a sequence of knitting stitches that form a design that will repeat regularly in the work; *in colorwork:* a design charted by different colors.

Picking up stitches: pick up stitches with smaller needle along edge of knitted piece, usually used for finishing, such as neck or armhole ribbing.

Ply: the number of strands twisted together in a yarn.

Purlwise: insert needle into stitch as if you would purl it.

Reverse stockinette stitch: *straight needle:* knit one row, purl one row, repeat; purl side is right side, knit side wrong side; *circular needle:* purl all rows.

Repeat: see *pattern stitch*; a repetition of knit stitches to form a pattern, usually indicated between asterisks.

Schematic: a small-scale drawing or diagram of the pieces of a garment. A schematic should show how the pieces are shaped and include the dimensions of each side.

Selvedge: an extra stitch at each side of a piece that acts as a seam edge when the pieces are sewn together.

Slip stitch: a stitch that is slipped from lefthand to righthand needles without being worked.

Stockinette stitch: *straight needle:* knit one row, purl one row, repeat; knit side is right side, purl side wrong side; *circular needle:* knit all rows.

Swatch: a knitted sample at least 4″ × 4″ that acts as a test for gauge, tension, stitch, and care of the yarn.

Symbolcraft: a way of visually charting instructions using a symbol for each different stitch variation.

Tension: the amount of pull on the yarn as one knits—will determine how tight or loose the weave is.

Thumbnail: a small sketch that communicates the basic shape and details of a garment.

Waiting: stitches held on a spare needle or stitch holder while another part of the garment is knitted.

Work even: work the same pattern stitch without increasing or decreasing stitches to required length.

Yarn forward: increase between two knit stitches by bringing the yarn forward.

Yarn over: making a new stitch by looping yarn over righthand needle.

Yarn round needle: same as "yarn over." Forms a hole in the fabric.

Yoke: a knitted extension of the sleeve cap that covers the top of the shoulder and attaches at the neckline.